ADVANCE PRAISE FOR
The World We Want

"Peter Karoff, the poet laureate of philanthropy, brings to life a number of powerful and innovative paths for creating a better world. This book combines inspiring stories, thoughtful analysis, and provocative questions. The people profiled here are determined to make a lasting difference; they must combine their passions and deeply held values with careful strategic thinking, entrepreneurial creativity, and determination. This is an art, not a science, and Karoff's treatment recognizes that. His insightful observations, analysis, and questions should help every reader take their own philanthropic art to a new level. By profiling a wide range of people and paths, Karoff assures that every reader will find approaches and stories that resonate and enlighten. *The World We Want* should guide a new generation of philanthropic entrepreneurs and engaged citizens as they seek to apply their knowledge and skills, as well as their resources, to the task of improving the conditions in which we live."

— Professor J. Gregory Dees, faculty director, Center for the Advancement of Social Entrepreneurship, Duke University's Fuqua School of Business, and coauthor of *Enterprising Nonprofits* and *Strategic Tools for Social Entrepreneurs*

"'Dare to be naïve,' Buckminster Fuller once said. In *The World We Want*, Peter Karoff, a poet and preeminent philosopher of philanthropy, offers us visions of a better world via a guided tour of idealism in America, circa 2006. His 'naïveté,' and that of the many accomplished activists he interviews, offers a compelling challenge to the cynicism and resignation that reign in much of the country today. A stirring read."

— Paul Grogan, president and CEO, the Boston Foundation

"Karoff has succeeded in giving the reader a view of a world we do all indeed want. Each of his interviewees speaks with passion and truth about a different tile in the mosaic of a whole world of humaneness and beauty. Would that we may achieve it. His poems, beautiful and moving, work as exclamation points for the chapters."

— James E. Hughes Jr., Esquire, author of *Family Wealth—Keeping It in the Family*

"It is tempting to approach a title like *The World We Want* with resistance. Who is 'we?' How do they know what I want? And then Peter Karoff introduces us, one by one, to his cast of storytellers, and we are irresistibly drawn into his concept—a poet's journey of possibilities and celebration, frustrations and reassurance. After all, we all have our dreams of a better world, and our own versions get activated and integrated into these inspiring accounts. By the end we are captured and engaged, and Peter's book has accomplished its purpose: a design experiment of hope."

— Kelin E. Gersick, senior partner, Lansberg, Gersick & Associates; management fellow, Yale School of Management; and author of *Generation to Generation: Life Cycles of the Family Business* and *Generations of Giving: Leadership and Continuity in Family Foundations.*

THE WORLD WE WANT

THE WORLD WE WANT

NEW DIMENSIONS IN PHILANTHROPY AND SOCIAL CHANGE

PETER KAROFF
WITH JANE MADDOX

ALTAMIRA
PRESS

A Division of
ROWMAN & LITTLEFIELD PUBLISHERS, INC.
Lanham • New York • Toronto • Plymouth, UK

AltaMira Press
A division of Rowman & Littlefield Publishers, Inc.
A wholly owned subsidiary of The Rowman & Littlefield Publishing Group, Inc.
4501 Forbes Boulevard, Suite 200
Lanham, MD 20706
www.altamirapress.com

Estover Road
Plymouth PL6 7PY
United Kingdom

Copyright © 2008 by AltaMira Press
Published in cooperation with The Philanthropic Initiative.

this book is supported by
literaryventuresfund
investing in literature one book at a time
www.literaryventuresfund.org

British Library Cataloguing in Publication Information Available

Library of Congress Cataloguing-in-Publication Data

Karoff, Peter.
    The world we want: new dimensions in philanthropy and social change /
Peter Karoff with Jane Maddox.
      p. cm.
    ISBN-10: 0-7591-1048-4
    ISBN-13: 978-0-7591-1048-9
    1. Social change—Citizen participation. 2. Social action. 3. Charities.
    4. Humanitarianism. 5. Community organization. I. Maddox, Jane, 1947– II. Title.
    HN18.K273 2007
    303.4—dc22
                                                   2006023833

Printed in the United States of America

™
   The paper used in this publication meets the minimum requirements of American
National Standard for Information Sciences—Permanence of Paper for Printed Library
Materials, ANSI/NISO Z39.48–1992.

To Jacob, Kaeli, Sophie, and Emma,
and the world they will inherit

CONTENTS

ACKNOWLEDGMENTS

I T HAS BEEN a journey, writing this book, which is one reason the book itself is organized as a journey. I owe much to a great many, beginning with the more than forty amazing people who agreed to share their stories. They are the soul and substance, and without them there would be no journey. My gratitude goes out to them and to the many clients of The Philanthropic Initiative (TPI) from whom, over eighteen years, I have learned so much, in more ways than I can count.

The extraordinary TPI family, especially our president and CEO Joe Breiteneicher, my valued colleagues, and the TPI board, have provided a level of intellectual stimulation and dedicated support that would be the envy of any writer anywhere. To be able to do this work has been a huge gift to me.

A particular thank-you to Leslie Pine, TPI Vice President for Program, who during one memorable discussion said, "Why don't you call it 'the world we want'—that's what it's all about!" The title set a high bar.

Barry Dym's advice helped enormously in the early stages of the book's conception and development.

Jane Maddox, far more than an editor, has been a talented partner in thought and execution, and I have relied heavily on her excellent judgment. She commented, edited, wrote, rewrote, and worried the book to completion. It has been a great collaboration.

This book, however, had another editor, one who didn't read a page. Marty Karoff has been my love for fifty years. She did not anticipate celebrating our anniversary year with me obsessing over wrestling this impossible subject to the ground, but in a sense it was for us. I want this book to meet Marty's deep, heartfelt concerns about the world she will be leaving to our beloved grandchildren. She is not optimistic and wants to be. I hope this book will make her more so.

CONSCIENCE

Caught in the dangerous traffic
between self and universe.
—STANLEY KUNITZ

I carve out a small space, a nest
Of sorts and lie my conscience down to rest.
As a gift it bears little resemblance to
The madness around me, those who think
They know everything, those who despair.

My own absurd, hesitant presumption is hope.

I watch the Osprey hunt the harbor at dusk,
It soars and glides to a frantic wing-beat
And like an acrobat hangs in mid-air
As flashes of silver scales below
Signal time to make a precision dive.

My own hesitant presumption is hope.

As an infant flails, wails, loss of womb,
Its wet, loud, pronouncement—I am here!
My conscience, not newborn, nor single-
Minded like the Fish Hawk, hears the cry
Of the wounded heart.

My own presumption is hope,

Even as deadly fog shrouds the backstage
It is no match, these awakenings are legion,
New dimensions of spirit and soul
Rise from sweet hearth and beloved earth,
Feminine and Divine.

My own hope
Lies in Mahler's 1st, from minor to major,
From darkness to Frère Jacques. So rise
Tired traveler, renew, seek secret places,
The great percussion of possibilities within.

Peter Karoff
July 2006

My Imagined Community

> *Light the first light of evening, as in a room*
> *In which we rest, and for small reason, think*
> *The world imagined is the ultimate good.*
> —WALLACE STEVENS

W E ARE IN what appears an ordinary room, furnished simply, except for bookcases that line the walls and a few comfortable chairs. Outside, the evening light is low, the windows admit only a sliver of silver, but we have the lamp and a fire burning. In this room the world might be imagined as "the ultimate good." We have gathered tonight, to plot our way into that realm, the domain of the World We Want, and to begin our journey. It is not the first time I have been in such a room.

I am reminded of Henry Hampton, who when producing *The Eyes on the Prize*, the historic PBS series on the civil rights movement, would fill a big room with people he recruited to review the rough cut of each episode. Scholars and activists from the movement, journalists, filmmakers, and folks who had been there—donors, regulators, politicians, and lawyers—all would come together for three intense days. By the end, the blatant errors of fact were caught; the plot, substance, and aesthetics of the film were refined; and it was ready for prime time or sent back for more work. Henry called that process "school," and it had a lot to do with why *The Eyes on the Prize* won so many awards and became the standard of excellence in long-form documentaries dealing with social issues. I am thinking of this room as a kind of school, and the job of those who are with us is to make sure this journey comes out right.

This of course is not *The Eyes on the Prize*; this is *The World We Want*, and if Henry Hampton were here, he might very well say, "But that is exactly what the Prize was!"

I met Henry in the 1960s and over time became part of the extended *Eyes on the Prize* family of advisers and board members. While there was always a very close bond between us, it wasn't until Henry died, much too young after a heroic struggle with first polio and then cancer, that I realized how much he meant. It is somehow revealing that the relationships we form are often deeply embedded in our lives in ways we are not aware of until they are no longer there. It may have to do with my own sense of mortality, but I sorely miss Henry. He was a great American. The world is less, and I feel more alone. It is one of the reasons I am on this journey, to capture a small precious piece of some good people and have them tell their stories. These are stories of discovery about self and about a vision for a better world. They are different for everyone, as it is for you, and it has been for me.

While I interviewed more than fifty people to prepare for this journey, the truth is I have had so many conversations with so many people over the years that I have lost count, and in the process I have collected hundreds of visions, even if I did not call them by that name.

The 2004 book *Just Money—A Critique of Contemporary American Philanthropy*, which I edited as a collection of the learning and wisdom of those who had led major private, community, and corporate foundations, was also a journey.[1] *Just Money* raised some important questions about the world we have but did not presume to answer them. Big questions that ranged from survival in the face of threatening global issues, the environment, weapons of mass destruction, and massive poverty, to trying to understand the paradigms of change and the cross-cutting trends that are transforming the energy and the flow of contemporary society. There were other questions about how we learn to listen better to the community of which we are part, about the need for visionary but practical ideas that work on the ground, and how we find within ourselves the courage, the will, and the strength of heart to confront those challenges.

Just Money was about the role of large foundations and organized philanthropy that, though influential and important, is only one player on a vast stage. The journey on which we are about to embark is a much broader one, one more open and inclusive of other players and more reflective of the complexity of the world we have. But I don't want anyone to think this journey will be a definitive overview of the world or the world we want, for there is far too much heterogeneity and vastness in such a subject. However, I do hope it sheds light and that the extraordinary people we will meet in the stories that follow not only answer some of these questions but serve as inspiration for others who are on their own journeys.

I have been most drawn to those in the trenches: dynamic social entre-preneurs, community activists, nonprofit leaders, and philanthropists who are changing historical notions of "the human condition" in Africa, Asia, Eastern Europe, Latin America, and North America. And the new breed of business leader who believes that profit and social benefit are not only compatible but essential. Beyond tinkering with what we must accept and what we can adjust, these actors on the world stage are transforming the mission itself. These are the visionaries and doers, the catalysts for social change, who are working for greater equity and less suffering around the world. Part of their brilliance is in their enthusiasm for sharing, but as astonishing as they are, I know there are legions of others with stories that have not been told. The truth is, every-one has a story. What is needed is for each of us to become conscious of our own roles, of what we can do to make the world a better place, especially those of us who for whatever reason are not yet actors in our own communities.

The philosopher Allen Wheelis has written, "We are driven to find mean-ing, and find it by discovering a necessary relation between our lives and some larger purpose."[2] It has been estimated that half of Americans are on a hunt for a higher purpose, a search for values, for connection, for community, for spirituality. For a purpose beyond work, beyond the sound bites of the evening news, away from the information overload, the minute-by-minute spin world that we inhabit. This yearning for engagement runs across the sociological divide of wealth and class.

What is missing, however, from many people's lives is the bridge between that yearning and what is called the public space. Very little attention, in our schools or in the media, is focused on what it means to be an engaged citizen of the world. What I am especially interested in are the unlikely connections, when social responsibility intersects with business and community, and in how we go about our individual, family, and professional lives. It feels para-doxical to me that, on one hand, we so cherish our private lives and, on the other, are so drawn to public ones. The same thing that motivates us, that pro-pels us down the path to community, is also what holds us back, what cautions us to not proceed at all. Yet the pull is great. The connection we feel is far more than social, it is fundamental to our humanness.

What kinds of people are in my ordinary room? Who are these vision-aries? Dreamers, realists, entrepreneurs, activists, spiritualists, secularists, pragmatists, ethicists, critics, cynics, and reluctant seers, all playing varia-tions on the same theme. They are engaged in a struggle of sorts, the conscious engagement and "shoulder to the wheel" that is a fundamental part of the world they want.

If there is a common persona, it is that of a seeker, someone who balances a deep belief in the human capacity for caring and for improving world conditions, with a healthy skepticism of oversimplified solutions.

What has emerged is a Scheherazade of themes, less a collective vision and more a pattern work that weaves together sets of experiences, all different but at the same time connected by similar strands. What has emerged is more like life itself.

At one end of the strand is the struggle of a single individual to be heard, the giving of voice to those who have not had influence, or a good job, the empowerment of a citizen—an extraordinary ambition for democracy that, practiced on a large scale, could change the world.

At the other end of the strand are huge systems and a vision of a world where silos are broken down and all the sectors work in unity to harness and integrate the resources of the market economy, the civil society, and government in the resolution of large-scale social dilemmas. At the heart of this union, there is collaboration, an intermingling of domains, fast-expanding networks of intellectual exchange and the adaptation of ideas to suit new purposes, new goals. Some call this the open source phenomenon, a technological reference based on a system and philosophy of sharing, shaping, and expanding what already works.

And in the center of this pattern work are the intersections and the visions that form the connective tissue that brings all the cravings and cares together.

I find the world is abuzz, the world we have. It is a world where the power of human connection is reinforced by will and the boundless capacity for caring. It is also a world with constraints, limitations, violence, and evil, and people need immense courage to face down the dark side of human behavior.

Here is a vision from Melinda, one of my most thoughtful soul mates:

"In the simplest sense, my vision for the world is what most of us want: a place where everybody has food, clothing, shelter, freedom, and opportunity. Less simply, it is a world where our public policies are considered with love and interdependence."

Here is another from Alan, who lives in Toronto:

"What I want is a society that is as rational and predictable as possible. You want societies where people have a combination of health, wealth, well-being, educational attainment, security and safety. Those are the commodities that allow people to live lives in a predictable way, where there's a good chance that if we work hard, they will be rewarded. Those rewards are the comforts of a civilized life. That's a reasonable set of objectives—peace, order, and good government—the Canadian ideal of America's life, liberty, and pursuit of happiness."

There are always underlying expectations at the beginning of a journey, that it will be valuable or enjoyable, and then there is the unexpected challenge as in this one from my friend Shirley:

"One of the very first questions that must be asked of leaders and participants in any movement is, Does everybody understand that we are coming to the table to work on our own stuff?"

Ideals and intentions must be more than words, left hanging in the air. If they do not lead to constructive action and real change, we are probably just wasting our precious time. Working on our own stuff, in Shirley's sense, means working within ourselves first, as the essential precondition, to going beyond ourselves—and that, along with the poem I wrote in honor of Henry Hampton, seems like a good place to start.

VILLANELLE
for Henry Hampton

The story is finished but it is not complete.
We have listened, we have seen, we have been told,
Accolades, applause, are no mean feat

Nor celebration, nor awards. So why do we weep?
Weep for the archives, the untold metaphors of gold.
The series is finished but it is not complete.

In a great land, a country we so yearn to greet,
The comings, the goings of color, bright, black, unfold,
Accolades, applause, are no mean feat.

In life, in love, in passion, there is no retreat,
We go deep within our soul and pray it will hold.
The story is finished but it is not complete.

Was it today or yesterday the prize was sweet,
Pain and vision magnified a thousand fold,
Accolades, applause are temporal receipts.

Gentle spirit, castles in the air, these are concrete
Around us, surround us, told, untold and retold.
The story is finished but it is not complete.
Accolades, applause, are no mean feat.

A Peddler Goes to Work

I am basically a peddler, a salesman, someone who loves to be loved and thus is intrinsically a mediator, a collaborator, and finder of middle ground. It is in my genes. My great-grandfather sold sugar from a backyard mill in Shepatovka, a small village in the Ukraine seventy kilometers east of Kiev. In America, my grandfather sold meat in a kosher butcher shop in Haverhill, Massachusetts. My father sold hardware and stove grates from a narrow, high-ceilinged store in Brockton until the first of the big discount stores mowed him over like a Snapper cutting through new grass. My brother sells stocks; my cousin, toys; and so it goes.

Among peddlers you often find a glass-half-full conviction that all one needs to prevail is to have something substantive to say, to be true to it, and to use good words.[3] Perhaps it is no surprise I became a salesman, but that I ended up in the business, if it is a business, of selling philanthropy was quite unexpected. I started out, while still in college and married with a baby, selling pots and pans to "hope-chested" girls, a line that for years I thought very funny—that is until my wife and daughters made it clear how hopeless I was. For many good years I sold life insurance, and I learned to listen to what people had to say, to what they held dear, to what they believed in. Later, I moved on to real estate investment and hawking my poems to small magazines no one knows.

I have a good friend who is a CEO of a large company, who loves to introduce me to "important" people as a "pot and pan" salesman who gave up on pots, tried insurance and real estate, now sells philanthropy, and has never really distinguished between them. In some ways he is right, but it is philanthropy that brought it all together.

Twenty years ago I left the plain vanilla business world and founded a nonprofit organization called The Philanthropic Initiative (TPI). Since its inception, TPI has been an unabashed, flat-out attempt to market the ethic, concept, and practice of strategic philanthropy, especially to those with substantial resources who are on the sidelines, those in the woodwork. TPI is a social venture that has been a unique journey in itself into the heart and soul of why some people are remarkably generous, and why others are not, and why some corporations are instinctively socially responsible, and others are like lumps in the desert sand. Most important, TPI since its inception has developed, guided, and managed the philanthropic investment of more than $850 million in a wide range of programs and initiatives, and we have seen firsthand the power of passion and values when joined with creative ideas. TPI has become a good place, not unlike the ordinary room where we began this journey, a place where it is possible to envision a world made better.

Starting TPI was in some ways a complete shift, but I had been warming up to it for a long time. Over the years, I was a board member and advocate, another word for salesman, for more than thirty organizations that dealt with racism, criminal justice, mental health, human services, community development, the environment, state government, and the arts. I learned firsthand that philanthropy and community involvement comprise the best "graduate school" experience in the world. The work, the people, the challenges afford opportunities and experiences unlike any other. The needs, on so many levels, are deeply compelling, just as their resolutions are difficult and sometimes uncertain. The work drew and engaged me, and over time I wanted more of it in my life. It was part of who I am long before TPI, and I am better at this "work" and feel more complete doing it than anything else I have done or could do.

The two decades with TPI have been a gift to me. My wife could comment, if she were not so kind, that if I had worked this hard all of those years I was in business, we would have a lot more money than we have. True, but I never cared about those businesses the way I care about this one.

My slant on philanthropy is personal and multilayered. It might begin with a song from my youth called "The Hokey Pokey," where you put your "whole self in." By whole self, I do not mean big money or even a monastic personal commitment, but I do mean a certain intensity, ambition, and clarity of goals. When I began the TPI journey twenty years ago, I thought that one could make philanthropy fit every aspect of "right" action that is not covered by government. Now I am not so sure. My friend John Abele, whom you will meet, has a business that makes medical devices that significantly reduce pain and cost. John makes the case that such an enterprise is as good an expression of love of humankind as one that feeds and houses the poor. In fact, John calls his company, Boston Scientific, a "for-profit philanthropy."

So, I have used the word *philanthropy* only because I haven't found a better one. There is a lot to like about the Greek root of the word, *philos*, which means "love." But to many people, the word *philanthropy* seems a bit dated and formal, even off-putting. It sounds like something right for Mr. Rockefeller, but not for me. Maybe a better word will come to mind or a fellow traveler will think of one, a word that encompasses love and goodness and says something about duty, charity, and giving back, about generosity of self and spirit, about fairness and justice, about doing the right thing.

If this sounds like a "clarion call," it is indeed an attempt to stimulate at least one more person to stand up and be counted, to make a difference, to give back.[4] A chance to motivate someone who has wondered for some time whether he or she could, should, might get involved. So that under the right circumstances, with terms and conditions that meet their criteria, this person will throw a hat into the ring for a cause he or she cares about and perhaps come to care passionately.

John Updike once said that he wrote his novels for that one reader who he knew was out there somewhere—a reader who was his soul mate, the essential counterpoint to him as a writer without whom there was no meaning to the writing at all. Tom, a friend of mine, met the famous novelist at a book signing some years ago and with trepidation in his voice said, "Mr. Updike, I just want you to know that I am your reader!" Tom may not have been the precise soul mate the author of *Couples* had in mind, but Updike did visualize an individual reader, as I do. One person whose generosity gene lies dormant, who is waiting in the wings, picking up signals, but biding time for an "ah-ha" moment, a wake-up call, a long-distance clarion call.

Clarion calls are, of course, suspect. We guard ourselves against overzealous advocates and professed enlightenment. From Elmer Gantry to the latest TV ministry revealed as charlatan, from political speeches ripe with empty promises, from get-rich promotions and pyramid schemes, we have heard it all. And yet these calls have moved me . . . .

When Franklin Delano Roosevelt said, "The test of our progress is not whether we add more to the abundance of those who have much, it is whether we provide enough for those who have little." . . .

When Patanjali (third century B.C.) wrote, "When you are inspired by some great purpose, some extraordinary project, all your thoughts break their bonds; your mind transcends limitations, your consciousness expands in every direction, and you find yourself in a new, great and wonderful world. Dormant forces, faculties and talents become alive and you discover yourself to be a greater person by far than you have ever dreamed yourself to be."[5] . . .

When Antonieta Gimeno, founder of the Latino Parent Association, received a Boston Neighborhood Fellows Award and said, "I accept this award on behalf of all the brown women," and the 150 people present, of which I was one, were moved to the marrow of their bones. . . .

As a teenager, I heard a dramatic call in a recording of the great African American baritone Paul Robeson singing "The Ballad for Americans."[6] "Who am I?" sang Robeson, "Who are you, mister?" the chorus responded, and in that magnificent voice came the staccato response: "Well, I'm the everybody who's nobody; I'm the nobody who's everybody." He sang of being the engineer, musician, and street cleaner. The carpenter, teacher, farmer, and office clerk and all the et ceteras and so forths who do the work. The Irish, Negro, Jewish, Italian, Greek, Turk, Czech, American, atheist, baptized Baptist, Lutheran, Catholic, Mormon, Quaker, Christian Scientist, and more. And, finally, in that pure and powerful voice, "I am America!"

Lying in the late afternoon on the living room floor of my parents' house, there seemed to be no worthier aspiration than to be that kind of American person. But when Paul Robeson, a member of the Communist Party, became a target during the McCarthy hearings, I could not reconcile what was happening with the romantic images in my mind and the perfect sentiments in that song. I was confused and not alone.

Growing up in the 1950s, I found these proud notions irresistible. If today this post–World War II era mood sounds ingenuous, the truth is that I am still conscious of its spirit in me. While the references may be different, the desire to participate and fully belong to a place is still intense. Robeson's vision of unity through diversity is still powerful and important, not only for the comfort and security of the displaced, of newcomers, immigrants, and refugees, not only for mediating rival groups and rival doctrines, but for the well-being of every person and every society around the world.

Certainly I did not know the words *public persona* at that early age, but I instinctively understood that living a life that is right and good demands more of us than living for our private selves.

This became horrifyingly clear with the assassination of John F. Kennedy in 1963. The murders of Martin Luther King and Robert Kennedy made for a troika of loss—gone the heroes, gone the innocence of the nation, a kind of death of the American dream. It felt as if the soul of the society had become deeply disturbed, and the "terror of shapelessness"[7] was palpable. Millions of Americans experienced this tragic intersection in the life of the country as both painful and profound.

At that time we desperately sought reasons and solutions for what was wrong. Many of us felt the need to get involved. This desire was not new in me; I had been working on community change, but it was the first time I really listened attentively enough to get the perspective right. I had already learned the hard way, as you will see, how easy it is to get it wrong.

Over the years, my personal aspirations have been similar to most people. I have wanted to be a good husband and father; they are roles I have loved with all my heart. I have watched my children become successful, happy adults, and I now go into raptures over my grandchildren. I have wanted to earn enough money, although what is enough has never been clear, and to find satisfying work that engaged me, which took a while to figure out. It

sounds pretty ordinary, but the truth is that nearly a third of the world's people do not have the basic "commodities" of life—human rights, enough to eat,
a home to live in, freedom from preventable disease, education for their children, and safety from violence and war. If everyone in the world had a fair shot
at satisfying life's needs, I would not be on this journey. Because, in the world
I want, their concerns would become ordinary achievable ones, just like mine.

It seems, though, that we have no choice but to explore alternatives and
resolutions, for the world today is precariously balanced between a disastrous
downward spiral and the real potential for the resolution of major social
dilemmas. For my part, I want assurance, evidence of renewal, of values and
spirit, of community and citizenship, of equity and opportunity, and of purpose and peace. These are aspirations many hold, and they run like a pure
mountain stream through these stories, through this collection of visions.

What I have come to realize is how inventive and constructive we can be
when we choose to be so. The alternative is to repress our fear and indignation,
ignore the dangers and injustices around us or else to simply accept despair,
which, despite the ambiguities, is simply unacceptable.

I had dinner recently with a good friend who usually manages to be wise,
sardonic, and funny all at once. This night, however, he was troubled by a
litany of discouraging observations. "The tax cut makes no sense. Domestically
we have lost our sense of balance and with it the political will to deal with our
problems. The implications from the Iraqi war are vastly understated. The U.S.
version of democracy will not automatically work in poor countries around
the world, yet we continue to pour resources into infrastructures that are inad-
equate. AIDS support is way out in front of the capacity to manage it. Around
the world we ignore the underlying economic, environmental, health, and
political realities. It has become a game of Russian roulette. Let me tell you, I
am not optimistic."

But then he went on to describe the important and constructive things his
friends and colleagues are undertaking—building an organization to serve children in Myanmar, working in the global environmental movement, single-
handedly greening up Boston, building and sustaining a new theater company,
having an impact on management education in China and Singapore, no less.

"We are awfully lucky to have the opportunity to be so usefully engaged,"
he said. "So many of the world's troubles arise from not having constructive
opportunities or from the sense that the only avenue is to blow oneself up or
target others. Terrorism is an occupation of last resort (a particularly narrow
call to action). We are fortunate to be able to do our part, but we could be
doing better."[8]

The counterpoint to this chat: On another night, someone else I know confessed, "Since I retired I haven't done much except have a good time. We have the money. We travel a lot, then there's the Vineyard in the summer. It's not that I feel guilty, but I wouldn't be averse to finding some nonprofit or community thing. I wonder sometimes if we are being selfish, but I really value not being tied to anything. Still, I wouldn't just want to write a check, if I do decide on anything I'd want to get involved.

"So, good catching up. Keep your eye out, will you? If you see something really interesting let me know. No promises, OK?"

I could only sigh. It made me think of the dramatic closing lines from Eugene O'Neill's *Long Day's Journey into Night*. Edmund, in one last attempt to find hope in a lifetime of despair says:

> Then the moment of ecstatic freedom came. The peace, the end of the quest, then the last harbor, the joy of belonging to a fulfillment beyond men's lousy, pitiful, greedy fears and hopes and dreams! . . . For a second you see—and seeing the secret, are the secret. For a second there is meaning! Then the hand lets the veil fall and you are alone, lost in the fog again, and you stumble on toward nowhere, for no good reason!

This momentary vision escapes Edmund, who is headed only for the abyss. He, like my recently retired friend, probably could have been doing a lot better. I think of these little vignettes, the bits and pieces of conversations we all have, as waypoints on an uncharted journey—the one that we navigate whether we like it or not.

As this call goes out, I wonder what extraordinary things we might accomplish together, and I know how very good it will feel to simply lift the veil and try.

The Hard Way

It is 1968, a week after the assassination of Martin Luther King. Cities across America have erupted in violence as black communities explode in anger and frustration. Boston is among them, and I have driven to Blue Hill Avenue in the middle of the area where the riots took place. I park and step inside a storefront with "Roxbury Development Corporation" on the door. "SOUL" is scrawled in soap across the plate glass windows. Carol, a tall, heavyset young black woman, is at her desk. She is the secretary for this struggling little operation that runs a Head Start project and rehabs apartments.

"You OK?" I say.

"Yup, at least we were not hit like so much of the block," Carol responds. "We were lucky." We talk about one of the vacant apartments, and as I am leaving I ask Carol what SOUL means. I will never forget the look in her eyes— sheer amazement that spoke volumes. How could this white guy who has been coming to this community for years, doing work here, supposedly one of the good guys, not know? "Soul means black," she said, "which is why we didn't get trashed when they were tearing things up last week." Carol turned away, her scorn evident. The phone rang, and I walked out, embarrassed. It was not the first time.

A year earlier, in a meeting at the local office of the NAACP, my colleagues and I were complaining about the lack of support in the "community" for our work. In the early 1960s, nine of us, all young professionals, white but for one Asian, and suburban, began a modest but earnest attempt at community development, a term not yet defined and promoted by the Ford Foundation and others. This was before the days of community development corporations and organizations like the Local Initiatives Support Corporation (LISC) and the Enterprise Foundation. Our target area was a thirty-six-square-block area in Roxbury, a very poor black neighborhood in Boston. The goal was to rehab apartments, rent them at a low price, and, at the same time, acquire key real estate to attract social service programs into the area. (Eventually a big new multiservice center would be created, and a former supermarket would hold the first Head Start project in the city, operated by our group.)

The idea was that we would fix up the houses and at the same time fix up the people who lived there. We never said it exactly that way or meant it that way, but our actions clearly sent mixed messages. We would drive into the city once a week and during confusing and endless Monday night meetings struggle to make these complicated projects work. For years, the one consistent complaint was "Where is the community?" From time to time, a neighborhood person would wander into our meetings and wander out. After more than six years, we had been successful in bringing onto the board not one community resident.

At some point, the exchange in the second-floor walk-up of the NAACP office became heated. We were challenged as to who the hell "we" were to be making these allegations about the "community." We were not part of the place and were known as patronizing at best and insulting at worst. In addition, we were screwing up the work—we were accused of being incompetent. The NAACP vice president, a man known for his temper, got so angry he suddenly stood up and threw his chair at me! We left the meeting angry ourselves, frightened, and confused.

At the time I didn't understand what was wrong. Now with the perspective of intervening years, our behavior, my behavior, seems outrageous, the hubris palpable. With the best of intentions, it was a fair question: Who were we, and what gave us license to presume so much in a community that was not ours?

The death of Dr. King had a powerful effect on our society, and among other things it led to a bright spotlight, *Time* magazine cover and all, on the long-neglected status of African Americans. Concepts like Black Power became actualized in many cities, including my own. Among the responses were new organizations in both the black and white communities dedicated to the support of economic and social development. One of those organizations was the Fund for Urban Negro Development (FUND). FUND led others and me on an unusual four-year odyssey into more than five hundred suburban homes. At highly energized 7:00 A.M. breakfasts, we engaged in a remarkable in-your-face dialogue about racism and the pursuit of social justice. It ended with a pitch for $1,000 and one day a week of time. We raised money for the newly formed Boston Black United Front, a bold attempt to build a broad-based and inclusive coalition of organizations in the black community. In its brief four-year life, FUND turned over to the community several million dollars for nonprofit organizations and economic and job development.

Perhaps more than money, we raised some consciousness. I learned how hard it is to talk about such issues in polite company, how ill equipped we are to hear things that we would rather avoid or deny. How hard it is to change our thinking. Those early mornings were filled with many awkward moments, sometimes confrontational and sometimes amazingly uplifting. Newly remodeled kitchens were unlikely settings to pitch the concept of social justice, the confrontation of racism in America, never mind the undefined and unsettling notion of Black Power. It was an unforgettable lesson in how our society did not then, and does not now, know how to talk about uncomfortable issues. If you want evidence, note the absence of the issue in the last two presidential elections. It took a hurricane to put the issue of race in America back on the burner.

Those breakfast dialogues were the first time I realized how many people of goodwill want to help, want to make a difference, but are also skeptical and do not know how. From 1968 through the early 1970s, more than 2,500 Bostonians joined FUND as a tentative first step toward standing up to be counted.

These experiences, even figuring in my naïveté, good intentions, youth, and a healthy dose of guilt, raised questions that I struggle with to this day.

These are not principally questions of what impact or results we achieved, which were modest, although that remains the unfinished business. Nor is it about my own motivation and ambiguous involvement, though I learned a lot from examining both. The bigger questions center on the immense difficulty in bridging different worlds. The life of a suburban family, with the means to remodel a kitchen, juxtaposed with a family living day to day on the street, whether that street is in São Paulo or Boston, is like night and day. Is it possible to talk across such great distance? Is it possible to relate, to listen as citizens? Making that happen may be the most important thing of all. If we do not get it right, what we want to accomplish will not work.

It is also about what we take away from such experiences, and what we do with what we have learned. It comes back to whether we choose to walk by or walk in.

It is discouraging but perhaps not surprising that this kind of mistake happens all the time, sometimes on a much larger scale. There is a neighborhood in Baltimore called Sandhurst. In the early 1990s, Sandhurst was the site of a comprehensive, neighborhood community development effort. Conceived by the Enterprise Foundation and funded by a number of national foundations, it was very ambitious. Unlike our rump effort in the 1960s, there were many sophisticated actors in the Sandhurst story. After investing a lot of money and experiencing several years of frustration, the project failed for essentially the same reasons ours had failed thirty years before. It lacked the filter, the lens of the community, and the voices of those most involved. Defining what the community is may not be easy, but it is the very first step in tackling any serious philanthropic or social change work.

And through it all, that hard question from my memorable night long ago in the NAACP office in Boston hangs in the air: "Who are we, who am I, to come to a place that is not my own and presume to do good works?"

It hangs there still.

We all begin our journey from a certain place and with a certain perspective. These experiences from many years ago are mine. They taught me many things, but perhaps the most important among them was to listen to the voices.

Reader's Guide Questions

1. Can you conceive of a "world imagined as the ultimate good"?
2. What draws you to seek some larger purpose in your life? What holds you back? What holds others back?

3. Did the author's story "The Hard Way" resonate? It was difficult to talk racism in the late 1960s. Is it any easier now?

4. Do you think of your life as a journey?

Notes

"Final Soliloquy of the Interior Paramour," from *The Collected Poems of Wallace Stevens* by Wallace Stevens, copyright 1954 by Wallace Stevens and renewed 1982 by Holly Stevens. Used by permission of Alfred A. Knopf, a division of Random House, Inc.

1. H. Peter Karoff, ed., *Just Money—A Critique of Contemporary American Philanthropy* (Boston: TPI Editions, 2004).

2. James Wallace, ed., *Virtues and Vices* (Ithaca, N.Y.: Cornell University Press, 1978).

3. These words are adapted from Robert Frost's definition of what makes a good poem—that the poet had something to say, was true to it, and used good words.

4. Clarion—the sound of a trumpet, loud and clear, rallying and rousing.

5. Georg Feurerstein, *The Yoga-Sutra–Pantanjali: A New Translation and Commentary* (self-published); also *The Yoga Sutras*, Microsoft Reader Series.

6. John Latouche wrote the lyrics to "Ballad for Americans," and Earl Robinson wrote the music. Billed as a modern cantata, it was published in 1940 when Paul Robeson debuted the work on national radio to a sensational response.

7. From the poem "Cellist" by Carl Rakosi.

8. From a conversation with William Pounds, professor emeritus at MIT, former dean of the Sloan School of Management, and senior adviser to the Rockefeller Family.

LISTEN TO THE VOICES

Midori

In each piece I play there lives a story created by all the lives that made this music happen. Of course, those included would be the life of the composer, lives of artists who have performed the work, as well as the lives of the listeners. I am a listener too, as well as a player, and each time I listen I have an experience unique in its time and space, an experience distinct, but not necessarily better from that of other listeners.[1]

THE VIOLINIST Midori Goto is wise in understanding that every player, irrespective of fame, position, and domain plays within the context of a broad and multifaceted story.

To be a good listener means putting aside our "presumption of brilliance" and subjugating one's ego, one's preconceived conceptions and prejudices. In this way listening becomes the bridge of learning between what we know, or think we know, and the knowledge we lack.

Who are the great listeners in the world?

Studs Terkel, who for over four decades listened to workers of all stripes and wrote books that are an on-the-ground sociology of our time and place. Alan Lomax, who in the 1950s took a tape recorder into remote rural communities, prisons, Grange Halls and bars, and in the process saved a generation's indigenous music.[2] Paul Simon, who went to South Africa and wrote music that caught so movingly the life and rhythm of that country. I think of Adrian Nicole Le Blanc's remarkable book, *Random Family: Love, Drugs, Trouble and Coming of Age in the Bronx*, the result of ten years of close observation and listening to the hard and unrelentingly sad life of two young women.

And I think of my father, whom people sought out and confided in. I remember as a kid working afternoons in his hardware store, how customers, men and woman, many of them with accents touched with Polish and Lithuanian, would stay and talk and talk. My father's warm, pleasant face, leaning toward the person, nodding sympathetically about who knows what.

Here is a family that listened carefully to the story of other families:

Paul and Phyllis Fireman have a family foundation. They and their son Dan are meeting with Sister Margaret and Nancy, two women who run a highly regarded shelter for homeless families. They have what seems to be a good idea, which is to help these families transition from the shelter into apartments—providing money for furniture and up-front rental costs. Three women who have made the journey from homelessness are participating in the meeting. The discussion starts out awkwardly, but gradually everyone warms up, and the women tell their stories. It becomes clear that it will take more than getting into an apartment to put them back on track. What they need most are jobs that can support their families. One says, "It would almost be worse to move into a new apartment and then get evicted and end up back on the street six months later because I couldn't afford the rent."

At the end of the evening, Paul turned to Phyllis and his grown children and said, "These families are not so different from ours. We always had money and other resources to throw at our problems. Enough bad luck, and this could have been us." It was a major revelation for the Firemans, and one that led the foundation to focus on education and jobs that would pay enough to provide real economic independence. It led them on a path that has at the end the goal of ending family homelessness in Massachusetts. They believe it can be done.

Melinda Marble also believes it can be done.

And she is not afraid of telling others what they need to hear. I learned to love that conviction and passion when she joined TPI in 1989 and pushed us to understand that people at the center of problems need to be at the center of their solution. That was her mantra when, as vice president at the Boston Foundation in the 1990s, she led this large community foundation's efforts in community development and the fight against persistent poverty. For Melinda, listening is not passive; it is the first step in enabling and empowering others.

"You also need a leadership commitment from influential people, and you need people in between who know how to navigate the horrendous complexities of making any real change happen, but you really must have key folks from the ground up," she told us.

Is there frustration in building that sort of constituency, with all the vying interests and agendas and different levels of expertise? "It is no more frustrating than dealing with a corporate CEO or public official. Everyone has limits. CEOs tend to think that if they decree something, it will happen. They tend not to be good at figuring out the messy stuff, or recognizing all the steps that need to happen in the process of change. Change is hard for everybody no matter where they come from. I've always been energized and moved by how people who have very few resources and have seldom been listened to can become so powerful when given their voice."

It was Melinda who arranged that memorable meeting between Sister Margaret and the Fireman family, and today Melinda is executive director of the Paul and Phyllis Fireman Charitable Foundation and the architect of the One Family Campaign to end family homelessness in Massachusetts.

Homelessness is a tough problem, and despite the economic boom in the 1990s, it has gotten worse. The rise in real estate prices has only exacerbated the problem of housing for the poor. On any given day, eight hundred thousand people are homeless in the United States, a quarter of those children—more than two hundred thousand. The shelter system has heroically attempted to put a roof over their heads, but the cost of this emergency response in human and financial terms has been great.

"Every day, I hear stories that convince me that extended stays in shelters do incalculable multigenerational harm. Listening to people in the throes of the problem is at the very center of any successful change effort. You may need to provide direct support, you may also need a systems change piece and a public information and engagement piece, but hearing those personal stories gives you the clearest picture of what needs to happen."

At the center of the One Family Campaign is a program that provides scholarships to formerly homeless women in Massachusetts. Education, mentoring, and leadership training are providing a path out of poverty. "We learned from them the limits of an emergency response. We began to understand the context of homelessness and became interested in going beyond shelter to real transformation and systems change."

People need a safe place to tell their stories, Melinda says. "When you are seeking big change, there is always something or someone who is being threatened. In the case of homelessness, an entire industry has grown up around creating shelter. It's managed by people who justifiably feel good about what they do. But we provided a safe place for people inside and outside the industry to get together and respectfully challenge one another to think about the problem in a whole new way."

Melinda is a natural for this work, but she describes falling into it. Although her family was never homeless, her dad was unemployed for several years, which made their economic life uncertain. Melinda experienced the stress this can place on families. Her mother, who was a social activist in a conservative community, had a huge influence on her, and so did the community.

"I grew up in a segregated part of Southern California where most of my elementary school classmates were Mexican or Mexican American farmworkers' kids. From an early age, I noticed they were treated very differently from me in school. Later I became aware of the racism that permeated every institution that dealt with them.

"Becoming a journalist and exposing injustice was the plan, but in college I fell into an internship with the San Francisco Study Center, a nonprofit that taught neighborhood people how to research their communities so they could take action on their own behalves."

She got interested in figuring out how to support local people who had agendas to push forward. She created a guide to understanding the city budget, wrote counter environmental impact reports on major developments, and trained people how to look at property records and find out who owned land in the neighborhood and what plans they had for it.

That led to an invitation to join the Resource Exchange, a unique Rockefeller Foundation initiative that connected small groups of young, multiracial neighborhood leaders with local corporate CEOs in San Francisco and other cities in the 1970s. "The dynamic was one of alienated children battling it out with their parents over dinner once a month. Many of us had never known a corporate person. They were like another species to us."

These skirmishes with big corporate chiefs took a lot of preparation. The "kids" had to figure out how they could work effectively in coalition and stand up to the heat. Before long, both sides had learned the value in the match.

"One of the most stunning moments for me came in helping start up a neighborhood association in a rundown area of rooming houses and strip joints in San Francisco called the Tenderloin. We were trying to convince the city that it was also a residential neighborhood, being overlooked, that deserved parks and planning. At one Resource Exchange meeting, I hosted a tour of the area. Tom Clauson, who was then president of Bank of America, looked up and saw his company's headquarters from a new perspective, looming over the block. 'My God, the whole neighborhood is in our shadow,' he said. It was an 'ah-ha' moment for him, and for me, a good lesson in the importance of getting people to see things up close."

In the mid-1980s, Melinda came east, bringing her practitioners perspective to teaching nonprofit training courses at Tufts University. Influenced by the work of John McKnight, who is now director of Community Studies at Northwestern University, she began to focus on how human service delivery systems took a deficit approach to people, describing them as a set of problems and needs instead of looking at their natural capacities.

"Every community, even the poorest, has assets, and building on those is the first step in community change. Yet institutions at every level diminish what people have to offer. Talking to the people 'living it' seems like such a common sense approach, but it's a step we often resist or do in a very shallow way, perhaps out of the discomfort of invading someone else's private life. My graduate students would rather theorize, or do anything except talk to the people involved. When I could get them off their butts, they would come back full of energy and interest."

Take the student who was trying to start a model recycling program and getting a lot of resistance from the city. "He was furious and full of reasons for why it was happening. I suggested he spend a day riding around on the trucks and talking with the garbage collectors. He did, and he figured out what needed to happen to overcome many of the institutional obstacles. He also saw that garbage collector supervisors, a relatively minor position in terms of city power, had the ability to thwart his plans. He set out to win them over, and he did.

"My vision for the world in the simplest sense is what most of us want: a place where everybody has food, clothing, shelter, freedom, and opportunity. Less simply, it is a world where our public policies are considered with love and interdependence. One way to get there is to radically change professional practice so that community building strategies take into account people's assets and what they have to offer. And we need to give people bridging skills so they will bring new partners to the table.

"What gives me hope, and what makes working in philanthropy one of the greatest jobs in the world, is the tremendous number of good people out there who are working hard to help others. They are what keep me from despairing. I hope their numbers will grow and that they are celebrated, made heroic, in ways that other kinds of heroes are. It seems almost as if they are holding the world together, holding a thousand streamers of light that are keeping the planet on course in some way.

"Nevertheless, I take a pretty clear-eyed look at the evil or injustice that exists; glossing it over or denying it would be a disservice. But given all that, I take joy in people's small efforts to combat what is wrong, and joy in the occasional victories. I do believe, with the Buddha, that living is suffering to some extent, and what you can do in the face of that is to minimize the suffering.

"I think about a comment from one of our scholars that when she was homeless she felt absolutely no one cared, but now she has become confident about the compassion in the world. Over the last couple of years, working under very difficult circumstances, we have helped make significant change happen in getting the state out of the motel business. We have done that in lots of discrete ways, like gaining access for more people to utility discount programs. We now have ninety to one hundred empty family shelter beds every night in the state, which is a huge shift. More importantly, the governor is for the first time shifting money from the shelter budget to prevention. So we are beginning to see movement in this giant system toward a goal that we could barely hope to achieve a few years ago. One of our One Family scholars, a woman who eighteen months ago had been homeless, just bought her first house!

"For real change to happen, people need to feel secure. One of the most useful skills we can develop is the ability to manage our own anxiety and the anxiety of others. This is not a standard part of professional education, but a lot of change comes from keeping people on the growing edge and making them comfortable enough that they can question their own assumptions and change their practice, stretch and do things differently. It is painstaking work to nurture that in other people, work that we don't talk about or understand well, but it is necessary. If I have a skill, it has to do with creating a safe container or atmosphere where people can feel comfortable enough to stretch and grow. That is a skill that we need to consciously cultivate."

Woman's Day magazine named Melinda as one of five to receive its "Women Who Inspire Us" award in 2003. In her response, she asked one thing of the magazine's readers: "The image you have of the homeless—a man begging in the street to collect money for alcohol—is not the entire picture. Many of those who are homeless are women and children struggling to get by, but most of us don't want to think about that.

"The face of the homeless is that of the battered wife who takes her children and leaves her husband and middle-class life," she says. "Or the immigrant mother who works two jobs and lives in a shelter with her children because she can't afford permanent housing. It could be me or anyone I know."

Melinda Marble's story is a perfect way to begin our journey of many stories because it illustrates the need to work with one family and one person at a time, while in the same breath working to change a whole system—in this case, the human service delivery apparatus, governmental and nonprofit—established to deal with homelessness. Bottom up and top down, on the ground and paradigm change, and all the intersections in between that inform each other, and yes, Melinda Marble, you are right, "change comes from keeping people on the growing edge." It is where we need to be.

Reader's Guide Questions

1. Are you a "good" listener? How so?
2. Melinda Marble believes those at the center of problems need to be at the center of their solution. What are the practical implications of that view for recipients and donors?
3. What does it mean to build on a community's assets instead of addressing its liabilities? How does that idea relate to "entire industries" that exist to serve social issues?
4. *Empathy* such as that Paul and Phyllis Fireman felt is powerful. But is it *essential* for social change or not? What could take its place?

Notes

1. Midori Goto, from program notes of Midori's concert given in Santa Barbara, California, in January 2002.
2. The *New York Times*, March 3, 2002, reported that one of those songs, "O Brother, Where Art Thou?" sung in 1959 by an inmate of Camp B of the Mississippi Penitentiary, went to the top of the charts in 2001, and the Lomax family tracked the composer down to give him a big check.

PARADIGMS OF CHANGE

PLAY ON WORDS

In a good play on words
Ideas seem to just emerge,
Fully formed long lyrical lines
From the chamber of a brilliant mind.
Hah! Don't believe it my friends!
Chaos—thousands, thousands of words,
Ideas, theories, notions carom off walls,
Tumble off the backs of one another.
Some drift lazily like hot-air balloons,
Bump gently up against the ceiling
Or as bats do hang upside down.
Others dash madly about like sperm
In passionate search of an egg to fertilize,
While those deemed worthless fall away
And die a slow lingering death.
How sad is the dismembered idea!
Once in a great while an event occurs.
Call it metamorphosis, transformation,
Inspiration out of the incomprehensible—
An idea is born and pops into plain view.
Such joy in the chamber of the mind
As all of those still stuck in chaos party
In everlasting hope their turn will come.
The birth of a good idea is rare indeed.
Even rarer are those who have the gift.
To those who do, we say Salut!

WHILE MY POEM is a bit tongue-in-cheek and pokes fun at those who purposefully set out to create new ideas, the salute at the end is a serious one. Paradigms of change do begin with a good idea. This is especially so with big change goals that aim to shake things up and transform or even revolutionize the way things are. They take great creativity to conceive and equally great drive and will to execute.

Any new idea or theory of change must answer many questions. How does a big new idea become concrete and real? How does an idea become a plan of action? How does an idea move from being on the margins to the mainstream? And behind all of these questions is the one most fundamental: how does change actually happen? Put simply, how does apple pie in the sky become something you can put a scoop of vanilla ice cream on and enjoy the taste of? Here is a somewhat less appetizing story about an incident in the early 1980s in Boston that represents one approach to change.

I was one of six hundred people in the middle of a middling lunch in the Grand Ballroom of the Sheraton Hotel for the annual United Way meeting. Suddenly things got more interesting and a bit dicey. Mel King, an outspoken advocate for the black community in Boston and a champion for the rights of poor people, interrupted the flow of speeches by dumping a few select bags of garbage on the head table. It was quite an attention getter, a tactile and noxious metaphor. To no surprise, Mel King seriously ruffled the feathers of a lot of Boston's most important people.

King's act was born of frustration, out of his desperately wanting to see change in the United Way's allocation of funding. While certainly outrageous, the garbage dump had more theater than substance. It did not bring about meaningful change. The action was based on the tactic of "disruption,"[1] a theory that is making the rounds in business and social policy that says, in general, interests become so entrenched that guerrilla action is necessary. It is, however, only one of many approaches to change.

The term *transformation* connotes huge change. Transformation is when the whole context shifts and people begin to think and act differently. Not all transformations, however, are about system change. If you have any doubt, ask the formerly homeless woman who graduated from the One Scholar program, got a better-paying job, and just bought her first house!

When we see "a unique opportunity that must be taken up,"[2] and we feel a sense of urgency or crisis, we are drawn to act, to stand up and be counted, though perhaps not as directly or dramatically as Mel King. Many people want to move mountains and many of them work to do so.

People are drawn to big change ideas for all kinds of reasons.

- Something is broken and cannot be fixed. It needs to be co-opted, circumvented, or overthrown.
- There is a huge opportunity to solve a market failure or create a new market that doesn't exist.
- You can't get there—"there" being a better place—from where you are today without something very new being added to the equation.
- You feel violated or angry or saddened by something that is very wrong and are compelled to face down that injustice.

When we think about change, we often turn to strategy and a careful analysis of the facts and circumstances. We look for the opportunity where the investment of available resources can most effectively be deployed. A strategic approach, in itself, is not change, but it can be very useful in bringing change about.

There are many kinds of change:

- Change for individuals with astonishing effects on their circumstance and opportunity
- Change in organizational capacity to accomplish big social goals
- Change for neighborhoods and cities to become better places for people to live
- Change in governmental policy through advocacy
- Change in whole systems and fields of interest
- Change in the way people think, in their attitudes, perhaps the most difficult kind of change of all.

Philanthropy is the resource with the least restraints, and thus it should be ideally positioned to be a change agent. But that is not the case. In a report on transformational philanthropy published in 2002,[3] a survey of foundations found that 95 percent of funding was directed to projects or work where the result was

- amelioration—lessening suffering within existing systems;
- adaptation—adjusting current systems; or
- restoration—returning things to their "original condition."

Even if more philanthropy was less risk-averse and more ambitious, it alone would not be enough. Both the market economy and governmental resources dwarf those of private philanthropy. Convincing government to do "the right thing" can result in transformational change in the well-being of society—witness the impact of the GI Bill or Social Security. Government is not viewed, however, as a source of innovation or as a risk taker, whereas the business community is. This is where entrepreneurs enter the scene.

Greg Dees, who teaches at Duke University's Fuqua School of Business, writes, "Put simply, entrepreneurs implement new and better ways of doing things. Entrepreneurs change the pattern of production by combining elements in new ways. The new pattern of production should be superior to the old pattern. They are, in a sense, innovators."[4]

What would happen if successful entrepreneurs from the business world became convinced that the market economy can and should address social dilemmas? What would happen if those who operate in the nonprofit space were to adapt competitive entrepreneurial approaches to their work? What would happen if these two forces were to bob and weave and join forces?

Let's find out, and begin with someone who has formed a company appropriately named for our purposes—Revolution!

Revolution—A World-Class Business with a Social Mission

"In 2005, I founded a company called Revolution, whose mission is to give people more choice, convenience and control over key aspects of their lives—especially their health care. The profits we intend to make will arise from our ability to advance the public good—whether building clinics where a sick child can be seen quickly and affordably on a Sunday, or creating online health portals where consumers can get reliable information about physicians, or providing people tools to better manage health care spending, or any number of other potential consumer-empowering innovations. Revolution's stakeholders are not just its investors but society overall."

This is the voice of Steve Case, who first burst onto the national scene as the cofounder of America Online (AOL) and the person responsible for building that company into an e-economy phenomenon. He was also involved in one of the largest and most controversial corporate mergers in history when AOL joined with Time Warner. When I first met Steve, in the early days of AOL long before it became a powerhouse, he talked passionately about his vision of how the Internet could become a transformational force for good. So we are listening to someone with a track record of taking new ideas and technologies and making them into large-scale enterprises that have changed the way we live.

In business life, he has always been attracted to bold ideas—what the authors of the management bible *Built to Last* memorably termed "Big Hairy Audacious Goals." The entrepreneurs he admires the most are the ones who swing for the fences, setting out to conquer brave new worlds that others can barely imagine.

"I am drawn to the same approach in philanthropic endeavors. It is idealistic, maybe arrogant, even crazy, but I'm interested in transformational change that lifts millions of people's lives. And to get there, I think we need to expand perceptions of how to engage in philanthropy—to bring in new actors and forge new alliances that maximize our collective abilities. After all, at its root, 'philanthropy' doesn't mean charity; it means love for humankind. Expressing that love shouldn't be restricted to giving money away, but should encompass a range of efforts that promote and improve human welfare.

"In the world I want, people would embrace a new paradigm for serving society, one that bridges traditional divides between the business and social sectors. For years, we've accepted the basic view that nonprofits' job is to fight for good and for-profits should help foot the bill. Yet, there's no real reason to wall off the roles of nonprofit and for-profit enterprises, when what really counts is what each can do to enhance people's lives overall. I want to help build a world where their roles are more fluid and synergistic, where businesses also have social missions and nonprofits are entrepreneurial, and together, they form a single, shining constellation for social change."

This notion may be heretical to purists in both the private and nonprofit sectors. But just as the birth of stars in the cosmos is a stormy, furious process, creating this new constellation for change will demand a degree of disruption, Steve says.

"As companies and nonprofits, donors and grantees, we all need to be open to bigger risks, bolder leaps, and new ways of doing business if that's what it takes to best serve our clients and best advance our causes. Because however unsettling the prospect of change, the status quo is untenable."

Is it untenable because the market is demanding change?

"Yes, one of the key things that drove AOL was to lower the barriers between technology and the consumer. To give the consumer, the citizen, more power. We leveled the playing field, connecting people to each other, a fundamentally democratizing process. At a certain point there is no turning back and it continues to drive the expanding use of the Internet. Those are the key things that attract me. Even though different industries or programs have different circumstances, the challenges are remarkably similar. I don't know why I am wired to think this way, but I am."

He may be wired to transformation, but "disruption" is part of the process, as he sees it. Disruption jars people and that is sometimes helpful. It forces people out of their comfort zones, which is necessary if you are trying to get them to think more broadly.

"Most large companies are structured to protect what is there and incrementally develop new business in a relatively risk averse way. The same is true of established nonprofit organizations and institutions. There is nothing wrong with that, but it does not interest me.

"Sometimes ideas are not ready for the mainstream, and that is a fascinating challenge. What interests me is to find the connections between ideas, books, people, different subjects and walk away from ten different meetings seeing the threads that tie them all together. OK, if something works there, maybe applying it over here will work. If it doesn't work, why not, when it seemed like it should have? Do you give up on it? Adapt it? For me, it is a matter of looking for those kinds of connections."

Steve speaks to the strains in the nonprofit world where too often even outstanding organizations are failing to reach their potential. They are not self-sustaining. They cannot scale up. They are competing for resources against like-minded groups, when almost none of them are serving all the people who need their help. And part of the problem is that even when nonprofits are doing pathbreaking work, the market mechanisms that would help innovative businesses grow to greatness—from mezzanine financing to management consulting—simply aren't available to them.

"I believe part of the solution for the challenges facing nonprofits is looking for ways to become more entrepreneurial, including, when appropriate, finding ways to generate their own revenue. That's why in my home state of Hawaii the Case Foundation has worked closely with the Hawaii Community Foundation to develop social sector leaders, for example, through a social enterprise training program for nonprofit professionals. The foundation also invested in the University of Hawaii business plan competition on the condition that it added a social enterprise category to support the next generation of creative nonprofit executives. And at the national level, we've been strong supporters of the Social Enterprise Alliance, which brings together social service organizations, funders, and investors to build a dynamic community of sustainable nonprofits.

"I've also tried to walk the 'entrepreneurial nonprofit' talk myself. In 2001, my family founded Accelerate Brain Cancer Cure (ABC^2) so others wouldn't suffer the sense of hopelessness we did when my late brother Dan was diagnosed with this incurable and largely untreatable disease. Brain cancer has for many years been viewed as a dead-end disease. As Dr. David Agus of Cedars-Sinai Medical Center put it, 'No cure, no hope, too few people afflicted, no funding.' ABC² took an aggressive, disruptive approach to alter this grim prognosis. We started from the goal we wanted to achieve: getting more promising drugs more quickly into the clinical pipeline. Then we developed a strategy to blaze a fast-track course to that end.

"ABC² used its convening power to break down the silos that separated government, academia, and pharmaceutical companies, bringing experts together from all these arenas to share and build support for promising research under way. It created financial incentives for scientists to spur pioneering research and helped them navigate bureaucratic hurdles to move their efforts forward. It invested in young physician-scientists who are building careers in translational medicine, with three-year awards to hone their expertise in neuro-oncology. The results are clear: Since 2001, the number of therapies in preclinical trial has soared from 20 to 120; clinical trials for the kind of cancer that killed Dan have multiplied from about 20 per year to 80 in 2004.

"ABC² also built coalitions beyond its narrow focus, so related organizations could combine and leverage assets for common goals. For example, a major problem for treating any brain disease is bypassing the blood brain barrier—the body's mechanism for keeping foreign substances from injuring the brain. In October 2004, ABC² convened a meeting of the other advocacy groups and funders to form a Brain Trust network and identify opportunities for collaboration. In April 2005, the Brain Trust launched a common award program to mobilize blood-brain barrier breakthroughs that can hold great potential for all of us.

"Now, ABC² has reached another stage in its development. It was launched, as many nonprofits are, to address a worthy social concern that the for-profit market couldn't or wouldn't. But, four years later, we've learned that success in accelerating a cure for brain cancer and other brain diseases demands tapping into the kinds of resources that only the for-profit market can provide.

"Philanthropies and government can effectively generate promising therapies and technologies, but there's a missing tier of funding and skills for therapies that are too far along for philanthropy but too young to attract corporate investment. As a result, good work is getting lost in the gap between the lab and the clinic. To bridge that gap, ABC² is exploring the launch of the Brain Trust Accelerator Fund[5]—a for-profit initiative that will invest venture capital in these critical stages of selecting, testing and advancing auspicious therapies. Designed to appeal to those who crave meaning as well as money from their investments, the fund will offer double return—profits, yes, and the priceless satisfaction of helping to save people's lives. As general partner, ABC² will invest a portion of its management fee and profits from this fund back into brain charities, ensuring the fund's financial success only further fuels the cause.

"ABC² is trying to model a new kind of nonprofit approach, including spinning off a for-profit venture that preserves a social mission. Yet, in the world I dream of, revolutionary social change can't be led by nonprofits alone. I dream of an even brighter constellation that also harnesses the power of the private sector and brings it to bear in a manner that serves society at large."

Some people are saying we are entering the participation age and the end points are starting to influence the center. Is that what Steve means?

"Absolutely, and that is largely driven by technology's capacity to level the playing field and connect people to each other and information they otherwise would not have access to. It is fundamentally empowering and democratic. That is what is driving people's use of the Internet. Initially it was kind of interesting, something else I could do with my computer, track stocks or pay my bills. It gradually became a whole new way to communicate—e-mail, instant messaging, and these things became an embedded part of people's lives. That is still the case and now it is moving in an incredible number of directions. So what was originally a crazy idea has become mainstream, and very quickly."

What one would love to see is a political will bounce from this democratizing flow of information and communication.

"I think I first became aware of this in 2000, but the [Howard] Dean presidential campaign proved how a candidate could build grass roots support and fundraise in totally different ways, and it didn't take long for all the other candidates to jump in. The next wave of political activity is absolutely going to be more Internet driven."

Steve may well be part of that. The traditional model for business leaders is first you focus on learning, then you focus on earning, and at some later point in life you focus on giving back, either by giving money away or by engaging in public service. That model has produced some philanthropic titans, but at forty-eight years of age, Steve has a different notion of giving back.

"I'm interested in a more integrated approach to business and philanthropy, one that blurs the line between profit making and community building and advances the aims of both. I want to help create a culture where entrepreneurs aim to do well and do good all at once, where our interests and ideals are not separate or sequenced, but part of the same bottom line.

"One option some visionary companies have adopted is weaving philanthropy into their corporate DNA. Timberland is an example, whose long-term strategic partnership with City Year has not only helped build a national youth corps, strengthen communities, and advance social justice but also reinforced the company's overarching commitment to make it better.

"Another approach is pursuing what my friend David Cole calls a 'holistic' business strategy—one that aims to add to the health and wealth of the community as well as the company. David is CEO of Maui Land and Pineapple (MLP), a landowning company with resort and agricultural interests in Hawaii. When I first invested in MLP in 2001, its unprofitable pineapple production was bleeding millions every year. Meanwhile, Maui was struggling with issues like youth unemployment, urban sprawl, and the rising cost of living.

"Today, led by David, MLP is transforming both itself and the community it shares. To give just one example, MLP is working with nonprofit partners, including the Case Foundation, to sponsor training in land-based arts for students at the local community college. David calls this 'growing the growers' while at the same time preserving Maui's natural beauty and reducing Hawaii's dependence on imported food.

"A third approach, and the one to which I've committed for the long haul, is building world-class businesses that also have a social mission. To my mind, the greatest reward of entrepreneurship isn't simply making money but making a difference in people's lives—and business today has an unparalleled ability to do that on a large scale.

"When my brother fell sick, I experienced firsthand the many inefficiencies, frustrations, and failures of the American health care system. I spent hours struggling to collect and decipher information to choose the best specialists for his care. I waited with him in hospital lines for blood tests he could easily have administered at home. Few things are more important to people than their health and that of their loved ones. Yet the health care sector, which will soon represent one out of every five dollars in the U.S. economy, today is working well for almost no one."

Many who have followed the health care crisis believe it's a hopeless case. Government has not cured the system's ills. Philanthropy clearly cannot, either. But Steve believes the private sector can play a transformational role by focusing relentlessly on shifting power to the ones who matter most: consumers.

"When it comes to health care, we are not looking for incremental change. The goal is to transform the way the system works, and there is no question it will be disruptive.

Twenty years ago, when people thought I was a little over the top, it did not strike me as far-fetched or futuristic to imagine a world where consumers were in the driver's seat, and had more choices in terms of information, communication, and entertainment. People were couch potatoes then, and the whole idea of interactivity struck me as logical. The same is true today in the health care system. I have no doubt that twenty years from now consumers will be more in the driver's seat, have more choices, control, and convenience. How we get there is less clear, but one way or another health care will change."

What about the role of government?

"My view is that government must set the basic ground rules, make the investment in the core enabling infrastructure, and then it needs to get out of the way and let the free market work. A good example is the Internet. The government made some initial investment in building the core infrastructure, which was initially for Department of Defense national security purposes. It was only in 1992 that the Internet became available for commercial development, and look what has happened. It's hard to know if it should have been done sooner or later, but you have to agree it has worked out pretty well.

"Generally my view is less regulation is better in the early stages. You just don't know what to regulate. The risk is that government overregulates and overreacts based on abuse from a few. It is probably wishful thinking, but I would like to see the private sector more responsible for self-regulation."

Clearly there are many social issues that will always need government or philanthropic support. How far can you take this idea?

"To some degree the question is irrelevant. It will happen to the extent it can happen, but I do think the entrepreneurial approach can be taken across the board, for profit and nonprofit. You can't do much in the way of social redemption with a heroin dealer, but almost every business has the potential to find an alignment with a social objective. There are those situations, and social needs, where the dependency on government and charitable dollars is just in the nature of the problem. There are also lots of situations that are in the middle and that could do a lot better in generating income. They will not all be hugely profitable, but they will be more sustainable, which for social ventures is very much on the asset side of the question. In my mind, I keep coming back to the idea that the business model is the best way to provide scaleable resources."

Steve has had an amazing roller-coaster entrepreneurial ride. What has he learned from that experience?

"I have had firsthand experience of what happens when the bridges that need to be built within an organization were never built, and how difficult it is for even a great company to interface with its own huge resources. Even when the ideas and assets are in place, you need the people with the right passion and commitment, or it can all fall apart. Having lived through that has only reaffirmed my conviction that the entrepreneurial approach is the only approach to achieve transformational change.

"And I think the real potential of organizations like ABC[2] and Revolution is that they don't just balance purpose and profit—they try to integrate and maximize both. In the world I want, sector-blending organizations will be the norm, and the potential to make our lives better and brighter is huge."

Is that what you mean by revolutionary?

"Exactly."

And so Steve Case has given us a vision of integration and light, one that is synonymous with hope. He is not alone in this quest.

eBay and the New Way

It is fun to be with Pierre Omidyar. In the first place, he is friendly, relaxed, open, and engaging. In the second place, he is a certified wunderkind, founder of the phenomenon called eBay, and he is worth, according to *Forbes* magazine, an amazing $10 billion. That he looks like a kid and is utterly without pretension only adds to the gestalt.

I first met Pierre at the World Economic Forum in Davos, Switzerland. We are now in a conference room at the Redwood City, California, offices of Omidyar Network, and once again I am transfixed. I have purposely taken off my tie and am trying to readjust my New England demeanor to match Pierre, who makes me feel like I am talking to an old and good friend. In a way, he has become such a friend to the 160 million people who regularly use eBay.

Pierre and his Network have come out of the flow of the eBay experience. We are here, as we were with Steve Case, at the crossroad, the intersection, between technology and the domain of money and social dilemmas. There is great ambition in this room.

"The elevator speech for Omidyar Network goes like this. The goal is to invest in initiatives that promote individual self-empowerment, whether it's economic self-empowerment, social self-empowerment, or political self-empowerment. We are looking for programs that help people to discover their own power. We believe those opportunities are extensive and lie in both the business sector as well as in the social sector."

An Omidyar *Network*—what does that mean?

"We chose the name very intentionally. We were thinking about others who want to impact the world, and how we could help them connect to one another. We are just part of it, part of an ecosystem that hopefully will help people think more about the world in innovative ways. To think about the role of business making the world a better place, for instance.

"When I look at eBay in more fundamental ways, the most exciting aspect is the economic self-empowerment that goes on that in turn has a social impact. More than three-quarters of a million people make their living on eBay, and we were not even in business ten years ago! Equally interesting, 160 million people have learned that they can trust a stranger. That is, I know, a very generous interpretation, and it's not the first thing that people would think of, but you can't conduct commerce without some degree of trust. It exists, and it seems to me important that it does exist. One of the really great side effects of eBay's business is that it helps people see that they have some-thing in common with other people who outwardly may be very different from them. It helps people find the connections that are so critical in the building of community.

"We didn't start out with any of this in mind. eBay was not founded as a nonprofit to create social impact but was started as a company, a for-profit in order to make money. But along the way, the business model by definition had to have this kind of social impact in order to be successful."

What Pierre describes is an example of the rule of "unintended conse-quences" and how we often back into results we did not in the least expect. It happens all the time.

A business that also became a community seems rare, but when you get down to it, the same types of things that make communities work make com-merce work.

"You have to connect with someone who shares your interest; you have to develop enough trust and confidence—not that you have to trust them with your life—but there has to be enough trust that you are willing to conduct a transaction. That in and of itself is a social benefit."

In an era that has seen the loss of trust in major institutions and across every sector of society, that indeed is a huge social benefit!

"When Omidyar Network started to explore the opportunities, what struck me was that we shouldn't do it just by focusing on the nonprofit world when the distinction between the nonprofit and the business sector doesn't really need to exist. If eBay has provided what I think is a really neat and tremendous value added to society, why not extend that concept? That is the premise for Omidyar Network, and it opens up a world of opportunity."

Most successful entrepreneurs who talk about their contribution to soci-ety will say, "My biggest contribution, more than any philanthropy, has been providing thirty thousand jobs." Is that what Pierre means?

"I think that is absolutely true, and it goes back to Adam Smith, who believed that given the right environment, business success is evidence of improving the general welfare."

Maybe Pierre is talking about "the Invisible Hand,"[6] but that is not created by intent or design; it simply flows secondarily out of the business activity, as in the creation of jobs.

"The social impact is typically not by design, but in the Omidyar Network way of thinking, it is a necessary condition of the business's success, or we are not interested. The Adam Smith example is, if the baker can sell a loaf of bread to the shoemaker and make a little bit of money doing it, the shoemaker has paid a fair price for the bread and is able to feed his family. The baker is able to take that profit and buy shoes. Clearly our modern economies are much more complex today than they were in Adam Smith's time, but the basic principle still holds true."

The principle may hold, but how far can it go? After all, a business is business.

"Today, yes, but if more people thought about the role of business in these terms, and looked for business models that can only be successful if they have a social impact, than we have shifted the social dynamics."

It is true that even a modest shift in the market economy would be significant.

"Omidyar Network won't do a deal unless we can see the social potential. For us to invest, we need to see the link between a societal impact and the success of the business. If the business success itself is clear evidence of the social impact, it makes your life a little bit easier. Measuring a social return is a very fuzzy and difficult thing to do. So, if you can say, 'The business can only succeed if it has a social impact, well, that's not bad.'"

OK, we have the baker and we have eBay. How do these principles transfer operationally for Omidyar Network?

"We have tried to distill the lessons into a couple of factors that we look for in businesses and nonprofit situations. There has to be a level playing field. There has to be equal access to information, to tools, to opportunities. It has to be open and transparent, and enable connections around shared interests. And the final point is that there has to be a strong sense of ownership among participants; people have to have skin in the game. Those four factors are the things that we look for before we will invest."

What happens to philanthropy in this dichotomy?

"Omidyar Network is an umbrella organization. We invest in the for-profit side as well as the nonprofit side. There are lots of great examples of nonprofits that also provide opportunity for individual self-empowerment that we'll continue to fund through our nonprofit checkbook. We really try to look at what the goals are and what the programs are doing.

What is the single biggest difference between the market economy and the nonprofit sector?

"If you want to reach scale, really large scale, I think you have to do it through the business sector, through the market economy. The economic model in the nonprofit sector for large scale simply does not exist. The only examples that I know of successful large-scale enterprises are commercial. There are lots of great multinational nonprofit organizations as well, but in terms of reaching hundreds of millions of people, the only way is through a commercial effort.

"There are other factors as well, such as the mind-set of doing business. The nonprofit-minded way puts doing good as the first priority. Of course that's the point, but I think that approach is inherently self-limiting, and it puts a constraint on an organization. What we are trying to do at Omidyar Network is to broaden the conversation. There is definitely a role for the non-profit sector, and there are many places where there are market failures, where the commercial sector cannot clearly operate effectively. So I do not in any way want to diminish the role for the nonprofit as well as public sector.

"In order for the commercial sector and businesses and nonprofits to function at their highest levels, they have to operate in the right regulatory environment, which is a critical responsibility of the public sector. My view is the primary role of government is to establish the conditions through which individuals can pursue their own self-interest and that this will inevitably lead to social benefit."

This is a very minimalist view of the role of government, even as it relates to establishing social policy, but Pierre has his rationale.

"As soon as government begins to try to tell people what they ought to be doing, even if well meaning, then it starts to limit the capability of our society to address our problems. I think the framers of the U.S. Constitution understood that idea. The Constitution does not tell you what you can or should do. It sets a structure, and it has certain limiting factors around what you can do. But overall it is an enabling document to allow individuals to create the society that they want to live in.

"One of my core beliefs is that people are basically good, so the notion of helping people connect to one another becomes incredibly important. It is because of those connections that they can manifest that basic goodness and work together around shared areas of interest. I know that might sound trite or naive, but just look what happened at eBay. If people weren't basically good, it just couldn't exist. I mean, you have $40 billion worth of transactions, and you know there is a whole lot of opportunity for people who might be basically bad. Every community has some people who are bad and basically take advantage of the community, but they are few."

We are in this really interesting time in human history where technology is enabling these kinds of connections on an unprecedented scale. And the strength of those connections allows people to have a greater impact on the world around them. That's a very exciting thing. It is sounds like an extension of open source thinking and acting.

"Open source in the context of the social sector, for me, has the characteristics of transparency and equal access. People can come together, and no matter where they are from, no matter what school they went to, what jobs they have held, they can actually interact with one another on a level playing field and contribute. So open source, in my mind, means you make your system open and anyone can show up, contribute their thoughts, and be respected for the ideas that they have."

Is this interaction similar to the principles of community organizing that earlier generations grew up with?

"I think there is some commonality with traditional community organizing principles, but it is also different in one important way. My emphasis is on something that we call 'bottom up.' This is a part of the business lexicon these days. At Omidyar Network we like to talk about self-empowerment. That is a very important semantic difference. It is not that we are giving power to an individual. It is that we are helping that individual discover that they have the power."

In what way is that different?

"Quite often advocacy efforts and organizing efforts have a certain agenda associated with them. They might be wonderful and I might agree with them but the way Omidyar Network thinks about things is minus an agenda. We just want people to have the tools they need to discover their own power to pursue whatever agenda they want."

Without being facetious, Pierre is assuming that the result will be more good than bad agendas. Some might disagree.

"There are certainly bad agendas, but I go back to my belief that you can trust people to be basically good. I think we are beginning to see social, class, and political connections grow, driven by technology. Blogs are increasing and evolving. More and more individuals are discovering their ability to have an impact around things they care about, and they are exercising that power. The wonderful thing is that once somebody discovers that power, there is no going back. You are not going to be able to take it away from them."

The picture that Pierre draws sounds an awful lot like democracy.

"I think so. I'm very passionate about the theory of democracy which cannot exist without individuals connecting with others."

Perhaps Omidyar Network's motto could be the opening lines of Walt Whitman's *Leaves of Grass*—"One's self I sing the single separate person/ Yet utter the word democratic, the word en masse!"

This is sounding good as theory. What has Pierre thus far found that exemplifies these ideas?

"One field that wraps economic self-empowerment, social self-empowerment, and political self-empowerment is microfinance. It is a perfect map to all of the things that we care about. It is giving somebody the tools—in this case capital—that they need to help themselves. It is not going in and saying, 'Well, you're poor, and therefore you need our help.' It is saying, 'You probably already know what you need to do to make your family better off. You just need a helping hand to get you there.' The loan gives you that helping hand."

I think Pierre has just expanded Adam Smith's theory from the Invisible Hand to the Helping Hand. I wonder whether Smith would approve.[7]

"He might not, but he would like the business model of microfinance because it is inherently a profitable model. The loan helps people get on the road out of poverty. And then it comes back to the bank and can be loaned to the next person. Microfinance can sustain itself, and therefore it has the potential to reach scale."

Microcredit is sort of a hybrid, though; it requires philanthropy or soft dollars to get it going.

"That has been true so far. All the models that we've seen have been hybrids, so one of the things that we are trying to do is to push that conversation along and see if that can be changed. The field is very exciting because of its promise."

Today there are more than sixty-five million people who currently participate in microcredit, which is a pretty significant number.

"Obviously millions of people's lives have been changed which is terrific, but there are more than three hundred million poor families on the planet. At the moment, the largest microcredit organizations don't have more than four or five million clients apiece. In order to reach scale—and I'm talking about three hundred million scale—you need to invest heavily in the creation of large, scaleable institutions. If the profitability potential in microfinance can be realized, then you can go to the financial markets and raise all of the capital you need. And then we'll get to the three hundred million clients sooner than you might imagine."

Microcredit most often empowers poor women, and in some societies that has led to difficult situations—and, in some cases, violence.

"That is of course very troubling, but hopefully those are rare incidents. The primary focus of Omidyar Network is on economic self-empowerment. It turns out the microfinance model demonstrates that economic self-empowerment often leads to social and political empowerment as well. We think that's fundamentally good for humanity, and hopefully over time the dislocations or disruptions that may be caused in a society will lessen."

In late 2005, Pierre and his wife Pam Omidyar announced an unusual $100 million gift to Tufts University. Both Pierre and Pam are graduates of Tufts and had previously funded its innovative University College of Citizenship and Public Service. The gift to Tufts, in addition to its size, the largest in the university's history, had unique conditions.

"We made the gift with the intent that the entire amount be invested in microcredit organizations. We expect Tufts to make those investments under the same market rate of return assumptions as the rest of their endowment. The annual return will be split; half goes to Tufts for scholarships and other university purposes, and half will be invested back into the microcredit field."

That certainly turns the established order on its head. The Omidyars have made a quantum leap. But won't it be hard for Tufts to make that rate of return?

"It will be challenging, but that's part of the goal, to show it can be done, and we believe it can. Tufts has considerable academic strength in understanding global issues, and that adds to the equation. It would be terrific if others began to think about how their major gifts could be leveraged to benefit the social issues they care about."

It *would* be terrific. In particular, private foundations are routinely criticized for not investing their endowment capital in the very issues that they support with grants. The raw numbers are telling. U.S. foundations in 2005 gave in the aggregate $33.6 billion to charitable organizations, but their endowments amounted to $510 billion.[8] That's a lot of capital that could be invested in social issues.

This really is a long way from corporate social responsibility as it's conventionally understood.

"I think corporate social responsibility [CSR] starts from the notion that the corporation is doing something that is bad that needs to be balanced by the good. And I think that notion is wrong; that is sort of twentieth-century thinking. I'd much rather see us change the environments and create business models that can only be successful if they have a social impact. Then you don't need a CSR program.

"What we're looking to do is move the needle beyond incremental change and achieve real step function change. It's the entrepreneurial desire to have an impact that really changes the way that people think about the world in some fundamental way. It does not have to be earth-shattering, but if we can get people to think more about how business can be a force for good, that could do a lot. That is what I mean by step function change."

People follow their passion. Pierre seems to be talking about other people's passion.

"My passion comes from seeing others get energized and having the tools they need to have an impact. It's a direct result of eBay. You can't live through the evolution of that community and meeting the thousands of people that come up to you and say, 'Let me tell you how eBay has changed my life,' without having a huge sense of being energized. That's been immensely satisfying."

So, here Pierre sits, admirably trying to maintain the demeanor of being just this geeky guy who fell into this position. Huge wealth, media spotlight—how has that changed this man? He seems remarkably in touch with himself, in balance. How does one keep one's ego in control?

"Try not to believe everything you read, I guess. I mean, it is a little weird, and I've always tried to maintain a low profile. We really value our privacy and our private life and try to stay grounded, but it is a challenge in this very celebrity-driven world. When Pam and I sat down and thought about what was happening to us, really overnight, in the grand scheme of things, it was overwhelming. The wealth generated through my shareholdings in the company was incredible. We felt a real responsibility to put it to good use. I mean, how could it be otherwise, when the source of the wealth had come from the kind of community that eBay represents? So the responsibility to that broader community to make sure that the wealth gets put to good use simply flowed. And it's not likely we can use all of it ourselves. There is a certain point where the level of resources goes far beyond what any individual or family could possibly need even into future generations. That certainly applies to us."

Pierre's view of wealth with responsibility is both logical and compelling. Yet, so many others with huge wealth have very different views and are focused mainly on its preservation. They do not seem to care; society, community, citizenship are not high on their agendas.

"I don't know that I would necessarily characterize it like that, especially in the case of entrepreneurs, who have built some wealth rather rapidly and are busy running their businesses. That's what they do, and in that way, they are making the world a better place. That seems to me appropriate. It takes time to actually sort it out and decide what you are passionate about.

"That is one of the reasons that I am so focused on thinking about businesses as a way to have a social impact. It would create opportunities for others out there to think about their world a little differently and might have an impact on their view of wealth."

It sounds almost subversive and it would be wonderful, but while we're waiting, there is a ninety-three-year-old person, who is on the same page in the Forbes 400 as Pierre, who writes me notes saying "not yet."

"Well, you know life spans are growing rapidly, and so who knows? Maybe that person will come around!"

Maybe he will. Let's hope so. Pierre has a clear vision for what he believes will work. What if he is wrong and these ambitious goals are never realized?

"My answer is that at the very least we will have demonstrated a concerted effort to engage in the world with these values. Others who come after us will look at our results and can say, 'Well, it did or didn't work out, but what can we learn from that?' At the very least we'll have made that contribution."

Can Pierre think up an ideal headline he would like to see ten years from now about Omidyar Network?

"I don't think it will be a headline: 'Omidyar Network had this impact.' If we're lucky and we are successful in ten years, we'll be able to look around and see that a lot more people are taking control of their lives, having an impact on issues they care about, and connecting with others who share their interests. See that we're living in a world where less and less you hear, 'I wish I could do something about that, but I can't. Why isn't somebody doing something about that problem?' People would have learned that they can have an impact, and they don't have an excuse anymore not to try. That is my vision for the work of Omidyar Network, and we won't get a credit or a headline for it in ten years. It'll just be something that has happened.

"The way that we're learning to do things at Omidyar Network is just one way to do it. There are lots of different ways. The important thing is to find something that you are passionate about. If mine is fueling other people's passions, find something you are passionate about and pursue it. Working together, I think, connecting with others who share your interests and finding those common bonds, we can all make the world a better place."

The afternoon sun floods the conference room where we sit. The cameras and microphones for *The World We Want* DVD are turned off, but the network is humming, the connection is made. Without trust and a strong belief that people are fundamentally good, the connection would be doubtful. That people are not only good but capable of extraordinary things when they have a values-rooted faith in themselves and in others is what our next voice, Bill Drayton, calls "the ultimate power of a first-class social entrepreneur."

Citizen Sector Jujitsu

"The transformation of the citizen half of the world's operations into a sector that is as entrepreneurial and competitive as business, and increasingly allied with business, is rapidly closing the business–social productivity gap. I believe this has the potential to deeply strengthen democracy and create a world that is radically different from the world we have today."

I have slipped into the back of a packed conference room at the World Economic Forum where Bill Drayton, the founder of the organization Ashoka, is speaking. It is not the first time I have heard Bill articulate his vision of social entrepreneurship, but its evolution from earlier versions is stunning.

"It all comes down to whether we can overcome the last three centuries where the two halves of the world's efforts, the market economy and the citizen sector, were divided one from the other. This was a historical accident, one that has created enormous dysfunction. If we can help catalyze their reintegration, the world will be a better place.

"The key is people coming together to provide a service or cause a change that is needed. It is not about a specific idea or field but about human beings, citizens being citizens, acting as citizens, exercising power. From the grass roots, bottom up. These social entrepreneurs have the capacity to build and change institutions and patterns of behavior. They are extraordinary individuals, the power of whose ideas cannot be overestimated. They have given themselves the freedom to define their role in life as causing systemic, continental scale, structural social change. And to think in unconventional ways free of today's categories. Their closest peers are the business entrepreneurs who have created new industries, who have thoroughly disrupted existing ones. They define themselves broadly, and they are fully committed to big, rich visions. Otherwise, they could never put all the pieces together. The synergies wouldn't happen. The different parts of the cathedral wouldn't fit together. The acoustics would be terrible. It takes high emotional intelligence and enormous ethical fiber as well as vision and entrepreneurial power.

"Moreover, every time someone succeeds in this field, they become role models that help empower other people to be full citizens. This goes to

Ashoka's long-term central goal—everyone is a change maker; everyone's a citizen is another way of putting it."

"Let me quickly sketch one of these programs to give you a sense of the power of this historic moment—the 'hybrid business/social value-added chain.' Now that the citizen sector is becoming more entrepreneurial and in many cases as competitive as business, it can partner with business to serve the public. With each side contributing what it can do best, the resulting joint production/distribution chains offer everyone one giant productivity advance after another. For example, commercial irrigation firms cannot serve small farmers because their cost structure is too high and they do not know the client.

"Ashoka has connected one of the biggest Latin piping and irrigation companies, Amanco, with a number of the large, skilled, rural citizen groups that Ashoka Fellows and others have built over the last decade. The company provides manufacturing, while the citizen groups provide the retail functions. Everybody wins big: (1) Amanco is first to break into a giant and highly profitable new market; (2) participating citizen groups get a markup that will give them both financial independence and the ability to give their clients access to this benefit, which gives them a big competitive advantage vis-à-vis other citizen groups serving small farmers; and (3) the farmers get more stable income and more sustainable and safe farms through water conservation and other environmental benefits.

"Once we have demonstrated these effects, and do so in other industries and services on which we are now working, competitor businesses and citizen groups will press forward. The jujitsu here is key: It's the competitive dynamic on both sides; the market side and the citizen/social side. It couldn't have worked ten years ago because the social side wasn't ready. It now is!"[9]

And the reason the citizen/social side is ready, or at least more ready, has a lot to do with Bill Drayton and Ashoka.

Over the last twenty-five years, Ashoka Fellows worldwide have practically defined the term *social entrepreneur*. Named for a tolerant and enormously creative early Indian emperor who turned from war to nonviolence, Ashoka has identified and supported more than 1,700 "Fellows," men and women in more than sixty countries pursuing large-scale change. It is a network that has transformed the lives of many millions of people.

Social entrepreneurship picks up on and extends the notion of blending the roles of the business sector and the philanthropic sector. While Bill does argue that the market economy long has been a major engine for social change, it is only when it is joined to the citizen sector that you get the jujitsu, a kind of problem solving genius that is new. Social change that is built on personal values, not decreed but lived.

"We are at a point of revolutionary change in a system that has its origins in the Industrial Revolution when the commercial side became entrepreneurial and competitive and ballooned in power and wealth. The social sector, the side concerned with public welfare, supported by taxes and protected from competition, lost ground."

Today, these concepts are much more advanced than when we invited Bill to speak at the conferences on global philanthropy that TPI cosponsored in the early 1990s.[10] The scale and ambition of this field, or perhaps better described as a movement, is much greater, as are the number of successful examples. Social entrepreneurship is no longer a theory.

Bill himself is a model for that kind of innovation. In the January 2005 issue of *Fast Company*, in an article titled "A Lever Long Enough to Move the World," Keith Hammonds called him "a seer and an audacious visionary of what will yet come." It should come as no surprise for those of us on this journey that Omidyar Network has invested $20 million in Ashoka, toward its goal to speed the emergence of an entrepreneurial citizen sector network.

Bill glows when he describes how social entrepreneurs go forward. He speaks of Rodrigo Baggio, who made possible hundreds of computer training schools based in and run by the communities in slums across Latin America and Asia. "Baggio convinced the Inter-American Development Bank to give him its 'used' (i.e., extremely valuable) computers, got the Brazilian Air Force to warehouse and transport them, and customs in Brazil to accept them. And he was only in his twenties, a very young unknown.

"Where others see a barrier, entrepreneurs see a logical solution. The work of social entrepreneurs flows out of the inner logic of their lives, from deep-seated values. Rodrigo saw the poverty around him and focused on the digital divide before there was such a phrase.

"That kind of inner confidence is remarkably persuasive. I believe that this values-rooted faith is the ultimate power of a first-class entrepreneur. It is a quality and force that others can sense and trust. Any assessment of Rodrigo's success that stopped with his ideas and his excellent (McKinsey consulting–assisted) business plan would not have penetrated to the core of his power. Too many assessments stop at this level and miss the underlying magic."

I am spending the morning to get caught up with Bill Drayton in his offices in Arlington, Virginia, with the Potomac River flowing past us as freely as his ideas.

"There is a gigantic perception gap that is holding this field of citizen-led organizations back. Few people see the extent to which the citizen sector is coming into its own. It began in the late 1970s and early 1980s, and productivity gains have been compounding aggressively. It really is growing vigorously; there are many more actors, and many now are highly sophisticated. Ashoka alone has twenty-one major social-business bridge programs across the globe with the huge potential growing as we sit here."

Bill looks like a wizard right out of Harry Potter's world. His form and features are angular, his formidable intellect is immediately obvious in the weight of his ideas, and his overall intensity is registered in shockingly blue eyes. He is in constant motion, and the flow of his ideas, associations, and metaphors just pours out, along with huge enthusiasm.

"I love the people I work with. I just returned from Brazil and several days with ninety-five Ashoka Fellows, twelve of their children, and two E2s (part of Ashoka's key Entrepreneur to Entrepreneur business-social program). You cannot imagine what it is like to spend time with this amazing group. Take Carlos, who grew up in the street and suffered terribly in childhood. He somehow got himself into the air force, did brilliantly, and then had this wonderful, simple idea for the air force to help street kids. Air force families tutor them, coach sports, and provide direction and a place to belong. There is discipline but also community and a chance for self-respect. Carlos wrote a book that has sold a million copies, and the idea has caught on with other military services in Brazil."

The selection process for Ashoka Fellows has been carefully honed over a twenty-five-year period. The foundation criterion is what Bill calls "ethical fiber."

"The key test is very simple. Do you trust this person? Do you deeply trust this person? Would you trust this person to be a babysitter with your infant? Would you make a deal with this person? Would you feel totally comfortable standing on a cliff edge alone with this person?" People only know how to answer these questions if they trust themselves.

When one looks at Bill, one intuitively trusts him.

"Talented young people need to know that this work offers them the chance to have a big impact. You also get great colleagues who are value driven, and there is no glass ceiling. When you go to a dinner party, people are more interested in you than the investment banker across the table! Moreover, salaries in the citizen sector are now gaining relative to business because we are closing the productivity gap. Not long ago, people thought the phrase social entrepreneur was an oxymoron. Now its significance and meaning is more widely understood, which in itself is a milestone."

A 2005 PBS program about social entrepreneurs, *New Heroes* with Robert Redford, featured eight Ashoka Fellows out of the fifteen who were presented. It was certainly gratifying to Bill, with one caveat that goes back to language and meaning.

"The program was wonderful, but I wish people would stop using the words 'nonprofit' and 'nongovernment organization' (NGO) in describing what we do. The Europeans saw something new and were struck that it wasn't a government, and the Americans saw something new and wondered why it wasn't a profit-making business. But defining us by what we are not holds us back. We are 'the citizen sector' made up of 'citizen organizations.' The key active ingredient is citizens caring and organizing to provide social change and/or services. Our most important impact is to draw others into this active citizenship—both by role model and by recruiting local change makers—to take our ideas and make them fly."

Changing how we talk about the sector could increase understanding and change perceptions about it, but language is just a tiny piece of the changes that Bill foresees. We could be looking at different kinds of democracy in the future, for instance.

"Every time you have a social entrepreneur, big or small, they upset things. They upset the existing way of doing things, and they upset the assumption that you cannot bring change. But, we can better deliver health care; we can change the whole educational system. We invite people in every community to become change makers. They, in turn, become role models for their family and neighbors. The citizen sector is also important to democracy because government is too big, too far away. You need an intermediary set of institutions. It makes the society systemically more citizen-friendly and democratic. Our sector is citizens, and it creates citizens."

The image of legions of informed and talented social actors exercising their citizenship is powerful. As a social movement, it would be transformational.

Bill was profoundly influenced by Gandhi and the civil rights movement beginning in his high school years. Then, in 1963 while a student at Harvard, he traveled to India and walked with Vinoba Bhave, the postindependence leader of the Gandhian movement.

"Gandhi, almost certainly the greatest social entrepreneur of the last century, changed politics forever. He understood that people could no longer be effective, accepted, participants in society merely by learning a set of rules. One had to master ethics based on empathy, which in Gandhi's terms means the ability to guide one's actions by grasping their impact on all those around them.

"Gandhi transformed politics globally by showing that people will make the right decision when given the choice of being a good person in society or behaving badly toward others so long as they are challenged respectfully and not coerced into accepting this. While people cannot be forced to recognize truth, there is a 'truth force' that reliably leads to the right decision. This 'truth force' has toppled empire after empire, and it was the engine behind our civil rights movement."

One can only wonder whether the truth force is linked to the notion "that people are basically good."

"However, many people and groups have not mastered empathy-based ethics, and this failure is very probably the chief cause of marginalization across the world. There is nothing more cruel or wasteful than this marginalization, which affects 20 to 30 percent of the population.

"Ashoka's overall goal, 'everyone a change maker,' is out of reach as long as hundreds of millions cannot even participate in society. It is hard to think of any other change that would affect the structure and equity of society as much.

"I've always been an entrepreneur, and I've always been fascinated with how institutions and societies work. And this work, Ashoka, is the ideal place for someone with those interests. The idea of specialization makes me acutely claustrophobic, and there is no risk of that here. We have the ability to bring things together, to see the whole picture; we have an effective community that increasingly knows how to think and work together."

Authenticity and *tenacity* describe Bill Drayton, and like every committed visionary, every dedicated artist, he is fueled by huge ambition, drive, and will.

"If you love something, you love it. If you have the privilege of doing this sort of work, with these sorts of people, good heavens! I learn amazing things every day."

There is the challenge of going to scale. Ashoka is a $30 million organization, but Bill believes that to fulfill its goals, it needs to double in size over the next five years. In the curious and often counterproductive funding world of organized philanthropy, Ashoka is literally a victim of its own success, as most major foundations do not fund recipients for more than a few years, no matter how successful.

"The architecture is largely in place. The citizen sector (including that infused by Ashoka's field organization) has reached an advanced level in North and South America, Europe, and South and Southeast Asia, and also in pockets of Africa and the Middle East. Each of these areas has thousands of citizen groups, second- and third-generation citizen groups that are becoming more competitive in their chosen markets. Institutional patterns of cooperation are beginning to emerge. Therefore, we now have a time window characterized by both significant maturity and continuing plasticity. The next five or six years are crucial.

"The answers to two big questions will determine how wisely the citizen sector and its entrepreneurial cutting edge will crystallize: Will we emerge as a globally operationally integrated field or not? Will the inertia of continued division win out, or will we be able to reintegrate business and society?

"We, and others, have many more programs that have passed our double test which is: important pattern change for the field, and a clear 'jujitsu' leverage way of making that change society-wide.

"At the same time, you're building a business social bridge where the lady in the flowery dress who runs the citizen group and the man in the suit who comes from the city have to talk with one another. They really want to talk because this is a big deal for both of them. So they will go bowling together, drink tea, or do whatever to work this out. That is the point when you are really tearing down three centuries of division, right at the heart of it."

The very idea of tearing down centuries of division through the means of a lovely lady in a flowery dress and a man in a suit sipping tea together is a stunning metaphor of convergence. I would love to see Bill Drayton make it so.

Reader's Guide Questions

1. Two schools of thought: one argues for big, transformational change; the other advocates for change one person at a time. What are the arguments for each notion?
2. Making profits from advancing the public good raises many issues. What is your assessment of the arguments made by Steve Case and Pierre Omidyar?
3. What are the upsides to bridging the traditional divides between the business and social sectors? What are the downsides?
4. Is the "entrepreneurial approach" the only approach to achieve transformational change?
5. Getting to scale is an argument in favor of market economy solutions to social issues. Is big scale always a good thing?
6. How do you respond to the proposition that people are basically good?
7. Bill Drayton believes the division of the market economy and the citizen sector was a "historical accident." Do you agree, or are the differences more fundamental?
8. Jujitsu as a concept is very different from disruption. Which do you think is more effective/powerful?

9. Does Drayton's enthusiastic description romanticize/idealize the social entrepreneur?
10. "Everyone a change maker" is a thrilling concept. The Internet has been proposed as one way to make that happen. What are other ways to engage the broadest numbers?

Notes

1. Michael E. Raynor and Clayton Christensen, *The Innovator's Solution: Creating and Sustaining Successful Growth* (Boston: Harvard Business School Press, 2003).
2. Comments from Ratna Omidvar, the executive director of the Maytree Foundation, established by Alan and Judy Broadbent.
3. Duane Elgin, Elizabeth Share, Mark Dubois, Tracy Gary, and John Levy, *Transformational Philanthropy: An Exploration*, a report, part of a fiscal project of Philanthropy for the 21st Century/Changemakers.
4. Gregory Dees, Bertelsmann Stiftung (ed.), *Effectiveness, Efficiency and Accountability in Philanthropy: What Lessons Can Be Learned from the Corporate World?* (Verlag Bertelsmann Stiftung, 2006).
5. For a fuller description of social investments that blend for-profit and social goals, see Jed Emerson and Joshua Spitzer, *Blended Value Investing: Capital Opportunities for Social and Environmental Impact* (Davos, Switzerland: World Economic Forum: March 2006).
6. One of the main concepts discussed by Adam Smith in *The Wealth of Nations* is that of the Invisible Hand. To put it simply, the Invisible Hand is an economic theory that states that if a market is left to decide how many products to sell and at what prices products are to be sold at, based on the demand of the consumers and providing that each consumer is allowed to choose from a variety of goods and services, based on the supply provided by industrialists, the market will run smoothly. The reason for this is that people (in general) wish to achieve the best for them and their families. They therefore work extremely hard, becoming productive members of society. The greater the productivity is in an economy, the more effective and prosperous the economy will become.
7. For a contemporary view of this subject, see David Warsh, *Knowledge and the Wealth of Nations* (New York: Norton, 2006).
8. According to the *2006 Foundation Yearbook* (New York: Foundation Center, 2005), assets of all active U.S. foundations were $510.5 billion.
9. *Jujitsu* is the weaponless art of self-defense where one uses one's own weight, strength, and talents.
10. TPI and the Synergos Institute sponsored several conferences on global philanthropy in the mid-1990s at Pocantico, the Rockefeller estate in the Hudson River Valley in New York.

C H A P T E R ④

THE LISTENING POST
Reflection and Radical Change

I AM BACK in the ordinary room to pause and reflect a bit on what we have heard. The fire has been stoked, and apparently I am not alone. The room has become a listening post for those who have joined this journey. I sense the restlessness in the air.

The almost evangelical pitch for the market economy as a servant of good is a hard sell, especially since the market has been the principal engine of modernization, in all of its ramifications, thrust on the world. There is just too much evidence to the contrary, from the devastation of indigenous cultures, to corporate greed and corruption, to multinationals stealing everything from water to wood, or doing business with outlaws and terrorists.[1] The culture of success in the business world, tough competition that can approach bloody combat, seems antithetical to the ideals of altruism, cooperation, and a social-benefit bottom line. The rhetoric from our free market friends may well be out in front of the reality, but on another level, both Steve Case and Pierre Omidyar are representative of the astonishing growth of socially responsible investments.

According to the Social Investment Forum,[2] $2.29 trillion, nearly one out of every ten dollars under professional management in the United States today, is invested with socially responsible criteria. The three principal ones are screening for various issues (i.e., environmental or tobacco, etc.), shareholder advocacy, and community investing. The big new dimension we have witnessed here is the purposeful efforts of well-capitalized, high-profile, and experienced entrepreneurs putting themselves, their resources, and their reputations on the line, not as passive investors but very proactively. These kinds of efforts—and Case and Omidyar are not alone[3]—if successful, could influence others in ways far beyond that of advocates arguing for responsible business behavior from a purely moral perspective. I also would not dismiss corporate social responsibility, as to a large degree it is the first step in making the corporation, especially huge multinational players, into enterprises more sensitive to community and societal impact.[4]

What is very new, however, is Bill Drayton's exciting depiction of an increasingly competent nonprofit/citizen sector able to partner with business in a large-scale way. What comes to my mind is the way the transcontinental railroad was built with two teams competing toward the same end. To a large degree it did not matter where in the continental United States they met. What did matter was that they shared the same end goal. Here we have market economy types and civil society advocates all driving toward the same goals. I love the way they are mixing it up.

I do wonder whether we are overromanticizing the entrepreneurs. They are hardly the only players; many other creative innovators share their passion for changing the world. It would be easy to bestow on Pierre, Steve, Bill, and others iconic status, but that is not what they seek.

The big deal here is the bridge making between domains, the linkages and connections between sectors, between the resources and the needs, between creative ideas and their implementation.

Are people basically good? Is Gandhi's "truth force" in evidence in today's world? Both assumptions are wonderful and arguable. If there is one intractable issue that tests them, and at the same time disturbs our soul, it is global poverty. That is why the Make Poverty History movement is so amazing. Let us go, then, and meet some actors who come from other perspectives who are part of that movement.

Make Poverty History

How large can a vision be before it collapses of its own weight? No vision tests that question more than the notion of making poverty history.

It is almost impossible to not be overwhelmed by the numbers, when we try to envision the scope, scale, and devastating effects of global poverty. With figures that are so incomprehensible, it is easy to deny or ignore them, even if it is dehumanizing to do so. Can it be true that one billion people live on less than $1 a day in this world? It's a fact. This is the level of extreme poverty that United Nations Millennium Development Goals seek to cut in half by 2015.

UN MILLENNIUM DEVELOPMENT GOALS

- Eradicate extreme poverty and hunger.
- Achieve universal primary education, ensuring that all boys and girls complete a full course of primary schooling.
- Promote gender equality and empower women, eliminating gender disparity in primary and secondary education.
- Reduce child mortality rate (by two-thirds among children under five).
- Improve maternal health (reduce by three-quarters the maternal mortality ratio).
- Combat HIV/AIDS, malaria, and other diseases; halt and reverse their spread.
- Ensure environmental sustainability.
- Develop a global partnership for development.

When we talk about this kind of poverty, we are also talking about hunger, malnutrition, preventable disease, and death. In other words, pain. More people are getting involved to try and change this dreadful picture, and the global infrastructure for change has begun to build. I believe more people will become involved, when they wake up to the nightmare and see that there is hope to end it.

In some ways, Ralph Smith is an unlikely person to have an epiphany, but that is what happened when he encountered the Make Poverty History Movement firsthand. We were discussing the World We Want on his return from Edinburgh, a visit that coincided with the June 2005 G8 meeting of the heads of state of the wealthiest nations. Ralph is senior vice president of the Annie E. Casey Foundation and the architect of Casey's immense $25 million-a-year investment in the revitalization of poor U.S. communities. He has been thinking about the issues of poor families and persistent poverty for a long time. It was the passion that caught him off guard.

"Sixty thousand people showed up at the Live 8 concert. Jack Straw, the British foreign secretary, made a dramatic plea for President Bush to bring the U.S. investment in ending poverty in line with the rest of the G8, and the roar was deafening. At the same time, two hundred and fifty thousand activists from all over the world were demonstrating in the streets, making it loud and clear it was time 'to make poverty history.'

"That night, shaken and stirred by the intensity of the crowds around me, I went up to my hotel room and read again with renewed focus the UN

Millennium Development Goals Report. The MDGs are very ambitious; among their goals is the aim to cut in half the incidence of extreme poverty by the year 2015. Nearly two hundred countries, including the United States, have adopted the MDGs since 2000. Progress throughout the world on achieving the goals has been uneven, but the very existence for the first time of world-wide consensus on these perennial social dilemmas is remarkable.

"As I sat the next day in a downtown bookstore and watched the huge crowds surge past, I couldn't help but be impressed with how directly the problem was stated, 'every man in the street, from New York to Nairobi can understand them.'[5] Unlike so many efforts in the U.S., the MDGs are not mired in euphemisms, not diffused in data-driven qualifications. There is a clarity that is too often missing from policy discussions. That was my take-away from this experience. What I shared with my colleagues back in Baltimore was this: No more euphemisms! Our job is to make poverty history!"

Later that same week, a letter to me from Amy Goldman, a trustee of the Better Way Foundation, arrived at TPI.

"How can we not try and make poverty history? When we first started considering making grants to orphans in Africa, I frequently heard 'the problem is too big; we can't solve it, so why try?' This is a classic American response to the inconvenience of international aid and perhaps also to the emotionally wrenching experience of trying to humanize the mind-numbing number of those affected.

"Some Americans delude themselves into believing that they do not have a connection to the orphan in Uganda, the grieving mother in Zambia, the devastated village in Banda Ache. Yet, I have seen that the mother who loses her child to HIV/AIDS in Uganda has lost everything. There is no solace for that grief. The strength to carry on in the face of such grief, to physically toil each day to feed one's remaining family is astounding. It is truly heroic. I don't think I could do what so many millions must do in our world—live with grief, poverty, and fear every day. Mother Teresa lamented the spiritual poverty in the U.S. That is truly a poverty we must all fight against, because our stunted compassion is an obstacle to action.

"In reducing poverty, it is important to remember there will never be justice without education. One motivation for making grants to support orphans and vulnerable children in Africa is that without education, these children grow into armies. Easily manipulated little souls have been transformed into killers by thugs like Charles Taylor and Idi Amin. Indeed, both Taylor and Amin started out as rootless children themselves. Could our work supporting education perhaps contribute to the stability and a peaceful outcome in the ongoing political chaos so many countries in Africa face? If there is any possibility of that, along with the great gift of improving and perhaps saving a child's life, how can we not try?"

The Global Actor: Linking People to Resources and Influence

Peggy Dulany gave her first speech about wealth and responsibility in 1992 at a gathering of the wealthy clients of a Boston investment firm. It was also one of TPI's first programs on strategic philanthropy, and we had agreed that Peggy should "tell her story," not only as an advocate for social justice but in personal terms. Peggy is the founder of the Synergos Institute, which is dedicated to the development of effective, sustainable and locally based solutions to poverty, but she is also David Rockefeller's daughter, and she was nervous. I may have increased her apprehension in introducing her, when I accused her of being "shameless" in the pursuit of her work. Half in fun and all in earnest, but there is no question that Peggy was, and is, a person who pulls out all the stops and is willing to share her deepest feelings and beliefs.

We were meeting in a big room overlooking Boston Harbor, and the sound system was terrible. Peggy has a quiet voice, and I remember the room was totally still. The audience hung on her every word.

"At seventeen I went to live in Brazil to do something socially useful. It did not start well. A newspaper, having heard I was in this tiny village, came through in a truck with loudspeakers blaring, 'Where is the Rockefeller woman?' offering to pay a sum to anyone who would find me. So much for being incognito. At that time I considered changing my name to escape this unwanted and intrusive celebrity.

"I started off giving injections in a clinic in a squatter's home where kids were going out and playing in the sewers. It was immediately clear that my work would not resolve the root problem that led there to be open sewers. But what I learned from that situation, the kernel that has stuck with me and has kept me at this work through the years, was that the people living in these settlements in absolutely minimal conditions have an intense desire to improve their lives and get out of poverty, and they understand better than anyone else what the solutions are. That has overshadowed anything I have seen since in terms of people on the outside trying to solve the problems of people on the inside.

"The will, the imagination, the creativity were all there, but something was missing. The connections to people with information, education, jobs and influence, people with decision-making power—the links— simply did not exist. I couldn't have articulated that forty years ago, but it has stayed with me ever since."

It led Peggy to establish the Synergos Institute in 1986. Synergos's mission is to provide those missing links in less developed countries between grass-roots leaders and political, business and philanthropic leaders, people who otherwise would not have access to each other. Peggy has seen the work evolve since the 1970s.

"Since then there have been changes. On the gloomy side, poverty has increased, a pretty discouraging fact. In some areas such as sub-Saharan Africa, the incidence of poverty rose between 1990 and 2001. China and India have achieved strong sustained growth and made major rapid progress in reducing poverty and certainly will continue to, but their population growth is still increasing faster than the number of people getting out of poverty. At the same time, in a number of countries, poverty is actually being reduced. Costa Rica, for example, is investing a huge percentage of its budget in the education of its people and not in defense. The programs that have been developed there and in many other countries are having an effect, which shows that it can be done, but the implications of population growth remain sobering.

"Divisions in the world are deeper now than in the past, which in some ways is paradoxical because communication is better, people travel more, and there are more opportunities for connections. Still, connecting is not simple. A traveler to a foreign country has little chance on his own of connecting with local groups doing good work on the ground and making a difference, even if they wish to do so.

"On the positive side, events around the world make the news more often, and people resonate with what they see and want to do something. Unfortunately, it is usually the disaster rather than the success that is covered, but the result is that people know more about the kinds of organizations that are doing work, at least relief work if not development work.

"It was fantastic that the world was able to agree on the MDGs. It is the first time that countries, civil society, and businesses have gotten together on very specific targets, and that is encouraging. However, we have not moved at a constant rate toward achieving them. And resources are not necessarily the major problem.

"For instance, Synergos is working on a major project with a number of partners including UNICEF and Unilever, to try to cut child malnutrition in half in India by 2015. Resources and solutions are not lacking. The government in India is providing $6 billion a year, there is a range of technical and educational community development solutions, and there are ways to reduce corruption, another form of solution. But child malnutrition is not going away, mostly because the stakeholders haven't decided which direction to go.

"You have the government with its various ministries at both the national and state levels—some good, some bad, some corrupt, some committed. You have government policy in place and a lot of money to spend on educating mothers and on getting micronutrients into the foods that families in different parts of the country eat. Basically a lot of the right stuff is being articulated and, in some cases, done. But probably a third to a half of the money is just disappearing. Then, at the grass roots, you have some very good organizations that may be dealing with five thousand, thirty thousand, a hundred thousand people. Those are huge figures, but with an overall population of 1.2 billion, they become a drop in the bucket.

"So there are a number of questions. One is how do you get the various government agencies working together with these grassroots activists who are doing good things and connecting with the community? How do you get the business brains, the corporate world, thinking about the systems issues and helping the systems to work better? How do you get the money that is available to actually get to where it's supposed to be going? And then the overall piece: once you have targeted the areas you want to work in, since you can't choose all of India at once, how do you get into those areas, both vertically and horizontally, and get them to come together to see the dimensions of the problem, see it in a different way by seeing it through each other's eyes so they can come up with common strategies, common solutions, and common commitment across all the barriers, whether vertical or horizontal or ideological?"

So, the question is not whether it is financially or technically possible, but instead, how do you get all the actors together and thinking collectively, to take concerted action.

Resources may not be the major problem in India, but Jeffrey Sachs, director of the Earth Institute at Columbia University, makes the case that if the United States in particular doesn't step up to the plate financially, the MDGs will not be met in anywhere near the agreed-on time lines. The United States has been slow to increase its support. It is hard to understand why. Peggy has some thoughts as to reasons.

"One reason may be the surveys that show the general public thinks the U.S. is giving about 10 percent of our gross national income (GNI) in aid overseas. In reality, U.S. official development assistance amounts to only 0.16[6] percent of GNI, an extraordinarily small sum. The UN's target, agreed to by thirty-five countries thirty-five years ago, is 0.7 percent, and the United States has never come close. The same incorrect perception exists in terms of philanthropy. Most people are surprised when they learn that of the $250 billion Americans gave in 2005, less than 3 percent goes abroad.

"At the same time, debt relief of the very poor countries has been on the agenda for a long time, and the major agreement by the G8 countries to forgive upward of $55 billion in debt owed by eighteen of the poorest countries[7] may be a sign of positive movement.

"Rather than it being a matter of the available resources, in my view, eliminating poverty is a question of political will and the willingness to work together."

According to the Global Monitoring Report,[8] what is needed to broaden progress is to get governments on board. In developed countries, this means living up to foreign aid commitments but also initiating policy reform in areas such as trade, capital flows, knowledge and technology transfer, and the environment. For developing countries, it will mean improving policies and governance to achieve stronger country-owned development strategies.

"You would think we would have the personal and public will to eliminate this kind of poverty, poverty where people live on less than a dollar a day. I have the sense that people feel there is a very narrow line between themselves and others. This can lead some people to demand action, but for others it may be easier to look away than confront it. Then there are the psychological factors. When people fear economic insecurity, even when they are reasonably secure, they can feel threatened or that there is never enough to go around.

"On the political side, different theories abound about what will make for positive change. You have a large group that genuinely believes that trickle down is the way that is going to get the bottom to come up. And another group that thinks that is false and that you must empower those at the bottom with tools and skills so that they can move up.

"People want to do something, but often they don't know how, even within this country. It becomes even harder to figure out what to do in Kenya or some other far distant place. We need more credible intermediary organizations like the Acumen Fund that was established with operational seed money from Rockefeller Foundation, to bring together a constituency of philanthropic investors who are tackling issues they could not undertake on their own. Synergos itself has organized more than fifty families, from eighteen different countries, committed to social investing in a Global Philanthropist Circle (GPC), all actively working on global issues.

"Philanthropy can have a very key role, even if proportionately small compared to government. In the dollars that flow with the members of the GPC, we have emphasized that the importance of what each family can do resides not only in their money, but in using their connections, influence, education, and talents on behalf of development. The impact they can have is particularly great in countries outside the U.S. where the percentage of people with money is smaller and whose wealth has a disproportionate influence.

"People who chose to use that clout have the potential not only to influence government but also to convene different stakeholders, including those affected by poverty who are not usually invited to the table. When they play that kind of convening and facilitating role, the synergies multiply and the impact is far greater than it would be from their philanthropic contribution.

"Philanthropists can also leverage their dollars. Take an example from South Africa. The Applebaum family, members of the Global Philanthropists Circle, started a Distance Education Program that is now going Africa-wide. They are also in contact with Brazil to get curriculum in Portuguese so it can be used there. This is really where philanthropists, using their minds and hearts and all their assets, have an opportunity to make a difference way beyond the money they bring. If they hit the right button at the right time, a relatively small investment can awaken a whole population to the possibilities of an entirely new strategy that other corporations, individuals and governments will invest in.

"Corporate philanthropy and corporate involvement is another avenue. I see an increase, but whether it is anecdotal or a sea change in how corporations are going to behave for the future is unknown. Let me give one example. One of the Whole Systems Partnerships [multisector collaborations of foundations and donors, government, business, and the civil society] that Synergos is participating in has to do with creating more sustainable food chains all the way from small local producers, through agribusinesses, reaching into government policies, through trade policies, to the large distributors of food. What is astounding is that right from the beginning eight agribusinesses signed on because they have realized that for economic environmental reasons, they must. The land is being degraded, and they cannot produce food as cheaply as they once did. There are also legal reasons tied to health. Some companies are in trouble for producing foods that are contributing to obesity, on one hand, and malnutrition, on the other. So, this sustainable food chain idea was something that basically came from business, led by Sysco, the large food distribution company.

"Often, it is when issues get grounded in genuine long-term self-interest that corporate policies shift in a major way. In Brazil, suddenly the business leaders took an interest in the issue of street children because of the related crime. It became so bad, they had to live with bars on their windows and send their children to school in armored cars. When you worry about your kids being kidnapped, it becomes very personal."

Another strategy is to focus on other development issues that relate to poverty. The Bill and Melinda Gates Foundation commitment in the hundreds of millions for health initiatives in the poorest countries is extraordinary. And Warren Buffett's $31 billion record-breaking gift to the Gates Foundation demonstrates his extraordinary belief in the Gateses' commitment and capacity. In a *Seattle Times* article interview, Bill Gates responded to criticism that he should just take poverty straight-on with the argument that if you simply find the cures and make the vaccines available, that will be the starter that addresses the poverty issue. We know that vaccine development and cures for malaria are absolutely needed, each month 150,000 people die from malaria, but there is more to it than just providing a scientific solution.

"Community involvement and process are both important," Peggy Dulany says. "It has been absolutely central to everything Synergos has done. One of my favorite development experiences, Gram Vivas in Orissa in India, has a focus on sanitation and health. That came out of consulting with the community, with women's voices very present at the table. Women invariably choose clean water, sanitation, and access to some kind of health care to reduce disease. The fact that they were the ones to choose the issue made them invest in it and made the systems that were developed work. That community involvement piece is applicable everywhere."

What troubles Peggy the most?

"There is still a lack of connection and lack of access to information, solutions, and how-to techniques. People need a menu of options The United Nations Development Programme is beginning to think of itself as a facilitator of dialogue, which could be a very interesting role for the UN because it has offices in 190 or so countries. It could be a center for dissemination of information if it saw that as its role. It could help marshal people of goodwill and organizations that have the skills that are needed.

"But closer to home, people who want to do something about conditions in another country need to choose a theme that really interests them—children or women or health or whatever. I would encourage people to apply their dollars to efforts that have a chance of engaging the communities that are going to benefit in designing their own solutions, rather than to top down applications. Because there really is the hope.

"But I don't think that the whole system is going to shift until there is a transformation of the human heart. That means starting with ourselves and then working outward, in mostly small increments. Mary Oliver, in one of her poems, talks about saving the one life you have to save, meaning your own. And she doesn't mean survival; she means self-transformation. So when I start to feel desperate about the entire world, I try to focus on whether it's possible for me to transform anything about myself and how I relate to other people that might make it more likely that other people might work on their own transformations and the way they relate to others. That is what it is going to take really to get to the bottom of this.

"I think we are all born with an individual soul and with a purpose in life, but the circumstances of our lives tend to shape us in ways that are not necessarily in accordance with our deeper purpose and meaning. In this culture, it happens all the time. We tend not to reflect much or to meditate or pray. The energy of this country is largely in doing. We spend less time in deep reflection or, for that matter, being in tune with nature.

"To me, it feels like our species has gotten awfully far away from where we came from. We can go deeper within ourselves and reflect on what the ultimate purpose is, and doing that can get us out of momentary worries—like the speech you have to write—that get us so anxious and so into a cycle of doing and worrying that we aren't at our deepest purpose."

Peggy Dulany's values and passions have found a home in the organization she started and the work that she does. Finding fulfillment out of one's "deepest purpose" is resonating on this journey. Getting the actors together and thinking together is the goal, and that takes work—but which actors?

We have heard intriguing arguments for the market economy and the citizen sector as domains that can influence social issues, but what about government? Is that role truly as negligible as some seem to be claiming? According to out next voice, government can be a great force for good, if one is willing to put one's shoulder to the stone.

A Shoulder to the Stone: Changing Public Policy

Alan and Judy Broadbent founded the Maytree Foundation to do their part in breaking the back of poverty and social injustice. In 2005, the foundation won the Paul Ylvisaker Award for Public Policy Engagement, an extraordinary honor for anyone, but even more so when considering the award group is American and the foundation is Canadian.

Thirty-eight years ago in a speech to what was the forerunner of the Council on Foundations, Paul Ylvisaker said:

The struggle between the haves and have-nots will dominate the next two or three centuries. What faith, what commitments, what elasticity, and what relevance do we philanthropists bring to this critical stage in human history? What we represent is the resilient margin of the industrial order, the most stretchable part of the world's status quo. The program question for us is whether we are stretching our resources and ourselves, as far and as fast as the situation demands. Not our own immediate situation, which is but a cozy corner in the walled castle of industrial affluence, but that universal circumstance which is the growing discrepancies between those inside the system and those without.[9]

He would be proud to have a champion and advocate for the have-nots like the Maytree Foundation as a recipient of the award named for him. Alan Broadbent is one of my favorite people in the world, someone I first met in the early 1990s at a time when the social venture movement was getting its first real traction. What makes Alan and Maytree so credible is the serious commitment to social justice expressed in highly disciplined, pragmatic and creative processes that have had a real impact on social policies that have a profound affect on the lives of the poor and the disenfranchised.

Alan described how he and Judy decided to focus on poverty when they created the foundation twenty-five years ago. Many of the efforts have centered on pressing immigrant and refugee issues. The foundation's work in this area has achieved critical mass. Real results are happening and long-term change is on the threshold, but it has taken time.

"In the beginning, Judy and I understood the need to have a rational basis from which to do grant making; otherwise we could say yes to every request and no to none. We didn't have enough money for that. Nobody does. So identifying our core values was important.

"We started with the belief in the value of political and social stability. We saw that three fundamental issues threatened that stability: wealth disparities between and within nations; mass migration of people because of war, oppression, and environmental disasters; and the degradation of the environment with its attendant social dislocation. We chose to focus on the first two of those issues, which in part dealt with one of the ramifications of the third.

"Poverty became our key focus. In many societies, poverty becomes systemic. It is embedded in the institutional fabric, into the social, cultural, legal, and economic patterns. Poverty is an unjustifiable burden to millions of people that also results in paralyzing costs to society as a whole. It perpetuates a vicious cycle by limiting opportunity and repressing the human spirit. The correlation between poverty and most serious social problems is a stunning indictment of any society."

Alan at first resists my request to elaborate on his vision for the future. He believes in rational thinking and planning, not dreaming. He grew up middle class, with no particular axe to grind or political cause to promote. Analysis, not sentiment or utopian vision, is what's behind his current passion for social reform. Yet you would have found him in the middle of protest politics, the antiwar and civil rights movements when youth and the 1960s proved a potent mix.

Ask him for his own assessment of his philanthropic efforts, and he says, "You get on with the work."

What motivates him? His response is this anecdote. "When Mario Cuomo left the New York governorship, he was asked by a journalist, 'What will you miss most?' He said, 'Going out every day and putting your shoulder to the stone. Some days it moves forward and some days it slips back, but it's the putting the shoulder to the stone.' This is what gives me satisfaction. And I do know what kind of world I want.

"It is a society that is as rational and predictable as possible. You want societies where people have a combination of health, wealth, well-being, educational attainment, security, and safety. Those are the basic public goods, the commodities that allow people to live their lives in a predictable way. These are things we owe each other as citizens, things best provided on a public, universally accessible basis. Once people can be confident that there is a solid floor under them, there's a good chance that if they work hard, they'll be rewarded. Those rewards will allow them to buy the additional comforts of a civilized life. . . . That's a reasonable set of objectives—peace, order, and good government—the Canadian equivalent of U.S. 'life, liberty and the pursuit of happiness.'

"When you get great disparities in wealth, all those things are threatened, and it renders too many areas of society unsafe. Another aspect of unequal wealth distribution is migration. If someone grabs your assets or you can't turn work into wealth, you leave. This has costs in human and social capital for the areas people are leaving and integration costs for the areas where they head. It's a paean to a rational society."

In the early years, the Maytree Foundation funded a great number of projects in community organizations that attacked poverty. Some were community-based adult literacy programs; others were parenting programs to give poor kids a better start in life.

But what Alan realized is that they were funding a plethora of pilots that in the end would collapse unless Maytree kept funding them. If it had less money to give or changed its focus, the limited good it was doing would end, and it would have left a very small footprint behind. Maytree decided it would be much better to show the importance of literacy, for example, and have government make it central to its mission.

"We could not help but notice that the greatest advances in the health of people had come from public measures: the separation of clean and dirty municipal water virtually eliminated the plagues that had periodically devastated populations, mass inoculation rid us of infectious diseases like tuberculosis and polio, seat belt laws reduced road carnage, and antismoking laws reduced the incidence of lung cancer. In Canada, social programs after World War II dramatically reduced poverty and unequal access to health care and education services.

"Canada is a country with a strong commitment to the role of government, more like a European country in that regard than like the United States with its governing mythology of not trusting government. So it was not unusual for us to look at public policy as a powerful and effective tool in the provision of societal goods. We began to think more critically about policy, about how it is made, who makes it, and how we could influence that process. We talked to as many people as we could who knew something about policy.

"In the end, we decided that we needed a Canadian organization looking specifically at poverty issues and at the gap between rich and poor. That is why we formed the Caledon Institute of Social Policy in partnership with Ken Battle, who was the head of the National Council on Welfare in Canada and, in my view, our leading analyst and commentator on poverty issues. Ken understood that social policy was driven by fiscal policy and that fiscal policy was ultimately expressed in taxation structure. He knew that any understanding of what was happening in social policy required an understanding of that complicated terrain, which most social policy analysts avoid."

Most think tanks are created by people with a point of view, and their pursuit of data is in search of things which will bolster that point of view. That is not the intent at Caledon, where there is a devotion to beginning with data, much of it census data, and seeing the patterns and where they lead.

Caledon is now nearly fifteen years old. It has had a number of policy wins, the most important of which was the implementation in 1997 of the National Child Tax Benefit, the first new social program in Canada in decades, which has significantly benefited families of poor children. Governments in Canada now routinely seek Caledon's view when they are developing social policy. The organization has become a respected participant in the public process.

"Caledon is not Maytree's only policy initiative, but we have learned our lessons at the Caledon school. Within our central Immigrant and Refugee Program, we have had significant policy engagement.

"In the public's imagination, communities of impoverished and politically oppressed people who have recently immigrated from abroad have become inextricably linked with poverty, and viewed as a tremendous burden and threat to security.

"But Maytree takes an asset-based approach to the issue. We believe that each wave of immigration has strengthened Canada and the United States as well. So accelerating the settlement of immigrants and refugees into our cities is a nation-building, not a remedial, exercise."

The foundation led the drive to change legislation to allow refugees in limbo—those who had been identified as refugees but had not yet gotten permanent resident status—to apply for and receive student loans from the government. This change will enable about ten thousand refugees across Canada to gain access to postsecondary education. Another major initiative was to create pathways to workforce and economic integration for skilled immigrants. Through Maytree's leadership, advocacy, coalition building, management capability, and funding, the Toronto Region Immigration Employment Council (TRIEC) was created as a regional public private council to dismantle many complex obstacles to full workforce participation by skilled immigrants and to bring employers directly to the table.

People talk a lot about the advantages of "leverage," and Maytree sees public policy as the biggest lever around. "Our attitude has always been that the government is us, not them, and we have a right and a duty to work with government to make effective public policy," said Ratna Omidvar, executive director of the Maytree Foundation.

As you might imagine, Alan believes that too much philanthropy is based on emotion, on empty vision. "A lot of philanthropy that 'turns people's crank' is lousy philanthropy based on personal satisfaction instead of whether it's good for others. It doesn't drill down, analyze, ask about good use of resources, whether it's sustainable. My view is if it isn't good for the community, it isn't worth doing."

What works in influencing public policy? This is my take on Alan's take:

Have a strong focus for your work. Having a deep knowledge is important, particularly in the complex or complicated policy areas, and a capacity to engage complexity is critical.

Strive for high quality in your analytical work. The diligence and rigor of the work must be unimpeachable. That doesn't mean the conclusions will be unarguable, but it will mean that your argument will not falter because the work is shoddy or superficial.

Make sure the work is "policy-ready." Create a workable solution. Policymakers need to see a way out of the swamp. Just describing the swamp is not good enough, because you run the risk of being part of the culture of complaint. Policymakers are highly aware of the limits of their capacity to act. As former Alberta finance minister Jim Dinning used to say, "Bring me something I can say yes to."

Be prepared to settle for less. When Caledon created and recommended the National Child Tax Benefit, it was delighted it was adopted but not so happy that only about 40 percent of the required funding was allocated. So Caledon complimented the government, on one hand, and urged them to do better, on the other. Subsequent budgets were increased to about 75 percent and then 80 percent.

Be relentless. Politicians and the public servants who work for them are used to living in short time frames. Often it is a twenty-four-hour time frame, or one news cycle. Old issues fall by the wayside unless someone keeps raising them. Ken Battle calls this approach "relentless incrementalism," and he credits much of Caledon's policy success to it. Major change takes time, often a decade, and you have to keep your shoulder to the stone day by day, month by month, year by year.

Don't demand the credit. Ralph Waldo Emerson wrote, "There is no limit to what a man can achieve, if he doesn't care who gets the credit." Credit is important for politicians or heads of organizations seeking to enhance their status with boards or bosses. Let these people "own" the solution. (Let them think it was their idea in the first place!) Besides, sharing success widely is most likely an honest expression of the reality of the effort.

Maytree has come to the point where it thinks of all its work in a policy perspective, even when it is making a simple grant to a community agency serving an immigrant group.

"We try to ask the question, 'How will this grant contribute to the creation of a long-term solution to the problem or issue at hand?'" In itself, that grant may not be the grand solution, but it should represent an important step along the way.

In a letter in support of the foundation as recipient of the Paul Ylvisaker Award for Public Policy Engagement, my colleague Joe Breiteneicher, president of TPI, had this to say about the Maytree Foundation after conducting extensive interviews.

"Maytree stakeholders and colleagues see it as the most relevant, effective and critically important foundation in Canada. As one foundation CEO said, 'Canada would be bereft if Maytree ceased to exist.' Maytree's unwavering focus on immigrant and refugee issues, its collegiality and fairness in treating grantees as partners, its collaborative spirit and unflinching involvement in public policy matters are central to its unparalleled reputation and impact. This is change making at its best, all that anyone could hope for in the real power of philanthropic leadership to do important things that endure."

Maytree's story is one of passion, mission, and strategy joined at the hip. In its clear success, it pushes back on the assumption that philanthropy is a messy science. What we learn is that people must come together to talk from multiple perspectives, to solve complex problems, and they must be open to unanticipated possibilities.

In all efforts there is always the on-the-ground process, an alchemy of events that gets you closer to the goal. It starts with bringing together the disparate players in the way Peggy Dulany and Alan Broadbent have done. With this mix of people and elements, things accelerate and you get more energy and potential than the sum of the parts could ever produce.

The theme we keep circling is how to utilize the power of collaboration in identifying, addressing, and ultimately solving problems. At one level collaboration is something we aspire to, but in affecting it, nothing is more practical or concrete.

It is the art of navigating between different perspectives, stakeholders and communities of interest and seeing that in those intersections there lies the potential for positive change.

Reader's Guide Questions

1. The "ah-ha" moments like Tom Clawson in San Francisco, Ralph Smith in Edinburgh, and Peggy Dulany had in a village in Brazil can be life changing. Have you had such a moment?
2. Trickle-down or bottom-up—can both approaches be employed at the same time?

3. Are you persuaded that poverty can become history? If not, what would make it so? Do you believe the Millennium Development Goals are the right goals?
4. Peggy Dulany believes the most important transformation is that of the human heart. Do you agree? If so, how does one make that happen?
5. Alan Broadbent talks about basic human needs as "commodities." Is there an advantage in taking this kind of inventory? What are the "commodities" essential to making your community a better place?
6. People view the role of government differently in Canada than in the United States. That being the case, is it possible to replicate in the United States what Maytree has accomplished?
7. Have you ever played an advocacy role in your citizen or philanthropic efforts? If not, what holds you back?
8. Alan's "shoulder to the stone" is supremely rational, and he resists ideology and sentimental vision. What is your perspective? What is your metaphor?

Notes

1. See the work of Global Witness, a UK NGO that works in Asia and elsewhere on corruption issues, and Corporate Accountability in Action, which is currently focused on the commercialization of water resources in very poor countries.
2. Social Investment Forum news release, January 25, "2006 Trends Report."
3. The investment firm Hambrecht & Quist raised a $200 million environmental fund in 2006.
4. The United Nations Global Compact currently has more than 1,800 corporations as signatories. It requires corporations to agree to a rigorous set of socially responsible criteria,
5. From the foreword of the *2005 U.N. Millennium Development Goals Report.*
6. Organization for Economic Cooperation and Development (OECD) data give U.S. development aid (ODA) as 0.16 percent of GNI.
7. Edmund L. Andrews, "Rich Nations Reach Deal to Drop Debt of Poor Ones," *New York Times,* September 25, 2005.
8. The "Global Monitoring Report 2005: Millennium Development Goals from Consensus to Momentum," issued in April 2005, was prepared by the World Bank and the International Monetary Fund in collaboration with the United Nations, World Trade Organization, OECD, and the European Commission.
9. Paul Ylvisaker, *Conscience and Community: The Legacy of Paul Ylvisaker,* ed. Virginia Esposito (New York: Lang, 1999).

INTERSECTIONS

SO MUCH OF what happens in life is at the intersection, the place where things come together, sometimes abruptly and sometimes in a stream. It is that moment of inspired synthesis, what Rakosi calls "a sweet pause," when potential seems infinite. Intersections are those moments when we make a decision to say something or to take an action, or perhaps we make no decision and the moment, the opportunity, passes by. What happens at those moments in time can determine the direction of our lives. What happens collectively is what determines the kind of world we live in, the kind of world we leave to our children.

The most interesting intersections lie between heart and soul, between passion and values, and between what we believe and feel, and what we say and do.

Intersections not only happen to us as individuals, but within a society. These are never isolated events, which is why Robert Frost in his poem *The Road Not Taken* wrote, in addition to the line that is so well known, this one: "Yet knowing how way leads on to way." Everything we do, or do not do, influences what comes next. Think of the impact on our lives of certain little actions, like asking someone to marry and that someone saying yes. Now that is an intersection of some note.

What happens in those intersections can determine how some people end up at a dead end and how some people end up in a wonderful place. Intersections are part of the connectivity of things, of the continuum of what is called flow. We have all had some kind of proof of the mere six degrees of separation within the whole gestalt of experience.

There is chemistry in the intersections that are most interesting, a flurry of sparks, a reaction and a combustion that can ignite and compound ideas and intuition into leadership and practice.

The problem is we often do not realize we are at an intersection when we are immersed in the flow of events. Ask any parent of a teenager how difficult it is to know when to say no. One of the great advantages I had as a father of three daughters is that my wife instinctively knew what was right in the moment. Thank goodness. Not only was I easily managed by my smart daughters, but I didn't have a clue I was being managed.

All kinds of decision points can be confusing and difficult. But there are times when we feel a jolt in the flow of our lives, in our community, country or world, and the collision is so obvious, so visceral that we have no choice but to notice.

The most interesting intersections are found in listening to others, to the unique voice of each indigenous person, culture, and community.

Sometimes the intersections that punctuate life's journey get a spotlight turned on them. That light might come from deep within us and be profoundly personal and spiritual, or it might emanate from a great or a terrible event. When that happens, we suffer, worry, dissect, analyze, dream, create, plan, and, with great trepidation, we act, giving what we hope is the right response. Or worse, we do not.

The intersections that are most interesting are those that bridge self-interest with a broader public purpose, where we play a role, where we stand up and are counted.

Parallel Tracks

Sometimes you have to find a way around a tricky intersection, just to avoid a collision en route to your destination. That's what John Abele did. Here is an e-mail I got from him that shows something about his nature and leads us into his story.

"Last week in Newport we discussed how to make the institute vision a reality.[1] Several strategies involve bringing together a small number of change agents, futurists, publishers, producers and experts for a conference I'm sponsoring. I want to call it 'Searching for the Butterfly' after the chaos effect. I'd love to share these ideas with you since they mirror your own objectives."

John is someone with a whimsical, inquiring kind of mind, counterintuitive to the core. He also knows firsthand a lot about process, especially the process of change.

I first met John in the early 1990s. We had dinner at the Concord Inn, an old New England–type place with wide creaky floor boards and a smoky fireplace— an odd spot for a conversation about the future. (I came home and told my wife I had just had *My Dinner with Andre*—the Louis Malle film with Wallace Shawn and Andre Gregory. Andre's ideas, shared over a dinner, are far-reaching for poor Wally, who is somewhat baffled but mesmerized. I played Wally to John's Andre.) Since that first dinner, I have had many such conversations with John, who, as he likes to say, is someone "always trying to see around the corners." ·

He is the cofounder of Boston Scientific Corporation (BSC), a pioneer in the less invasive medical device industry that has transformed medicine and surgical procedures, a company that twenty-five years later has revenues of $10 billion.

When I asked John that first evening what his role was at the company, he did not talk about his scientific or management contributions to the company's phenomenal growth but gave a reply that has stayed with me. "I am the company ethicist." So when John talks, I listen, or, as an alternative, spend a day searching for butterflies.

John told me an interesting story about the challenges of the early days of developing and marketing of what ultimately became a whole new way to practice medicine.

"The problem was cultural and had to do with the prevailing medical view that the larger the hole the surgeon made in the body, the better it was because you could see what was going on. And here we were proposing you did not need a big hole at all and, in fact, could save a ton of money, and provide the patient with much less trauma and pain and significantly earlier recovery. All very good if we could actually deliver technically, which at that time few believed possible, but so foreign to the culture of organized institutional medicine that the resistance was huge. Now I admit it sounds like a *Saturday Night Live* skit. 'A bigger hole is safer for the patient. The better you can see, the better the patient is. If something goes wrong we can fix it more easily.' I would argue that damage was a self-fulfilling prophecy, and you are left with this big hole that has to heal with all of that complication.

"But that was the culture, and we were marginalized, which is the natural response of any establishment to a new idea. It is just like the human body when it takes a foreign object like shrapnel and immediately encapsulates it and pushes it to the side—that is what happens to you when you confront the power structure in any professional society or the powers that be in any culture.

"What we did, what we had to do, was to go forward on parallel tracks outside organized medicine. We started with individual doctors who were excited about the potential and independent and smart enough to ignore the conventional wisdom. It was at that time that Boston Scientific and others in the industry realized the imperative to develop highly sophisticated demonstration, teaching, and conferencing methods that would be independent of the establishment. By design those demonstrations and conferences were inclusive of a wide range of experts and especially included those who were highly critical.

"Everything was on the table for analysis and debate. The whole range of technical issues and quality of life and ethics issues were part of these discussions. Since technology does not spring whole out of a box and takes years of an iterative development, this open and transparent process was part of what built confidence. We listened carefully, and we constantly integrated the feedback. As a result, credibility came not from Boston Scientific or the medical societies, but from leading physicians who had practical, hands-on experience and already had credibility with their peers, growing numbers of whom participated in this process. At a certain point, the number of physicians utilizing or demanding these amazing new technologies and procedures became greater than those who were not. It had become normative. As a result, what was a parallel track to the established order merged and became over time the established order. There were lots of bumps along the way with many dead ends and mistakes, but this strategy ultimately prevailed, and the result for medicine and for patients was, and continues to be, truly transformational."

One can see why Abele calls Boston Scientific a "for-profit philanthropy" because at the end of the day, the company's products reduce human suffering and reduce costs. Who can argue with that?

It is also why he believes that "social dilemmas need to be looked at through the lens of parallel tracks, especially if the goal is to transform and bring about change." There is always a protectionist culture that surrounds the conventional order composed of organizations, associations, and bureaucracies, most of whom have vested interests in maintaining that culture. While direct confrontation is a strategy, John believes, "change agents have a better shot at success if they develop and organize constituencies from within those cultures that do not agree with the establishment."

John has applied his unconventional notions to other efforts as well. He is chair of Project FIRST, a nonprofit program that creates teams of high school students who design and build robots and compete with one another for prizes and scholarships. FIRST is an amazing undertaking for these students, and the work of building a robot is a very rich mix of math, physics, design, electrical engineering, manufacturing, and marketing, but it is even more a lesson in team building.

FIRST is not an "odyssey of the mind"–type experience but instead very tactile and hands-on. It appeals to kids who learn best when they are working with concrete rather than abstract problems. FIRST has successfully defied conventional wisdom that says teams of weak students from very poor urban schools cannot compete with peers from expensive suburban schools—they do and often win—and that today's kids who live for MTV and instant gratification will not commit to such a demanding project. They not only commit and follow through—they love it!

The kids rise to the high expectations FIRST has, along with its high drama and showmanship. (If you ever get the chance, go and experience first-hand a FIRST competition; it will blow you away.) Students learn they are capable of amazing things, but to achieve them, they need to work with others. On one level, FIRST is a game and a competition, but to win big, participants must cooperate with those they are competing against.

"The social dynamic is phenomenal. One-third of participants are female, it's mixed gender and multicultural, and who works with whom constantly shifts. It is an intensive experiential learning activity. Mentors help with key elements like design management built around teams. In designing and building their robots, the teams do not compete one-on-one but in alliance against alliance. Many times alliances change, and there is an incentive to know your competitors. It is a fascinating dynamic I call 'coopetition.'"

FIRST does not rail against the prevailing youth culture in our society, which some see as negative and others defend, but instead offers a compelling alternative track building on what is positive and potential filled.

John told me that his mother always took the other side, no matter what the discussion or argument. "I must have picked up that trait by osmosis, because I am always drawn to the other side of a question. It is why I disagree with conventional approaches to social dilemmas that polarize, instead of bringing opposing forces and stakeholders together, even if that takes some doing."

At Kingbridge, his state-of-the-art conference center in Toronto, John Abele is pushing the envelope on how advanced conferencing techniques can be adapted to other domains, including philanthropy.

"Too much philanthropy is polarizing, which just reinforces the status quo. We tend to live in our own silos, and unless we open things up, change is not possible. Deep learning only takes place when we are confronted with a mix of countervailing views."

He acknowledges that profitable dialogue has its challenges. "There are often pontificators impossible to turn off and other people who speak entirely in innuendos and euphemisms. To cut through some of the puffery and bombast, you have to be a benevolent despot, something wealth enables one to do.

"There are a lot of questions in regard to wealth. From a societal perspective wealth aggregation, corporate and individual, is a tremendous asset because it distributes power. If the government turns you down, you still have a lot of options for your ideas. It is another kind of market and is part of what makes for an open source society, one more likely to survive. But wealth and being listed in *Forbes* magazine is not what constitutes success. What you do with wealth is what defines you, and you never completely get there. The end goal is to provide value for society. That can happen in business, as I believe it happened at Boston Scientific, and it can happen in philanthropy."

John is on the board of Amherst College, and while he respects and loves this excellent school from which he graduated, he feels there is a moral dilemma when it costs $65,000 a year to educate a student. "I think an Amherst owes society something in exchange for that kind of cost. Those who come out of such elite institutions run the risk of not being prepared for the real world. I don't mean Amherst should spend less, but I think the obligation is to do something that is visually productive for society." It has led him to endow an intensive community service program at the college that he hopes will be part of every undergraduate's experience.[2]

When it works, Abele believes that philanthropy can be very effective in pushing against established authority and in bringing together those who would otherwise not talk. "I worry about any situation where there is a 'body of Gods' that makes rules by pronouncement. An awful lot of philanthropy, certainly well intended, suffers from that problem. What is so unique about philanthropy is that it can act without some of the conventional restraints. Philanthropy can be a convener, an introducer, a bridge to common ground, and it can encourage others to expand the dialogue beyond the usual.

"There is no need for outside consultants to take this over. You have to own it." At Kingbridge, he encourages the business groups, nonprofits, and state agencies that participate not to use "expert" facilitators but instead to select one of their own to lead the session or process.

Openness, transparency, and seeing around corners is what Abele believes will lead to a better world, which makes him part of the open source movement that is changing the way we interact.

For John Abele, and others like him, this flow of energy is close to bliss. "To me there is a parallel in all of these things, the power of learning and seeing relationships. It is seeing the patterns that I find most stimulating and most useful in terms of actually implementing things. It is where change can actually happen."

That is why I look forward to my next dinner, whenever, with John Abele. I might also like to invite Henry Izumizaki along, because he would make a fine addition. Henry is about working outside the system, too, and his life is filled with parallels, parallel universes that is. Starting from the streets, he traveled out, up over and back before he went and did it again.

Downward Progression

Henry Izumizaki is a kind of rebel against the established order. And, like John Abele, Henry's iconoclastic is born out of frustration and the experience of helping people to grow and take control over the process of change.

He is in TPI's offices to meet the extraordinary women, all formerly homeless, who are running the One Family Campaign to end family homelessness in Massachusetts. This is the team that Melinda Marble and her colleagues are supporting. They are fascinated with what Henry has to say.

"My first servant job thirty years ago was a street worker in San Francisco where I met any number of schoolteachers, principals, social workers, police officers, and a whole host of nonprofit types. What struck was how ineffective so many of the efforts were. I wanted to change the system and that led me to a job in the Mayor's office. At twenty-eight, I became the highest-ranking civilian in the San Francisco police department, heading up one component of civilian crime prevention. It meant working to organize neighborhoods.

"The rank-and-file police hated us. We were organizing blocks in the nine precincts the police department covered in the city, nearly five hundred blocks in my three years. The folks we were working with had big complaints against the police—lack of respect and response and those kinds of things.

"If I had lunch with a young person we were working with in Chinatown, for instance, I'd be accused of hanging out with cop killers when I got back to the department." Henry's approach was outright incompatible with the department of police.

"They would mark crime spots with pins on a map, go in and sweep the streets in the Tenderloin district where most incidents occurred, and crime would get dispersed. In a couple months, everything would be back where it started. 'We *apprehend* criminals; we don't prevent crime,' an officer told me when I noted the lack of success. So, I went into the Tenderloin and we organized the Northern Market Planning Coalition, coordinated a lot of services for people, helped create a sense of neighborhood, and got one police district to be responsible. We made great strides. But it was political, and after a while we were out."

For the next nine years at the San Francisco Foundation, Henry tried working the supply side. "I thought I'd see if a grant maker could accomplish more than an insider or an agitator. We were able to start a lot of things, low-income housing development, different forms of community organizing and a whole host of model projects, but without the kind of change I wanted to see. Something was missing."

It was the mid-1980s, and the Oakland public school system was in trouble. The district was bankrupt and heading into receivership. Its superintendent had resigned, and four leading candidates who were offered the job declined it. The board of education invited Henry and a few others from a consortium of local colleges to get things turned around. "We were able to involve the community in developing a whole new plan for public education in the city, one not based on a single savior."

So far, so good. But the new superintendent coaxed Henry into the system to help implement the new education plan. "I couldn't resist. I thought, well, here's another opportunity to make change in an important social system."

Pure frustration followed. "Systems can be misguided and unable to change for many reasons, including the fact that things have already been negotiated away."

He wanted to get deeper into smaller organizations, organizations working on the ground directly with people. The chance to organize Oakland's Empowerment Zone initiative looked like the opportunity. "It was based on community-building teams, residents working in their own neighborhoods, identifying needs and issues, and then developing solutions. It was a continually moving target of work projects, developed by the folks most involved.

"All of the resources of the federal government could be applied without category to solving problems in the urban core and some rural places. It came out of a huge federal program that was meant to coordinate efforts from Human Services to the Department of Justice. The problem was that run through HUD; it was a mess. And the implementation, working with the city, was another mess."

Henry kept returning to the idea of how powerful community organizing is. He looked at developing grassroots constituencies. The models he found were oriented to specific issues, not designed to develop the holistic life skills that people need to grow and to take control over the process of change. That knowledge finally led him to cocreate with Judith Rosenberg TEAMS [Transformation through Education and Mutual Support], which is based on a straightforward idea that seems to work.

TEAMS addresses the entire range of social problems that affect low-income communities with a unique approach that leads to effective, systemic change. Our work does not focus on community deficits or imported change. Instead we think in terms of developing the capacity of low-income people to solve their own problems, and realize their own problems, and realize their own opportunities, through self-development and mutual support.

"We are invited into a neighborhood and we interview people—crossing guards, school receptionists, even the kids—to find out who they trust most in the community. 'Who would you go to for help?' We hear the same names over and over again. Those are the people we invite to come hone their leadership skills on behalf of the community and become part of a support action team.

"We pay them for their work to reinforce the fact that what they are doing is of value and we have expectations for them as professionals. This may involve teaching them how to file their taxes and document their mileage and meeting expenses, things they can teach others.

"Typically, groups meet for quite some time. One Latino immigrant community group has met weekly for six years. To start, we talk a lot about the importance of goals. Some folks have no idea what that means. One woman said, 'I'm supposed to keep the house clean, have supper ready, and get the kids off to school.' So we begin to explore a little.

TEAMS begins with small projects like cleaning up a yard, doing immunizations directly, providing physicals for the kids so that they can participate in sports, or bringing dental services into the neighborhood.

"Each time the group accomplishes something, they come back and review it. What worked, what didn't, who's doing all the work? Why did it go down that way? Over time, they get better in doing. In six years, one idea evolved into the Monument Limited Liability Corporation, a Latino nutritional health catering business, and an ever-expanding list of community-conceived, community-controlled, and community-run programs.

"What I have learned is that change, to be real and have legs, is really dependent on the people who are intended beneficiaries. If they are not ready, no amount of resources, or policy changes, or interventions by people who want to be helpful is going to make any difference."

Many people, including several whose stories we have heard, believe that change can come from multisector partnerships, where government, business, and nonprofits collaborate on major systemic issues. Henry Izumizaki, however, is wary.

"Even if they promise better coordination, or greater efficiencies, the problem is that they are run by professionals, paid to go to meetings, and represent the interests of a particular organization or institution. Points can be argued ad nauseum with no meaningful results. Good leaders change, not to mention the political dynamics, and you are back to square one. That is why I believe in being in control of your own destiny and not reliant on outside resources or services."

Remarkably, scaling up is more realizable than it might seem, through efforts such as TEAMS. "What we do is relatively cheap. Our organization operates on less than $350,000 a year, yet we've got all these economic development ventures going on with hundreds of people involved, and many different partners. That's the key. We help them negotiate and keep it all going. Our organizational philosophy is to grow wherever we are working, and then let the people run with it."

As an example of what doesn't work, Izumizaki describes a county government, working unsuccessfully on its welfare program. "Finally, they throw up their hands and decide to go see what the community wants. So, they drop down to the community and ask, 'How would you do such and so?' By and large, the result is something that looks like a one-stop shop. You've got the public health nurse and the food stamps, the probation officer, and the welfare worker now under one roof. All that has been accomplished is that a woman on welfare now goes through *one* door and in the course of *one* morning is abused and disrespected by four different agencies, when before it would have taken at least a week."

The group in the TPI conference room has not lost interest!

"The natural response to problems is to try to fix them in the familiar way. But some things are not fixable. Horribly bad systems that have evolved over time are immovable. The question should be, 'How would you do what needs to be done?' If people are given space and time to think through their own lives and situations, and given the opportunity to think through solutions that do not depend on anyone else except their neighbors, that's where you get innovation. That's what we do. We don't have people protesting that the welfare department needs to be doing something. Face it, that's a waste of time. We say, 'Let's think through what the problem really is and figure out what you can do about it with whatever resources you have.'

"What I am advocating is still at the margins, but there is growing awareness, particularly outside the U.S. In this country, the proliferation of nonprofit institutions, the nonprofit industry, has become part of the problem. Its very existence reinforces dependency. In Central America, for example, there are not as many institutions, so people have to rely on people to do things.

"American philanthropy just exacerbates the problem, I think, because it basically exists to fund nonprofit organizations. There has been a huge proliferation of nonprofits and many of them are not connected into the constituencies they serve.

"Philanthropy needs to adjust how it operates and focus much more on grassroots leadership development, but it is easier to spend gobs of money. You can sort of shift big money if you have big organizations to gobble it up, but it is harder to do a good job distributing it over smaller areas.

"At TEAMS, we build people's capacity, changing individuals as opposed to institutions. Is it possible that even successful efforts to change the institutions serving poor people don't do enough to empower the communities themselves? That's what we think, and that is why we have developed a fundamentally different approach to community change."

The meeting in the TPI conference room is over, but the lessons remain.

Henry Izumizaki is a long-distance runner, and over thirty years he has covered a great deal of ground. He does so in his rambunctious but workmanlike way. Henry is a gifted community organizer, and because his observations are all hard earned, they are easy to admire.

Yet his conclusions disrupt the prevailing norms of philanthropic and nonprofit practice. They also bridge differing views about who bears responsibility for poverty and for ending it, and the role of the poor in the process. Henry does not blame the poor for being poor, but he does urgently want the poor to take control of their own lives, and he has no faith in the capacity of large governmental systems, police departments, school systems, and welfare and social service agencies to do it for them.

Henry has a clear antidependency and anti–social service bias, something that is shared by many others, as I saw at a lunch we hosted for a group of recent winners of the Boston Neighborhood Fellows (BNF) Awards Program.

One of TPI's most gratifying initiatives, the BNF program each year celebrates six unsung heroes in the city of Boston. The Fellows are a wide range of citizen activists—passionate neighborhood organizers, street workers, advocates for immigrants, cops on the beat, priests, nuns, social workers, teachers, "ordinary people doing extraordinary things." Funded by an anonymous donor, each Fellow receives an unrestricted gift of $30,000, more than $1 million to date. You cannot apply for this award. Some of the most delightful phone calls we make each year are to the stunned recipients, who often express disbelief that they would even be considered. Later, the BNF award is indeed presented to these amazing people by the mayor of Boston in front of a large and boisterous crowd, and it is one of the best evenings of my year.

Not long ago, twelve recent Fellows joined us over sandwiches for an informal conversation about the state of the city. One began by attacking what he felt was an inequity in services to the Hispanic community, which elicited a series of heated exchanges. One woman said, "Forget more services. That's what is wrong with the system. I want opportunity to get an education, a job, and to own the problem, man." It was quite a lunch, and it ended with someone saying, "My beans are different from your beans, so don't put me in your pot!"

It was the kind of conversation John Abele and Henry Izumizaki, and others, would have appreciated.

The Izumizaki vision for the world is where people do in fact discover their own power, and thus it mirrors the aspirations of Omidyar Network. How fascinating to think of these lines converging, one that goes one city block at a time, and one that travels at light speed around the globe.

Henry has been TEAMS president for the past five years, and he is now moving on to the Russell Family Foundation and the Threshold Group in Gig Harbor, Washington. He will be the director of learning and strategy, working on the local leadership and international peace issues.

Reader's Guide Questions

1. What have been the major intersections in your life?
2. What have been the major intersections in the life of your community?
3. John Abele talks about his mistrust of "a body of Gods." Have you ever had such an experience, and if so, how did you handle it?
4. What do the theories, disruption, jujitsu, and parallel tracks share in common? How are they different?
5. Polarization is a growing problem in our society. Is there anything we can do about it in our own efforts?
6. John makes the case that wealth, since it represents another market for ideas, is a democratizing force. Do you agree?
7. Are there systems that you feel are "so broken, they are irredeemable"? Have you ever encountered, worked within, or gone around, one that was broken?
8. Henry Izumizaki's approach is incremental—how is it also systemic?
9. Have you met people like Henry—dedicated and in for the long term? What are some things that people can do to stay passionate and committed?

Notes

1. Kingbridge Centre and Institute is John Abele's 120-room conference center in Ontario that provides special services and research to businesses, academia, and government.
2. In 2006, the Argosy Foundation made a gift of $13 million to Amherst College to establish a Center for Community Engagement.

OPEN SESAME
Networks and Open Source Solutions

Open—Of a space; not enclosed or confined: not walled, fenced, or otherwise shut in; to which there is free access or passage on all or nearly all sides

Open Sesame—an unfailing means or formula for opening secret doors and gaining entrance; an allusion to the tale of *Ali Baba and the Forty Thieves* in the *Arabian Nights*

IS OPEN SESAME a fantasy? On one level, sure, but the capacity of creative thinking and sheer human willpower to unlock doors is magical and very real. You have seen it in your own experience. It is what we are experiencing on this journey.

The theme of openness is a drumbeat. Breaking down silos, crossing domains, blending seemingly contradictory values, standing up against dogma and rigidity, seeing around corners, telling the truth to ourselves and others, and deep listening are examples of that beat. This represents a transition in the way we think and act in our relationship to the world. It emanates from our inner condition, the yearning, fears, and the hopes present within. And it is thrust on us by the sheer complexity, pace, and stress of a world that moves faster than we can comprehend. While there is exhilaration, confusion and insecurity are by-products. With all the new doors opening on the improvement of the human condition, at the same time there are signs that some old portals are closing.

This phenomenon of change has many names: *open source*, *open space*, and the *flat world* are three terms for it, but at its core, it is characterized by a flow of ideas, data, services, products, and markets that move more seamlessly across an ever-widening and inclusive landscape of participants. Whether this movement is the Open Sesame of our generation is to be determined, but there is a great deal within it to like.

What is especially interesting and new is that in many domains, the old model of competitiveness, survival of the fittest, is being challenged and in some cases replaced by new models of collaboration. There is a growing movement, for instance, of "cooperative studies," led by Howard Rheingold[1] at Stanford, that is based on the notion that cooperative arrangements, interdependencies, and collective action in areas such as biology, technology, commerce, sociology, and society are propelling alternative ways of thinking and acting. It is what John Abele calls "coopetition." There is a real resonance in these themes with the term *open society*, which for many of us expresses the way we want the world to be—a place that acknowledges and combines all of these elements and interdependencies. The question for those interested in social change from any perspective is, What does this phenomenon teach us, and is there an opportunity to rethink the way we do things?

The Open Source Movement

The economics of peer production, of collective action, especially the power of distributed computing, have radically shifted the knowledge—economic equation. The big example, of course, is the Internet, which has provided an open platform for immense economic development and wealth creation, as well as changing the way we live.

Most significantly, the development of workflow platforms software has allowed people in India to do tax returns for U.S. citizens living in Omaha.[2] The person who takes your order for a hamburger at a McDonald's in Missouri is actually nine hundred miles away in Colorado Springs. This is creating profound changes in communication, the sociology of work and global economics.

In his book *The World Is Flat: A Brief History of the Twentieth Century*, Thomas Friedman traces the economic and technological implications of an interconnected world on the geopolitical future, and they are huge. These terms and ideas are becoming mainstream. Christopher Lydon, a popular public radio commentator, calls his program *Open Source*, "an interactive discussion about art, culture, books, politics, and spirit." WGBH, the Boston PBS station that produces Lydon's show, is "streaming live" over the Internet most of its output. In fact, TPI's conference series is one of many that are now video-streamed out to national and international audiences. Those videos are available for three years via the WGBH Forum—a wonderful shelf life extension of what would otherwise have lived only as a ninety-minute conference. All of this is part of a new and transformational flow of ideas, information, and services.

No one owns open source technology, but everybody can use it, adapt it, and license the adaptations. In these respects, open source technology, networks, products, and ideas become part of the commons, the public space that is available to all.

Those who work in technology live in a world where the competitors, customers, and allies constantly shift, something that completely changes your attitude. In technology, people have learned that to yield is often more profitable than to resist. Remarkably, they have also learned it is sometimes more profitable to give something away for free rather than charge for it.

These are counterintuitive notions, yet they work because they extend concepts and approaches that would otherwise be limited, and through that extension these become even more "profitable" over the long term than if they were kept exclusionary and proprietary.

The Tough Case for Cooperation

American values have always been based on concepts of mutuality, on inclusion, on access, on opportunity, on the making of level playing fields. From that perspective the intersections between the themes of openness and cooperation and philanthropic and nonprofit practice should be natural, but they are not.

First, the very notion of a collective effort pushes against the fierce individualism that is also an entrepreneurial American trademark, one that is increasingly being adapted globally. Few donors are attracted to collaborative action. People want their own thing. Few nonprofit organizations easily yield organizational ambition for a greater social gain. Being proprietary is a cultural norm.

Major foundations have jointly funded projects and programs for many years, but those who have been involved in such collaborations describe how different cultures and decision-making processes have made those partnerships labor intensive and difficult.

Donor intent is considered a prerogative. How could "private" philanthropy be otherwise? Fund-raising practices reinforce transactional philanthropy by "selling" the name on the building, the chair, or the program, which only accentuates the ownership aspect of the process.

The fierce competitive nonprofit landscape contributes to the problem. Colleges and universities are caught up in the *U.S. News & World Report* annual rankings. The notion of becoming a "brand" along with the whole panoply of corporate and management science practices are gaining currency within the nonprofit world and these often reinforce proprietary behavior. Terribly weak economic models for smaller, community-based nonprofit organizations increase the challenge of working collaboratively. As we have seen, social entrepreneurs are highly valued as innovators, but they are also, by definition, independent and strong-willed individuals, not characteristics that lead instinctively to collaboration. In the main, the nonprofit world lacks the market forces that compel technology companies to think collaboratively. Some funders have tried to create that market force, but a recent article in *The Stanford Social Innovation Review*[3] documented the practical problems and pitfalls when foundations make funding conditional on partnerships. If there is not a good fit between a nonprofit's goals and strategic direction, collaboration for collaboration's sake doesn't work.

Add to these issues the lack of transparency that continues to plague the foundation world and the enormous duplication of effort. The flow of ideas and the management of knowledge that is the hallmark of the open source movement are frequently missing in philanthropic practice.

Yet we have heard some evidence that defies these generalizations. If we were to look for common denominators from our expert witnesses, I would suggest it is the belief that collective action leads to less segmentation of issues and more holistic ways of solving problems.

Opening up the existing constraints of conventional philanthropy is one answer to these questions. Listen to Lucy Bernholz, who has tied these themes together around the building blocks that are leading to more open philanthropy.

The Building Blocks of Open Philanthropy

Cho chiwengi pano nchakutose
"Whatever happens here, happens to us all."[4]

"I have been fortunate to live most of my life with only distant, filtered knowledge of war, disease, famine, and despotism. This is not the case for much of the world's population. Unfortunately, few of us who live far from these realities see how close we really are. When we recognize the small size of our planet and the human dimensions of global connections, we act. We see this in relief efforts and in diaspora philanthropy. The single most significant shift for the next century, the defining feature of the world I want, is one in which we base our actions on an understanding of just how connected we really are."

This is the voice of Lucy Bernholz, researcher, thought leader, and vision maker. I am not surprised that Lucy sees the interconnectivity of the world we have, but why is it so hard to grasp?

"It is because we have not changed the way we think about change, even as the change is all around us. The truth is our environmental, social, and economic ties to people across the globe are as fundamental to our well-being and happiness now as were the village communities of yore. What happens to one truly happens to all.

"Bound by locality, we used to try something out on a small scale, get it 'right,' and then find ways to replicate what we had built. These steps have been the holy grail of 'scalable' social change efforts. Decades of public and philanthropic strategy and countless millions of dollars have gone into pilot projects, target communities, and dissemination efforts. And still we wonder why nutrition programs that worked in South Africa fail in South Philadelphia or environmental practices that succeed in Haiti don't work in Peru."

Are you saying that we need to change how we think about where change happens?

"Absolutely. Instead of funding local pilots and trying to scale them, we need to build global and let local happen. To do this, we need to focus on funding interoperable pieces of solutions and supporting local communities to deploy the appropriate mix for their situation.

"Some of the biggest technological changes to come along in recent years don't do anything other than let millions of people interact using a common set of protocols. Everything from podcasting to social tagging to playing SecondLife are systems that allow people to exchange ideas quickly, broadly, and at ridiculously low costs (usually free). What these examples have in common is that the tools are interoperable, allowing the content to be locally made and locally relevant, while also globally available.

"Imagine if philanthropy focused on helping communities cocreate solutions and work together. For example, CompuMentor, a global nonprofit technology provider, relies on users of its website to create the taxonomy they need for finding tech support.[5] Community organizations 'mash up' public health data with Google maps to depict regional variations in diseases and mobilize their constituencies. These kinds of activities are made possible by openly shared, interoperable systems. Such systems, perhaps exemplified by Creative Commons' licenses for sharing intellectual property, are exactly the kinds of building blocks that the social sector needs today."[6]

Is this totally new, or are there existing models?

"There are many models, many of which predate the Internet. For example, music and dance are inherently portable forms of political and social expression. They cross cultures with ease, and creators can quickly learn the basics of a genre and riff it into something indigenous. This is how we get rap from poetry, modern dance from classical ballet, and postimpressionist painting.

"Cultural expression is built on fundamental codes—rhythm, notation systems, alphabets—that are learned and then adapted. Creative recombination is the key to new expression. From the rhythms of Africa that pervade Caribbean music to the satirization of classical ballet that defines Mark Morris's choreography—art thrives because it breaks shared protocols."

What a wonderful metaphor!

"Thank you, but the truth is every domain relies on some kind of code to express and communicate the work. These codes make up the grammar of each discipline, as balance, strength, and rhythm are to dance or vowels and consonants are to an alphabet. They are the smallest pieces—the basic building blocks—that must be mastered so that proficiency and improvisation can happen. Understanding these pieces helps us see familiar systems in new ways. It helps us see the changes occurring in these systems at their most fundamental level.[7] What philanthropy needs to focus on are the building blocks that allow local communities to use global systems for idea exchange.

"To make this shift, funders in fields from the environment to media are assessing core elements of why they do what they do.[8] The old order of 'pilot first; evaluate and replicate later' hasn't worked well. In the connected, flat world we now inhabit, we can expect this approach to fail even faster.

"Funders are now trying to build for big and allow the small to emerge. The Capaciteria website (www.capaciteria.org) demonstrates some of the possibilities. The site provides always-on access to capacity-building tools—information that can be maintained, ranked, and edited by the site users. Everyone can be both a provider of the content and a user of it. This strategy is built on an exchange system of equal communities. Every participant adapts the experiences of others, improves them for their place and time, and puts those revised ideas back out for the next community to use. Philanthropy that supports this approach to change is what I would call open philanthropy."

You make this flow sound almost organic. What are the building blocks of open philanthropy?

"Another metaphor is helpful when considering a profound shift in practice. Think of LEGO™ blocks. Countless structures can be built from LEGOs because the pieces all connect using a common set of posts and holes. LEGO does not limit the user to a predefined end. Even as the company sells boxed sets that contain everything you need to build a helicopter or a giraffe, it also has stores where you can buy just the blue rectangles or yellow squares that you want. LEGO has built the system; you decide what to do with it.

"Compare this to jigsaw puzzles—another system of interoperable pieces waiting to be assembled. But puzzles have only one right outcome. Philanthropy has been funding jigsaw puzzles. We need to shift to LEGOs—funding basic interoperable building blocks that communities can fit to their situation."

Lucy is not the only one who finds LEGO a useful metaphor. Eric von Hipple at MIT's Sloan School of Management, in his theory of "personal fabrication," argues that the leading edge of innovation in manufacturing is increasingly coming from the customer. His examples run from surfboards, to kites, to surgical equipment, and then to LEGOs. When LEGO Mindstorm came out with a new embedded microchip product, users went wild and created a free website that quickly advanced the technology way beyond what LEGO had envisioned. The company had three engineers working on the product, and all of a sudden there were thousands of user-engineers conducting "personal fabrication."

"The parallel to LEGO's blue rectangles and yellow squares for philanthropy will be the assumptions we bring to the work and the way we expect our investments to catalyze broader change. I can think of at least seven emerging building blocks to make philanthropy operate more effectively in our globally connected world. This discussion, and the journey it is part of, may best serve to jumpstart a collective identification process—we will continue to define open philanthropy as we create it. These seven building blocks of open philanthropy are [as follows]:

1. Facilitate adaptation—don't hinder it.
2. Design for interoperability; local specificity will follow.
3. Build for the poorest.
4 Assume upward adaptability.
5. Creativity and control will happen locally.
6. Diversity is essential.
7. Complex problems require hybrid solutions.

"The lessons of alphabets and choreographic notation shape the first building block of open philanthropy: *facilitate adaptation—don't hinder it.* Building blocks are not mandates. They are the pieces that must be put together in order to do something. Alphabets build languages with millions of words. Philanthropy can organize its work around practices and principles that lead to success, rather than funding models or pilot programs.

"The second building block, *design for interoperability; local specificity will follow*, requires exchange mechanisms that operate everywhere. In order for ideas to be locally adaptable, they first need to be available. This opens us up to ideas from unusual places or sources, new applications of old strategies, or the cross-fertilization and repurposing of tools from one arena to another."

What are some examples as they relate to social dilemmas?

"Think of it as using the same kinds of cultural systems that let two or three enthusiastic sports fans get a hundred thousand other fans to stand and 'do the wave.' The rules of the wave are universally understood—it takes only a small (and very vocal) catalyst to get one going because three key protocols are in place: first, people know how to do it; second, they're in the right place to do it; and third, peer pressure. The crowd is always free to stop or morph into doing the Macarena. The protocols of doing the wave are universal, yet every crowd of spectators controls how it plays out at a given event.

"In terms of philanthropic investments, we see analogs in those that have made possible the Public Library of Science, which puts scientific research findings into the public domain for anyone to use. The data are available for anyone to analyze, try new methodologies, and draw new conclusions or challenge those claimed by others. Similarly, open-access journal projects, public databases of cultural research, and self-generated knowledge sources such as those used by Jews around the world to trace genealogy are all magnificent community tools that function because they operate off of clear, transparent, and accessible common protocols."

This kind of freedom of movement assumes a reciprocal relationship between funders and recipients that does exist because we have seen some examples, but it is seldom the case.

"Right, it is almost a direct contradiction to most philanthropic practice, which attempts instead to teach selected sets of schoolchildren the Macarena rather than tapping into the exchange system that exists every time a crowd gathers at a sporting event.

"Codes that facilitate sharing and global systems of exchange are a big part of open philanthropy. The third and fourth building blocks, *build for the poorest* and *assume upward adaptability*, address the directionality of change in a flat and connected world. If we really want social actions to spread from place to place, we need to design them for the least resourced situations. The reason is simple: solutions that work in the toughest conditions can be adapted where greater resources are available. Once a health intervention or agricultural practice is successful in arid and poor conditions, it can spread to places where clean water is prevalent and electricity is available. We know that this doesn't work in reverse—things built for the rich may be incapable of being adapted for the poor. It is easier to adapt 'up' the resource chain."

There is something inherently right about the notion of beginning with what works for those with the least.

"The principle of 'building for the poorest' is beginning to take hold in philanthropy. In 2005, the Bill and Melinda Gates Foundation announced $437 million in awards for health innovations. The idea was to support risky research that would 'concentrate on projects for the world's poorest people.'[9] For example, vaccines that need no refrigeration are critical for tropical climates. Once such vaccines exist, there is nothing to stop them from being useful in places with refrigeration—they can easily be 'adapted up' the resource chain. As we practice sharing ideas globally and promoting their local use, we also need to ensure that the ideas are adaptable."

Perhaps that is what both Pierre Omidyar and Steve Case meant when they said that once launched in this new networked direction of interconnectivity, there is no turning back.

"I'd agree with that and argue that it should inform governance, in that the fifth building block notes that *creativity and control will happen locally*.

"Simply put, globally distributed practices cannot be managed from the top down. As Friedman notes, flattening 'is not simply about how governments, business, and people communicate, not just about how organizations interact, but is about the emergence of completely new social, political, and political models.'[10] Friedman finds examples of how the forces of 'flattening' have reorganized journalism, restaurants, graphics arts, and medicine. In almost all professions, there are pieces of the work 'where we can digitize and decompose the value chain, and move the work around.'[11] And where it can be done, it will be done.

"Philanthropy will be no exception. The basic tools of philanthropy—knowledge, contacts, and finances—are ripe for this transition. Almost every tool in the philanthropic toolbox may soon be produced, distributed, or rated according to the rules of a flatter world. We can anticipate new providers of retail philanthropic products, syndicated data and knowledge sources on areas of philanthropic interest, and a rapidly intensifying shift toward metrics of success.

"The sixth building block addresses this issue of new players in the field. It draws from biology, evolution, and systems theory and notes that *diversity is essential*.

"In open systems, diversity matters. Biodiversity keeps ecosystems healthy, and diversity of information, experience, background, and participation is critical in open philanthropy. As James Suriowiecki argues in *The Wisdom of Crowds*, 'The simple fact of making a group diverse makes it better at problem solving.'[12] In practice, this would lead to philanthropic decision making in the vein of Ashoka's Innovation Award and not the traditional program officer corps.

"The seventh characteristic of open philanthropy addresses the issue of diversity in regard to how philanthropy works with other sectors. This is the idea that *complex problems require hybrid solutions.* All around us, the roles of the public, private, and community sectors are shifting. Philanthropy needs to help build social innovations and finance systems that are robust hybrids of all three sectors. Ideas may be incubated in the community sector, evaluated by market tests, and ultimately monitored and shared by licensing systems that accurately reflect the source and movement of ideas."

You make the best blend yet of how the sectors can and are coming together.

"As philanthropy begins to adapt to the world around it new patterns will emerge. Think about community philanthropy that puts both the idea generation and selection processes in the hands of the community. This is what the Skoll Foundation has done with its community portal, socialedge.[13] Similarly, Oodle uses the matching possibilities of a Craigslist-type forum to help people find places to donate their clothes, furniture, or electronic equipment.[14] These are early examples of open philanthropy.

"There are several current examples of nongovernmental action that demonstrate these principles. In addition to changing copyright laws,[15] we see the use of common codes in low-power FM radio, VirtualPharma, Social Venture Partners, and emerging standards for socially responsible corporate behavior.[16]

"One likely result of recombining the core pieces of philanthropic practice to capitalize on new exchange systems is the launch of new vehicles for giving. For example, a new service called Fundable (www.fundable.org). Marrying the Internet's power to aggregate information to social networking tools, Fundable lets people create group actions for giving. Or buying. Or investing. Or supporting a political campaign. Although the software was designed to help groups of people do one thing, it immediately became apparent that the same steps can be used to several different ends. By going back to the core of how we work, we both unearth outdated practices and identify new ways of working.

"The search for basic rhythms and notations of philanthropy should accelerate the move to hybridized systems, where all three sectors are involved in defining problems, creating solutions, and implementing strategies. The more we rely on action from the core of these sectors, the more we will spark new combinations and new rhythms. We will be building new hybrids as we go. And will be better able to act positively on the ties that bind us."

Lucy Bernholz's building blocks juxtaposed to Henry Izumizaki going block to block create some interesting images in my mind. They are the technological equivalent of the continual feedback loops that develop when the same community group meets week after week for years, and refines and improves the work that they do. John Abele once gave a speech that included a slide of an African warrior in elaborate and full ceremonial dress, holding an enormous spear in one hand and a cell phone in the other. How long will it be before Henry's TEAMS will be instant messaging and podcasting to each other? High tech and low tech may have more in common than we realize, and Lucy is certainly right—"whatever happens here, happens to all."

Let the game of LEGO-philanthropy begin!

Before we do, however, it is time for a reality check. I know of no one better for that job than Dave Bergholz, who brings us a different mix of metaphors around codes of conduct and attitude. It is to him that we turn next.

The Amaryllis and the Skeptic

Dave Bergholz takes magnificent photographs of the plants he and his wife Ellie grow in their garden and of the winter amaryllis that splash their home with breathtaking oranges and reds. The photos have been displayed at galleries and the Botanical Garden in Cleveland, where he lives, and he is thrilled with the response to the work. A flamboyant amaryllis in full bloom gives a spectacular boost to one's spirits, something we all need. Dave's own spirits are dampened too often by pessimism, he says, though he thinks of himself as a basically optimistic person.

He's a complicated man. In another exhibit, his inner demons materialized as he reflected on his fourteen-year assignment as executive director of the George Gund Foundation. The installation, *The Archaeology of Philanthropy*, placed on view his collection of more than a thousand meeting attendance labels, two thousand daily schedule cards, annual calendars, and other detritus of his life in philanthropy, "revealing his valiant personal struggle against both obsession and chaos."[17]

He is also one of the most intuitive people I know in the field of philanthropy. Recently retired, he demonstrated at Gund what a large foundation can and, he would argue, cannot accomplish in the life of a community. Prior to that, he led an innovative national initiative in public school reform and had an extensive career in the operating side of the nonprofit world. In fact, that is how I first met Dave. In 1989, TPI was helping to develop what became the CVS/Pharmacy Innovations Grant Program, and we obtained his advice and counsel. His expertise was critical in the design of what became a major investment by CVS over fifteen years in more than 160 school districts across the country.

With the issues that threaten the globe, he wonders how anyone could not be worried. "Even though scientists differ in their opinions about the risks, global warming and rising levels of carbon dioxide could trigger sharp and painful shifts in the Earth's climate. Considering just two of the major problems, environmental degradation and exponential population growth, never mind a glacier meltdown, is enough to sour any conversation about the making of a better world."

How can anyone not be troubled? Where is the evidence that there is the vision, and the will, to confront these huge, overpowering forces? This is where Bergholz starts, not because he wants it so, but simply because his gut and intellect tell him it is so.

And if he is right, how can there be a realizable view of a better world to come? Yet Bergholz rises to the challenge to prove himself wrong. "I guess I am at a point in life where I do have some beliefs and opinions that for me shed some faint light on the dark corner."

"The problem begins when we delude ourselves as to our own capacity for good and for improvement. We do some things, many things, beautifully but there are many other aspects of human nature that are not at all beautiful. We are far too rapacious, greedy, and violent. Can we change? Change is hard, and we are a species enormously gifted but often out of control. I see secularism and humanism as being among our best qualities; for other people, it is faith and spirituality; still we lean toward tribalism and in its current guise fascism."

I wonder aloud how Dave juxtaposes those views and his gorgeous and hopeful amaryllis.

"To find the beauty and to be in the presence of the positive, amazing mystery of the world around us is my best simple-minded answer to the existential dilemma we have before us." It's the Bergholz version of positive deviance, the notion that the way to escape despair, or move an agenda forward, is to concentrate on the 20 percent that works best and not the 80 percent that is dysfunctional. The amaryllis in full bloom clearly trumpets what works.

That said, and on the record, so to speak, Dave continues. "One piece of the puzzle of what might make a 'world we want' is technology with its still developing capacity for producing change, especially in terms of interconnectedness and the creativity it spawns. Technology is an art form, and like all art, it enhances our humanness. There is a broad humanitarian dimension to the role the technology will play that we are only beginning to understand and master. Along with the obvious negative effects of technology on our lives, I look at how it enables people and removes restraints and this as fundamentally progressive. What I would labor toward, as a citizen and as a foundation leader, and vigorously promote and nurture, is the world of progressive ideas."

What do you mean by a progressive idea?

"Democracy is one, maybe the big one, but there is great value in the exploration and development of other innovative ideas of all kinds. Ideas about the use of information sharing, or about the centrality of arts and crafts in human development and fulfillment that can lift the individual up and provide the intellectual and conceptual foundation for communities and societies to sustain themselves and prosper in the fullest sense of the word. The question is, How do you capture hearts and minds so that they lead to expansion, to the extension of human capacities, rather than contraction and self-interested parochialism?

"We are great at bonding together as a tribe, a family, and a community of interest, but too often it is an exclusionary experience. The secular and spiritual beliefs that could bind us often become the vessel for ill will and even evil. We need to turn those powerful yearnings and the ties that flow from them into positive, expansive interactions."

What comes to mind as Dave talks is the line from the old Shaker hymn— "Till by turning, turning we come right." What he is suggesting is that this duality, this capacity for positive and negative social interaction, good and evil, run side by side. How to "turn" or merge those two tracks is a strategy question that keeps surfacing, and, even more important, it is a moral question.

"One way to keep the course is to build upon the positive aspects of the rule of law. There is something comforting to me about a courtroom. It represents a structured way to be fair and equitable. It has order and enforceability. There is due process, which is necessary. For example, at a local planning commission meeting the other night, a complicated and contentious development project was being considered. I was struck by what a good example this democratic experience is of how to productively come at a problem, somehow sorting out the issues and then resolving them. Hardly perfect, but it gets you there in a responsible and ethical manner. Yet, we are increasingly distrustful of public process in resolving problems and turn to so-called market solutions—what sells, what represents the most technically efficient means to get things done—to solve our dilemmas."

But doesn't dialogue, in the way that Martin Buber defines it,[18] do the same thing? And doesn't community organizing, with its protocols and process, get you to the same place with order and agreed-on results?

"Those approaches are in the same vein and useful, but there comes a point where there is a problem, a big disagreement, and you have to challenge and confront it. There is no judge or jury to make that decision. One such experience happened here in Cleveland with my struggle with the United Way. It was over the funding of the local Boy Scout organization at the time the national organization had adopted a policy and had sought and obtained high court approval prohibiting homosexuals from being scout leaders. That was unacceptable to me and to the Gund Foundation trustees. Our stand bothered a lot of people, and there appeared to be no way that dialogue could help resolve that situation. Those are tough calls, and I wonder if there are not better and less rancorous ways to adjudicate this kind of situation.

"My work at the Gund Foundation was most productive when we focused our resource and energy on leadership identification and development. Leadership is what energizes people to come forward and become engaged. I do not mean just the names, the top-down elitist leaders, but widespread engagement of all the parties at interest who come together to confront the issues that make a city or a community or even a nation work for the broadest constituency of its diverse citizens.

"I've always been suspicious of philanthropy. On so many levels, it is an enormously productive way to seed, to organize, and to support necessary organizations and many foundations do good things. But let's face it, it is sometimes a hell of an elitist way to bring resources to bear on complex issues that should be resolved as part of an extended public conversation.

"I spent most of my career on the money-raising rather than the grant-making side of the table. My livelihood was significantly dependent on the largesse of the wonderful world of philanthropy so my criticisms of the field should be couched within that context. No matter the pleading of well-intended foundation staff that they have the pulse of the community they serve, it is basically a privileged and isolated business. The gap in equity between grant seekers and fund grantors is wide and profound. It can be lessened but, from my perspective, never overcome. My first mentor said to me forty years ago that philanthropy is at its best when its resources are put to use in strengthening public institutions, not just in largesse directed toward private institutions that have been a part of a donor's life.

"Frank Karel, former communications director of the Robert Wood Johnson Foundation, put it best when he said that 'philanthropy does not rest easily on the bosom of democracy.'

"Today, given how daunting it is to define the 'world we want,' we must be careful to remember that it is the *we* that is important, not just the movers and shakers of philanthropy. The advent of widespread big-box philanthropy raises my level of suspicion about the productive role that private giving can play in helping to lead us toward a better future.

"In my special area of interest, the improvement of this nation's public schools, the power of enormously resourced foundations in setting the course of the conversation is alarming whether I agree with the path promoted or not. This is more a reflection of the increasing divide between rich and poor in this nation than it is a sign of enlightened debate about a community-determined course of action to improve outcomes for our children. Foundations should, from my perspective, be about helping this democracy effectively check and balance its excesses rather than choosing up sides, particularly a side that may be about diminishing rather than strengthening public involvement.

"What I would love to see, and what would make a huge difference in philanthropic quality, is far more accountability and transparency. A willingness on the part of foundations to better understand their role in this democracy of ours and to take these learnings to advance the public as well as the private will would be most beneficial."

Dave Bergholz continues his late-bloomer photography career, as well as aspects of his civic life that are both deeply involving and somewhat hopeful, but he ended our conversation in a discussion of his work on public school issues with a reference to the recent obituary of Kenneth P. Clark, the famous psychologist who was influential in helping to end school segregation. "Dr. Clark thought his life had been a series of 'magnificent failures.'" Dave is a reluctant pessimist, but in retirement he is trying to live a life that does not duck that condition of mind and still treasures small victories and the glories of nature.

When someone is as involved as Dave has been in the difficult work of education reform, there is bound to be some lingering frustration, though the work he accomplished helped organize local education funds that funneled more than $1 billion into three hundred school districts and brought improvements in teacher training and curriculum development and greater citizen participation in decision making. Still, lasting reform requires huge system change, and that job remains incomplete. And that is always true.

If we could all do as well in our own "magnificent failures" as have Clark and Bergholz, the world would be that much closer to the world we want.

It is time to dig deeper. We have moved from big, transformational ideas to the intersections and parallel tracks that opened up the sources and protocols of philanthropy, and now we arrive on the ground where the real amaryllis grows.

Reader's Guide Questions

1. Do the new topics that abound—open source, open space, and flat world—represent a new philosophy about thinking and working together? Or are they just trendy terms?
2. Has your life changed as a result of the new information technology?
3. Do you agree with Lucy Bernholz that philanthropy needs to change from a "jigsaw puzzle mentality" to an interoperable "LEGO mentality"?
4. Lucy presented seven building blocks of open philanthropy. Can you think of a time when applying one of more of these principles would have been beneficial in your community or work?

   Facilitate adaptation—don't hinder it.

   Design for interoperability; local specificity will follow.

   Build for the poorest.

   Assume upward adaptability.

   Creativity and control will happen locally.

   Diversity is essential.

   Complex problems require hybrid solutions.

5. If you, like the author, do not know how to do the Macarena, would you like to learn?
6. Do you agree that "we delude ourselves as to our own capacity for good and improvement," or are we "far too rapacious and violent"? Can we/ societies be both?
7. Have you had a stand-up-and-be-counted experience like Dave Bergholz's with the United Way and the Boy Scouts? If so, what did you do?
8. Are you suspicious about philanthropy? Do you worry about "big box" philanthropy? Can philanthropy ever be nonelitist?
9. Dave has his amaryllis—do you have something equivalent?

Notes

1. Howard Rheingold is the author of *Smart Mobs: The Next Social Revolution* (New York: Perseus Books, 2002). His work on cooperation can be found at Stanford University at http://cooperation.smartmobs.com/cs/node/8.

2. From Fareed Zakaria, "The Wealth of Nations," *New York Times Book Review*, May 1, 2005, a review of Thomas L. Freidman's *The World Is Flat*.

3. Francie Ostrower, "The Reality Underneath the Buzz of Partnerships," *Stanford Social Innovation Review*, Spring 2005.

4. Proverb of the Tongan people of Malawi.

5. See posting by Marnie Webb of CompuMentor at www.omidyar.net/group/compumentor/news/11/.

6. Creative Commons is supported by individuals, the Center for the Public Domain (www.centerpd.org), the John D. and Catherine T. MacArthur Foundation (www.macfound.org), and the William and Flora Hewlett Foundation (www.hewlett.org).

7. See Claude Lévi-Strauss, *The Elementary Structures of Kinship* (New York: Beacon, 1971) (original 1949).

8. See David Bollier's blog (www.onthecommons) and the work of Public Knowledge (www.publicknowledge.org) for information on the Commons. Other sources include Common Assets (www.commonassets.org), "The Future of the Commons"; Robert D. Hof, "The Power of Us," *Business Week*, June 20, 2005; and the interview with Yochai Benkler, "The Sharing Economy," *Business Week*, June 20, 2005. Howard Rheingold is the author of *SmartMobs: The Next Social Revolution* (New York: Perseus Books, 2002). His work on the technologies of cooperation can be found at Stanford University via http://cooperation.smartmobs.com/cs/node/8.

9. Donald G. McNeil Jr., "New Ideas in Global Health Get a $437 Million Boost," *New York Times*, June 28, 2005, www.nytimes.com/2005/06/28/health/policy/28gate.html.

10. Friedman, *The World Is Flat*, quoting David Rothkopf, former senior Department of Commerce official, 45.

11. Friedman, *The World Is Flat*, 15.

12. James Surowiecki, *The Wisdom of Crowds* (New York: Doubleday, 2004), 30.

13. See www.changemakers.net and www.socialedge.org.

14. See www.oodle.com, which lets givers and organizations identify what they have and what is needed.

15. See www.creativecommons.org. See story on the rise of open source software in Brazil in Julian Dibbell, "We Pledge Allegiance to the Penguin," *Wired*, November 2004.

16. Many of these examples are discussed in Geoff Mulgan, Tom Steineberg, and Omar Salem, "Wide Open: Open Source Methods and Their Future Potential," DEMOS, United Kingdom, www.demos.co.uk. Paul Hawken is leading efforts to set standards for socially responsible investing at www.naturalcapital.org, and metrics for corporate social responsibility are discussed at the World Economic Forum,

www.weforum.org/site/knowledgenavigator.nsf/Content/Corporate+Social+Resp onsibility, and The Keystone Report from AccountAbility, available at www .accountability.org.uk.

17. See www.spacesgallery.org.

18. Martin Buber conceives of true dialogue being possible only when there is an "I-Thou" relationship. The image of the self is incomplete without the image of the other. Martin Buber, *I and Thou*, trans. Ronald Gregor Smith (New York: Free Press, 1971).

ON THE GROUND

B ACK IN MY ordinary room, I am trying to assimilate the many ideas
about change we have heard. I feel the need to be more concrete and
less speculative. It has been said that "execution trumps strategy,"[1] and
I am with those who believe that T. S. Eliot was right when he wrote "between
the conception and the execution falls the shadow." Ideas are one thing; making them work is another. Despite the best plan in the world, some things cannot be predicted in advance. There are many unknowns, and there are always
unintended consequences that surprisingly and all too frequently provide the
most interesting results.

And yet the future may in fact be upon us. Many of the innovative ideas
we have been hearing about are evident in work under way. Utilizing the tools
of the market economy on community-based issues is a reality. The elements
of collaboration between the sectors and open philanthropy, even some of
Lucy Bernholz's lucid building blocks, are in play and being worked by thoughtful practitioners and activists, as we will see. And there are people who take very,
very, seriously the concerns about attitude that trouble Dave Bergholz. So let's
go check it out.

After I put more wood on the fire, that is, take a deep breath, and take a
step back.

Much of life's experience is indirect and composed of images. Sometimes the
images are very powerful, burned forever into our consciousness, like the picture of JFK shot in an open car in Dallas, or the second plane bursting into
flames as it hit the World Trade Center. More often they are the things we see
each day on television or in films or that come into our minds from books and
newspapers or simply in talking with friends.

These are the fleeting images of the "walk-by" part of our lives. The infinite collage of a world that is hurting—a homeless person huddled in a doorway on a rainy city night, a child with a bloated stomach in a Darfur refugee camp impossibly juxtaposed with a world that is beautiful—children building sand castles on South Beach in late afternoon, or Midori Goto playing the violin.

These images synthesize with the "walk-in" part of life, the day-to-day flow that comes from family life, student life, work life, community life, church life, and all the things that we do that define who we are. Some of these are of our own making, and some come by chance, but every one of us is conditioned in these multiple ways. It is that which prepares us, makes us ready to receive and to respond, or not. This is the soil in which our values and passions grow, out of which evolves our belief system whether or not we articulate it in those terms. It is the beginning of wanting to become involved.

Some people are receptive, open, and curious all through their lives. Others are not; they raise shields, hide behind gates, turn off, sleepwalk by, and remain silent in the face of demonstrable need. Some act, instinctively, naturally, and in the process grow, become more grounded, more generous, transformed, some word we do not yet know. Others do not. The point is we have a choice, and it is of our own making.

Street Scenes

Jim O'Connell was set on becoming a country doctor. He loved Vermont, its mountains and lifestyle, and he planned to practice there. Twenty years ago, as a Harvard-trained resident at Mass General Hospital (MGH), he was on a sure track. Then, to his surprise, he fell in love with something else—homeless people, whom he now doctors where they live in shelters, on the streets, and under bridges in the grave corners of Boston.

"I was enamored, really, with the old drinkers—homeless men, mostly—who came in off Charles Street and the Esplanade to a once-a-week continuity care clinic we residents did at MGH." There were all sorts of problems—broken limbs, toes being lost to diabetes, and so on. Several had cancer, and Jim cared for them in the hospital as well as at the clinic.

Just before he was to leave MGH for a prestigious fellowship at Memorial Sloan Kettering Cancer Center in New York, his chief of medicine, John Potts, asked him to stay on for a year as the program doctor for a new outreach project being formed by a coalition for the homeless. Thomas Durant, a legendary MGH doctor and humanitarian, also leaned in, and Jim agreed, thinking

Boston Health Care for the Homeless (BHCHP) would be a short stint, kind of an urban Peace Corps. He put his coveted fellowship on hold.

Jim knew little about homelessness except what he had learned at the MGH clinic, but he helped create a program that would spark federal legislation and become a model for health care for the homeless throughout the nation. The Boston program today, with fifteen doctors and 250 employees, provides medical services to roughly nine thousand homeless men, women, and children each year in shelters, on the streets, and in a ninety-bed respite care facility for those undergoing chemotherapy. It has seventy sites, including a trailer at Suffolk Downs racetrack where migrants working in the barns get medical attention. It may soon have a new home. A huge capital campaign is underway to enable BHCHP to renovate what once served as the city morgue.

From senior resident in charge of the intensive care unit at MGH, managing chaos and some of the sickest people imaginable, Jim moved to Pine Street Inn, a homeless shelter in Boston. It had an excellent nurse's clinic, but he was to be its first full-time program doctor. He felt prepared; he felt he knew next to everything.

"I walked in expecting they would be thrilled to meet me. Instead, they sat me down in a folding chair and read me the riot act. I should sit and watch; they would teach me the art and science. They made me soak the first few patients' feet. It was biblical."

Barbara McInnis, a nurse who had worked with the homeless for years, told Dr. O'Connell he would have to figure out how to slow down. "Nothing happens quickly, but only as you build relationships," she said. It was a foreign notion for someone trained to run, comfort, diagnose, and treat an intensive care patient in fifteen minutes, but it defined the culture that was needed for the new program to be effective.

I first met Jim through a mutual friend[2] who was chief of medicine at a state hospital in Boston that opened one of the first homeless shelters in the city. Also, in a classic "six degrees of separation" manifestation, my son Tom Karoff is now a resident in medicine in a hospital in the Bronx as a direct result of witnessing Jim minister to the homeless. Tom worked as a social worker for several years on the Pine Street shelter van that circulates the city. He told me about "this amazing doctor," and I immediately knew who it was. What makes Jim so truly amazing is his hell-bent desire to befriend and care for people many prefer not to see.

"Looking at homelessness is like holding a prism up to our society with all its shortcomings refracted, not only in health and mental health care but in housing, education, and corrections. Failures are interrelated and complicated.

We had excellent clinics in the hospitals and in the shelters, but we were not getting to many people living on the street, 10 percent of whom are mentally retarded, most of those with IQs below 60.

"I think it is a contradiction to expect health care where there is no safe housing, yet keeping these folks in housing is difficult because of the intense services they need. They have no skills for apartment living. Their doors are open to everyone and anyone including drug dealers who prey on them. Even when systems are working, you always see the edge of where it can all fall apart. Hospitals do pretty well caring for the immediate needs of homeless people, but when a longer term treatment plan is necessary, patients just don't have the capacity to keep it going.

"Closing down the mental institutions without providing enough support created huge problems, as horrifying as those back wards were. Throw in the added wrinkle of civil liberties, and you get people like the dear eighty-year-old man I know who should not be out on the streets. Even with the best of community services, I can't get him to come in. We need to be more creative in developing the right kinds of community support. The current federal effort to end chronic homelessness will merely scratch the surface, but the concept is right. Get people into supportive housing, and then get to work on their problems."

The Robert Wood Johnson Foundation grant that started the Boston Health Care for the Homeless program in 1985 envisioned that it would be a four-year program that would work its way out of existence. It was meant to be a catalyst to get this work into the mainstream health care system. That has not happened, but O'Connell has ideas for how it could.

"The model for geriatric care is a good analogy for approaching homelessness and healthcare. In the mid-1960s, before Medicare and Medicaid, when an older woman came to hospital with a broken hip, we would take care of the injury and then send her back to her third-floor walk-up with its impossible bathtub and, often, a rebroken hip. So geriatric programs began going into the home to figure out ways around the obstacles. Now these home care programs are everywhere.

"Similarly, we should not be creating a new system for the homeless. We take care of a homeless guy who comes in with a fractured wrist, but we need to go out and see the circumstances he is living in and change those to make it continuous health care. We've been trying to do this at MGH for twenty years, but it is still not the norm.

"The original project funded by Robert Wood Johnson and Pew Charitable Trust was a nineteen-city program. It became the genesis of the Stewart

McKinney Act of Congress that made health care for the homeless a legal right. Now there are federally funded health care for the homeless programs in every state, 165 throughout the country. The Boston program was the model.

"Massachusetts was blessed. Under the Dukakis administration, it was the one state that matched the grant so BHCHP ended up with double the federal funding of $200,000 a year for the first four years. Also, the academic medical centers in Boston genuinely bought into it. Oftentimes, doctors who take care of marginalized populations do so at the risk of their own professional standing, sad to say. In contrast, I was given a clinic in Mass General, and I remain part of the hospital. That kind of arrangement is rare."

Community action played a big role at the start of the program. To get the initial grant, every city had to have the buy-in of the stakeholders. In Boston, eighty-eight people, a coalition of shelter providers and homeless people, worked with the city and the hospital.

One thing they agreed on from the beginning was that health care is an issue of justice, not charity. It is a right, not a privilege. They decided there would be no use of volunteers, student doctors, interns, or residents, and no research. The lives of homeless people were marked by fragmentation. The idea was to bring some continuity into their health care.

"I hated those decisions at first. I had just finished my senior residency and was at the top of my game. Many of my friends, doctors, and specialists wanted to volunteer; it felt crazy not to let them help. I also thought the research piece should be allowed because we needed to prove outcome.

"Ultimately, however, they were good decisions. We were forced to evolve, to hire full-time doctors, fully privileged at Boston hospitals, who could meet the muster and be available twenty-four hours a day. A homeless person can go to the doctor and get medical attention and support. We can find you under a bridge, and if you need cardiac surgery tomorrow morning at Mass General, you will get it. We can break through all sorts of barriers, overcome all sorts of obstacles. But it happens quietly under the radar screen, and it is not happening everywhere as it would be in the world we want."

What is the solution? "While I am a huge proponent of universal health care, it alone will not solve this problem. The poorest of the poor have free care access to the health care system right now. Of people living in shelters, 70 percent have Medicaid, and 80 percent of street people are covered. The inescapable fact is that insurance is not answer enough. Much like housing, it is part of the issue, a necessary but by no means sufficient part of the solution. Most of these people have access."

What they are missing, along with a home, is family to speak for them. A woman who works in Haiti with pioneering doctor Paul Farmer of Partners in Health rode one night in the outreach van with Jim delivering blankets and food along with medical help. She told him that the abject poverty compares with Haiti's, but the poverty of spirit and utter desolation here is worse. It can defeat anyone, but Jim tries to break through, little by little, building trust directly with a familiar face.

"Take Greg, a very sweet and handsome young black kid I tried to coax out from under a bridge for years. He had a whole set of problems and a dense stutter that made it hard to understand what was going on. I finally got him into the McInnis House, a respite care facility, and learned his last name. He wanted to call his sister, also homeless, but didn't know how to use a phone. He never went to school, grew up chaotically in foster homes, and escaped at fourteen to live under the bridge. He has nobody; he's got nothing. So, what do we do? How do you figure out support for a life that is meaningful or enriching? We got him into a rooming house with five others, got a case manager one hour a week through the Department of Mental Retardation, and we tried to visit him often. After six months, it all exploded because he can't live with structure. He ended up back under the bridge.

"When you first start working as a doctor, you get really angry at a system that would allow people to be in this position. These people you care for—it is not their fault. It is a system problem we have to fix. You get discouraged because you feel that you are not going to change the situation; it is so big, and you're just a doctor. But you stay with it because of how close you become to the people you care for. You get attached and do what you can."

What you can do is sometimes confounded by systems failures, particularly in the coordination of care. Jim has primary care patients who live on Boston Common, a park with five corners each covered by a different Boston hospital. Someone who takes a spill inevitably has separate charts at Beth Israel, Boston Medical Center, New England Medical, Mass General, and Brigham. Complicating care even more, he can't look up his patients' records in the mental illness or substance abuse systems, which are separate and paid for in different ways. "The substance abuse system may be helping one of my patients withdraw from cocaine, with no knowledge that he is at risk of heart disease. It is not impossible to design and put in place a more coordinated and efficient system.

"Doing good health care doesn't cure homelessness, and I've had to learn that my niche is to work hard promoting health care for the homeless the best we can. We have to acknowledge that the solution needs to be much larger. A solution for Greg, where he could be part of something, a job he could handle, some life experience, would be so wonderful. For that we need some incredibly creative thinking. The vision I hold for the world I want is a very large tent, and people who happen to be struggling would have a health care system that is able to take them on, just like we have taken on the elderly. Programs like ours would be part of the mainstream."

Jim O'Connell is unusual in his chosen work, but he is not alone. We are about to meet another person who is also quite precise and clear about what needs to be done to help bring Dr. Jim's beloved people off the street.

If We Are Serious

I vividly remember the first time I met Frank Melville, founding chair of the Melville Charitable Trust. It was 1989, and we were in the offices of Peter Goldmark, then president of the Rockefeller Foundation. Frank and the other trustees of this new foundation had come in for some advice. "We are interested in the issue of homelessness, but all we know is what we read in the *New York Times.*"

What followed was a six-month TPI tutorial of learning, listening to policy experts and practitioners, and making site visits to programs. It was—just to make the link—Melinda Marble who put together the curriculum for the tutorial for the Melville trustees, and her sensitive guidance played an important role in trying to understand how the trust could work with any degree of success on such an intractable issue as homelessness. At the end of this initial process, Frank and the other trustees made a fundamental policy decision. Feeding and housing the homeless was the responsibility of government, and the job of the trust was to focus its resources on the systemic root causes of why people are homeless and to begin that work in its home state, Connecticut. It was a vision that has stayed remarkably the same for sixteen years. I would say it was a promise of intention that has been kept.

"I don't think of myself as a philanthropist," says Frank's son Stephen, who has succeeded Frank as the trust's chair. "The money I'm giving away is not my own. I only joined the trust's decision board after it had settled on its mission and approach, and I have only recently become its chair. I have a day job as a university professor, and that continues to be the primary way in which I identify myself. It is also true that the word *philanthropist* still makes me uneasy.

"It is not that I don't love my fellow humans, at least not exactly. But I am drawn to those thinkers who take the human capacity to betray the human to be a deep fact and inseparable from whatever ability we might also have to transform ourselves for the better. If you find this mood a more or less permanent color of your world, you're likely to distrust your own dreams or visions of better and best."

Steve does not pretend to be operating without any kind of vision, some strong aspiration toward a distinctly better world. What he tends to do is tamp that vision down—to say, for example, that what he is shooting for is just "some minimal level of decency," and, as he puts it, "decency calls for no vision particularly larger than the world you've actually got in front of you. Homelessness in America is a scandal, there for the seeing and naming. Saying so invokes standards we already share, and so the main demand on vision is for a certain steadiness, a willingness to stay focused." He knows that for some people this would feel like being stripped of purpose and passion, but for him it sets the terms of a job worth doing.

Of the eight hundred thousand individuals and families homeless in America, two hundred thousand are chronically homelessness. They confront severe mental illness, drug addiction, or long-lasting illnesses such as HIV/AIDS, and many are victims of trauma. They are people who become homeless on multiple occasions and often for years on end. They cycle through shelters, jails, emergency rooms, and treatment centers and end up living on the streets at a tremendous cost to themselves and to society. Chronic homelessness cuts across a multitude of issues from housing, to health and health care, to mental illness, to child welfare, to prisoner reentry, to poverty and community development. No single funder or provider can hope to solve it alone, and the involvement of both the private and public sectors is essential.

"The Melville Charitable Trust wants to put an end to homelessness, to the extent of our power in the matter," says Steve. "We are not inclined to think of our actions as having some inherent 'philanthropic' value. We are at times quite acutely conscious of the way in which too great a faith in the goodness of charity can become a tacit commitment to keeping in place the conditions that demand it.

"That, of course, is the rub—one of the rubs, anyway. If we are serious that we mean to put an end to homelessness, then we must play our part in creating a social fact that will exist, and continue to exist, wholly independent of us. We must put ourselves out of business or at least out of the business we're currently in. I find it useful to think of the trust's work as being an attempt at a redistributing agency and doing so in such a way that the trust does not end up holding any particular power."

The trust has been proactive whenever it has seen a need that wasn't being met, according to Bob Hohler, CEO of Melville Charitable Trust. It discovered early on that the housing and services groups in Connecticut lacked an infra-structure that would enable them to learn from one another, work collaboratively, and plan strategically. The trust funded and has continued to fund coalition efforts in housing, homelessness, investment, and legal services that have had sig-nificant influence in shaping action and policy on local, state, and national levels.

The trust recognized that the shift of federal welfare and support services to the state level would invariably result in imbalances and inequities that would penalize the homeless and the voiceless. So for several years it became the largest source of private support for consumer legal services in Connecticut. The result was the first statewide legal services collaborative in the country. This collaborative has played a key role in challenging and softening punitive agency regulations and protecting such rights as access to affordable housing for the mentally ill to health care for mothers and their families.

Some of the trust's support has had a resonating impact far beyond the projects it funds, Hohler says. It was a loan of $245,000 to the West Hartford Interfaith Coalition that was the linchpin of the coalition's ability to sustain litigation against the Town of West Hartford. The coalition challenged the town's zoning denial of its plan to build affordable, limited equity housing. It was the first community-housing group to use the state's new Affordable Housing Appeals Act, taking the case to the Connecticut Supreme Court—and against all predictions, they won a unanimous victory, fundamentally changing the course of housing law in the state.

"Often we think of power as something one needs in order to act," Steve says, "and of course much of our activity does involve giving our grantees the power to do something. But power is also a consequence of action. Any action generates effects, and power is a question of who is in position to gather up those effects. I am powerless when the effects of my actions are irrecoverable by me.

"This seems to me a good way to look at various aspects of the world we live in. Philanthropy—socially transformative philanthropy—seen this way, means attending not simply to particular programmatic actions but also to their unexpected consequences and to how those consequences create or baf-fle further agency. With respect to homelessness, there is no clearer contrast than that between the shelter system as a charitable means of continuing homelessness and permanent supportive housing as a means of ending it.

"More generally, this way of thinking offers a way to make sense of the language of 'capacity building' and 'empowerment' that is threaded through all of our efforts. Capacity building, for example, is not simply a matter of adding something to subjects or institutions already in place, but sometimes crucially a matter of creating new subjects or institutions that gather up, make sense of, or continue the effects of earlier actions. I'd describe the Partnership for Strong Communities in Connecticut as an institution that emerged along a path like this, one of those moments or places where the effects of earlier actions demanded a certain consolidation if they were to become more than isolated acts scattered across an untransformed field.[3] The inevitable drift of such movement is, I believe, toward policy and advocacy. My impression is that philanthropy is frequently wary of moving too far in this direction, but without it, the community on whose behalf we claim to act remains essentially voiceless and to that extent also powerless."

Vital advocacy and education innovation have been part of the trust's work, including support of Partnership for Strong Communities. A working coalition of key statewide housing and homeless organizations, the partnership has played an increasingly prominent role in raising public awareness, supporting pilot programs, and advancing policy solutions to end homelessness, create affordable housing, and build healthy and economically vital communities. The Melville Trust also played a key role in building a collaboration of nine national foundations, nonprofit organizations, and financial institutions that galvanized leadership and dollars to bring an end to chronic homelessness across the country. So far, the Partnership to End Long-Term Homelessness (PELTH) has dedicated more than $50 million in grants and loans to the Corporation for Supportive Housing (CSH), the National Alliance to End Homelessness (NAEH), and other groups working to end long-term homelessness.[4] PELTH aims to leverage at least $50 million more from other national and locally based foundations, financial institutions, and businesses. In addition, it serves as a knowledge center for best practices in housing and service initiatives to stimulate grant making and increase public and private sector financing for the costs of supportive housing.

"I take the connection of voice and agency here seriously; it is a connection we make all the time. 'Promising' is a prime example of speech that counts also as action: my promise is not a report on my feelings or intentions but a binding act. Failing to keep my promise is not excused by my claiming simply to have changed my mind. Furthermore, promises are social acts that must be made to, and received by, someone else.

"Philanthropy is ultimately a promissory activity with responsibility for the kinds of failure or misfires promises can run afoul of. It is, for example, a problem if there is no one to secure your promise or if people refuse to hear it as a promise. Homelessness in the United States is not a problem private charity can solve. There is a great deal philanthropy can do—our more or less regular activity of nurturing leadership and ideas, piloting projects, leveraging funding, making new collaborations possible, filling in gaps in government support, and so on—but in the end all this unfolds in the interest of creating a sort of elaborate and detailed promise that can only be secured at the massively stepped-up scale of national policy and resources.

"At this time, it is not at all clear that there is any real political will to secure such a promise. A government that once seemed to be seeking a certain kind of partnership with the private sector seems more and more intent on reducing everything to mere private activity. At times this feels like an argument over the sense and good of charity—whether it is best taken as its own reward, the giver's redemptive act, or as social action, a giving that matters in its consequences. The current mixture of religious sensibility and entrepreneurial faith makes the kind of work we mean to do hard, and it makes it easy for private charity to be satisfied with the simple human good it does and can all too easily continue to do."

Getting a clear understanding of the problem is one way to sustain a vision for change, and hard numbers help, Hohler says. Recently, policy makers woke up to evidence that "supportive housing" can be a cost-effective solution to long-term homelessness. In New York City, a day of supportive housing costs $31 compared with $164 a day in jail, $467 in a psychiatric hospital, or $1,185 in a community hospital. When formerly homeless individuals use supportive housing, emergency room visits drop by 58 percent, emergency detoxification services fall off by 85 percent, jail time is cut in half, and earned income is 50 percent higher.

One of the trust's most successful collaborations has been with the CSH. With trust funding, the CSH brought its model to Connecticut, and it led to the first-ever statewide funders' collaborative to match the start-up grant of $450,000. This initial outlay has generated approximately $30 million in state and private foundation funding—with many more millions of investment and development dollars on the way. It also produced a first-ever state government cabinet group to focus on service-enriched housing.

Steve's "sense of philanthropy—of the kind of action it performs and the kinds of risk to which it is exposed—is no doubt historically quite specific and distinctively modern: secular, wholly social, and, I believe (here, creeping and glimmering, comes the vision), profoundly democratic. Of course, I will say that last bit in more or less the same breath that I will also say that nothing is more democratic than the betrayal of democracy. Democracy, if it is to be anything more than an exercise of numbers, must surely be the simple, ongoing responsibility for social fact continuously informed and driven by the sense that it is yet to be achieved, that we still too often leave one another's promises unmet.

"Such a notion of democracy strikes me as close to what the philosopher Stanley Cavell calls Emersonian perfectionism, the willingness to hear within whatever self one may have the demand that there be a next self, and so also the willingness to hear within the apparently achieved terms of our democracy the clear claim of the social and political lives we do not yet have. Like Cavell, I'm prone to insist this cannot be a matter of knowing what the future perfection of our selves or our lives might be. What one acts upon has no deeper ground or principle than can be discovered in one's best attention to the present's failures of itself. The world we want must be this one.

"These remarks, all too clearly given over to the abstract and academic, are no doubt driven by a desire to knit up where I can the gap between my day job and the philanthropic life I'm still finding my way through. To me, it is important to pick out and insist upon the permanent and irreducible political dimensions of serious philanthropic activity—thus underlining both the limits such activity should continually press toward and the nature of the field in which it finds its responsibility and standards. We must answer to a present in which the general feel for the social and the political is as near to the breaking point as it has ever been—as if private philanthropy has now to bear an unheard of responsibility for the actual terms of a possible public life."

Stephen Melville tends toward systemic and thoughtful reflection. Bob Hohler speaks directly from the heart of concrete facts and experience. Bob has worked with the trust virtually from its inception, bringing to it his life-long passion and commitment to social justice. Here, then, is Bob's moving personal perspective on homelessness, which is a striking witness to the disparate terms by which two people might find themselves joined in promotion of the common good.

"My brother and I are sitting with our parents around a battered card table with two drunken legs. We are playing whist. The room is full of a blue haze from the handmade cigarettes my father and mother intently smoke as they mull their hands. We are barely able to read our cards, as the room is lit by only a small table lamp. The shades on the two front windows of our third-floor walk-up are tightly drawn so as to not show any light to the outside world. We are, in effect, hiding.

"My father, his hands trembling from a recent bout with delirium tremens, has just dealt a new hand. My mother is pleased with what she sees and has a small round smile on her face. My father, who is my partner, is smiling, too.

"Looking over the card players from a place of honor above the living room mantel is a cheaply framed, rotogravure picture of Franklin Delano Roosevelt. A strip of palm, placed behind the photo after Palm Sunday Mass, has now dried and droops over the great man's eyebrows. The late president appears to be staring at us through a bush in the gloom. Some pious households in this old Boston neighborhood might have the pope on their walls, but we belong to that sect, made up of working poor families, for whom FDR is the patron saint.

"As the bidding begins, the doorbell rings, and this sends a stiffening shock through both parents. With a strong 'shhh,' my mother leans over and whispers to my trembling father, 'What should we do?' I lean in and say, 'Answer the door?' which earns me a pair of grim looks.

"'Let's see if they go away,' says my father. The doorbell rings again. My mother reaches over and turns out the light. She gets up, goes to the window and pulls the shade back a sliver of an inch. 'I don't see any strange cars out there.' From experience we've learned that bill collectors nearly always arrive by auto. 'It may be Lucille,' my mother's best friend. 'Should I answer it then?' I ask her, anxious to turn on the light and get on with the game. 'OK,' she says.

"Life is a series of choices. Isn't it? Do you take a train or a plane? Do you walk or take the elevator, open the door, or leave it shut? Ninety-nine percent of the time, the choices are inconsequential, no cost attached. But sometimes the train goes off the tracks; the elevator gets stuck halfway between floors; the opened door reveals a process server who hands you a piece of paper and says, 'Give this to your parents. This is an eviction notice. Tell 'em they have twenty-four hours to clear out of this apartment.'

"That night is etched in my mind, because it was the last night that we were ever together. With appalling swiftness we were separated from our furniture, clothing, photos, books, and toys, that treasured picture of FDR—all sucked into storage—never to be recovered. And with the same appalling swiftness we were separated from each other—my father to a shelter for homeless men, my brother to the apartment of a kindly friend of the family, and my mother and I and a kid brother to a shelter for women and children. We never came together under the same roof again."

Bridge Builder

"Ultimately, what do we all want? We want a world at peace, a world in which there is opportunity for all. I believe that can only happen in a world that intersects at all levels, so every person is vested in the success and well-being of everyone else."

When I first met Elyse Cherry in the mid-1980s, she was a smart, young lawyer at Hale & Dorr, one of Boston's major law firms. The firm's partners had a reputation as big-deal power brokers and money makers; they were also thought to be mavericks, especially as related to their prodigious pro bono work on messy social issues. Elyse's and my meeting concerned a complicated financial problem faced by a mental health clinic that was trying to set up shop in a residential neighborhood—and Elyse was clearly the smartest person in the room. As I recall, she solved our unsolvable problem on the spot. I was impressed that this woman, incidentally a lesbian, was working so comfortably and successfully in what was then a white male wingtip world. As it turns out, the dichotomy is entirely typical of her.

That Elyse, a dozen years later, traded her upwardly mobile career as a partner at Hale & Dorr for the excitement of connecting low-income people with the mainstream economy through lending and investment, is not a surprise. It is, however, a gift and a great example of what can happen when first-rate talent goes to work on real-time social dilemmas. If there is any trend worth watching, it is the steady stream of trained and gifted people who are becoming social entrepreneurs.

A Citizen of Many Worlds

Elyse naturally bridges disparate worlds; she has throughout her life. She grew up and attended school in Revere, on the outskirts of Boston. Many consider this blue-collar town rough, but Elyse experienced it as "a wonderful city with a strong supportive community." From there she went to Wellesley College, an entirely different kind of community, where remarkably she also thrived; I suspect she was simply borne along by both her prodigious intellect and her disarmingly nonconfrontational attitude.

"I am most comfortable moving among worlds," Elyse explains. "I really love to stand at the intersections, to participate in the traffic of ideas, to combine the values and goals of parties on all sides of the table. Perhaps this stems from my early experience meshing Revere and Wellesley, but it is what I do all the time. If you leave your past behind, you run the risk of leaving behind important parts of yourself, too."

Today Elyse is CEO of the nonprofit Boston Community Capital (BCC), an organization she cofounded in 1985. The BCC mission is based on a belief, one that has become a constant theme on this journey, that low-income people are motivated, capable, and smart enough to sustain and manage the resources needed to improve their own communities—they just need access to those resources. BCC provides the access.

"Downtown" businesses have the resources to provide training and develop skill sets that are not often applied to community undertakings. When they are, it is sometimes at the expense of community values. From the outset, Elyse believed the answer lay in merging the two. She has done just that.

Closing the Access Gap

As Elyse describes it, "BCC's business is to support healthy communities where low-income people live and work; primarily, we engage in socially responsible lending and investments. But part of our goal is to create neighborhoods where people can have experiences that cross economic lines. We are not interested in keeping people in ghettos; ideally we would like to see people living in mixed-income communities across our entire country."

BCC helps build these neighborhoods through a Loan Fund and a Venture Fund; each bridges the financial gap that divides low-income communities and opportunity by offering access to capital that area residents would normally be denied.

Indeed, Elyse and her colleagues started BCC with $3,500 earmarked for loans to people building affordable housing in low-income areas. In the subsequent twenty years, the organization has committed over a quarter of a billion dollars to low-income communities through more than four hundred loans and equity investments, financing affordable housing for more than eight thousand families; strengthening more than two hundred community organizations, child care centers, and schools; renovating inner-city commercial space; building businesses and creating jobs.

While that track record alone is impressive, Elyse's background in corporate finance has led to a steadily expanding product line that goes far beyond conventional real estate lending.

"One of the initial products we pioneered is a simple line of credit, the sort of loan people in the mainstream economy can get easily from a bank or even a family member. Our lines of credit are generally in the $250,000 range and are intended to solve a particular financial challenge. For example, an agency may have a grant committed, but only half of it in hand; they need the money to keep the project moving, so we offer a onetime bridge loan. Other organizations have seasonal cash flow, and we can smooth out the peaks and valleys for them. "Many smaller community-based groups have difficulty establishing banking relationships that provide such short-term financing. Because we work exclusively in these neighborhoods, we know how to underwrite the risk and how to make loans that are both useful and get repaid in a timely manner."

Lest you assume that BCC is just a lender to these communities, don't; not only does it offer strategic advice, when needed, the group also creates neighborhood ties to existing banks. For example, it pools lines of credits and loans, then sells them to a bank; it also contracts with other lenders to participate in such loans, eliminating much of the expense of underwriting.

"In addition to building our own balance sheet, we can leverage other people's balance sheets. So we often create deals that enable us to expand our impact."

The result: the community group gets the loan; traditional banks increase their presence in the neighborhood; BCC frees cash to lend to another project— *and* creates a bridge between the community and the mainstream bank.

With Increased Scale Comes Increased Impact

The total amount of capital in the community investing field nationwide is still small, in the aggregate about $13 billion. There are ten to fifteen large players, of which BCC is one, and many smaller organizations. To increase their impact, they all need to increase their resources. One effective tool has been the New Markets Tax Credit, which BCC has deployed successfully nationwide.

"We currently manage $70 million in tax credit enhanced loans which, in addition to providing below-market loans to projects located in distressed areas, also provide additional resources to nonprofit allocatees, expanding their ability to pursue their missions. We hope to steadily expand that distribution."

Ultimately, Elyse envisions a shift of scale for the entire industry—moving from being project based to being system based. "In community development, people typically focus on financing a single project, and, once it is completed, turn to the next one. I believe that low-income communities should be like any classic market; we need to create systemic and efficient market mechanisms that allow our community development finance industry to lend or invest billions rather than millions."

Fueling the Economic Engine

Of course, diverse communities need businesses as well as housing. And Elyse's 1997 transition from volunteer board chair to full-time CEO was prompted both by the opportunity to expand BCC's scale and the decision to develop the Boston Community Venture Fund. Elyse saw an untapped niche: investing in local entrepreneurs from low-income communities, where access to capital is not easy to acquire even when opportunity and talent is in place.

The BCC Venture Fund looks for a "double bottom line" of financial and social return for investors. Although community development venture capital is a novel concept, there are a growing number of investors who share the fund's goals. Indeed, the fund is now two funds, totaling over $21.5 million in investments from banks, foundations, and individuals.

BCC's strategy is to invest in companies in which the social return emerges directly from the business model. "We use an all-inclusive test for selecting our investments. We find companies with a solid business reason for existing, and then look for inherent social returns, asking, Does this company have the capacity to create jobs for low-income people? Is it headed by a member of a minority group or a woman? Will it provide goods or services that serve low-income communities? Does it have strong environmental benefits? We consider management strengths and our own ability to add value.

"Most importantly, we ask about financial return: If the business cannot create a financial return, nothing else matters because there will be no wages or benefits. It is an interesting challenge."

Interweaving Disciplines

Of course, financial mechanisms are only one tool for leadership. A substantial part of Boston Community Capital's value entails erecting bridges across seemingly unrelated disciplines. As Elyse explains, "Isolation is the hallmark of unhealthy communities and organizations; conversely, the broader our networks, the more effective we can be." Indeed, BCC endeavors not only to stand at the intersection of disparate constituencies but to actively reduce the silos that form within them. BCC's Green and Sustainable Development initiative is a perfect example.

"The true cost of housing includes not only the expense of a mortgage, but of maintenance, including utilities. Anywhere we can substantially lower utility bills, housing becomes more affordable. And we cannot wait for the federal government to take the lead. Green and Sustainable Development is a classic situation in which eliminating silos can have a substantial impact on outcomes, because success demands the integration of many areas of expertise: alternative energy technologies, construction codes, zoning, historical preservation, public policy—and financing. BCC brings a unique and recognized ability to coordinate the knowledge and activities of these experts, as well as to create true markets for their products.

"This work on Green Development will support a continuing trend of joint venture partnerships between nonprofit entities and for-profit entities— partnerships which unite the grassroots community-organizing expertise of nonprofits and the development expertise and equity of for-profits."

BCC staff share their expertise in many other community initiatives, too. "Although civic leadership is technically outside most of our official job responsibilities, it is a personal value for many staff members and a means of furthering BCC's mission. So, we encourage staff to participate in the community by offering flexible job schedules, mentoring, and organization-wide support for such efforts. Through this volunteer work, our staff is able to fortify and extend networks, reduce the silos that divide our natural mission allies, and learn about new programs and concepts in our communities.

"Membership on the advisory board of Northeastern University's urban-focused School of Education, for example, offered an important window into the challenges facing public schools, pilot schools, and charter schools and helped us to better underwrite loans to educational institutions. Similarly, membership on the board of directors of the Massachusetts Cultural Council or the Center for Women and Enterprise have helped keep us apprised of opportunities to finance artists' live/work housing or new business initiatives. Involvement in social enterprise and venture philanthropy organizations provides insight into funding trends and gaps in programming for underserved communities. And participation in town government provides an unparalleled appreciation of the benefits and challenges of building, integrating, and maintaining affordable housing."

Of course, even within an organization such as BCC, silos and stasis can sneak in. BCC is aware of this danger and proactively challenges it. "We encourage creativity within our organization, eliminating boundaries and trying to stay flexible enough to respond to new ideas, and directions; 'we've always done it that way' is never an acceptable reason for pursuing outmoded approaches."

Communities without Boundaries

Recently, I met with Elyse in BCC's offices on the top floor of a beautifully remodeled old building in the Dudley Square area of Roxbury. In the 1960s, this area was completely derelict; what a total transformation today. At BCC, there are sophisticated financial skills at work, and equally important, there is extensive community involvement: Its board has community representation. Its loan committee involves the community through the lending and community relations staff. Its employees work closely with, and are a major resource to, the community development corporations that are the area's principal developers. "At this point," Elyse proudly says, "BCC works with nearly every significant financial institution and community development nonprofit in the region."

So how does BCC's work—and your financial wizardry—connect to the world you want?

"Financing is just the mechanism. It is what I understand, so it is what I use to work toward a better world. I believe that to actually achieve a better world, we all must be committed to the goal—and we must learn from the here and now to recognize and overcome the true impediments. BCC keeps me in the here and now.

"I also believe that boundaries are the largest impediments we face today. People talk about gay rights, equal rights, and choice; those are critical concerns, but I have come to think that they are primarily symptoms of larger issues.

"When people are imprisoned by boundaries—be they of nationality, tribe, religion, class, gender, or sexual orientation—they can rationalize negative behavior. Destroying the environment of those on the other side, or not educating their children, or not worrying about their political representation is less troublesome. It is easy to ignore problems that belong to someone else.

"We are working to change that.

"I want a world in which people cross interpersonal boundaries freely, without fear of repercussion. When people have a stake in many worlds, they are far less likely to make choices that are going to have negative impacts on other people, because those people stop being 'other.'

"So, for me, the core issue is getting people to open themselves to all of these other worlds. And it can be tough; it takes a conscious decision to cross boundaries.

"Dialogue is critical. I also think that forming organizations that are consciously perched at the intersection of communities is important. At least, that is why I do what I do.

"Of course, there are personal rewards, too. I get to live in a very rich soup of different ideas, ideals and values."

Elyse Cherry is grounded in the "here and now," but she has a powerful vision and plan for what could be. Listen now to Jack Murrah, who for over twenty-five years has demonstrated how to coax a vision out of an eroding city, flat on its back.

The Long-Distance Runner

"The more I think about the question of 'standing up,' the more it seems an inevitable part of any loving relationship that you have with your community," said Jack Murrah, president of the Lyndhurst Foundation. "If that is the kind of relationship you have, you mostly affirm what is good and encourage it to be even better; but there will be moments when you cannot love without dissent. Some parts of community (never mind ourselves!) are not worthy of affirmation, but those parts are in need of acknowledgment, and even if they are beyond amendment, they remind us to go forward with greater humility."

The Lyndhurst Foundation of Chattanooga, Tennessee, has an unusually persistent record of loving engagement with its hometown, and more than once in the past thirty years, it has stood up against the prevailing climate and pointed to a better way. Given its origins in 1938 and a forty-year history of anonymous and conventional grant making, it was, in many ways, an unlikely agent of change. But when Jack Lupton, son of the donor, saw his community slipping into despair as its economic foundations gave way in the late 1970s, he was determined to use his family's philanthropic resources to help revive the city.

Lupton hired two teachers, neither of whom had any experience with philanthropy, to run the foundation. He told them he was not interested in tweaking individual institutions but in restoring a sense of unity and confidence in the city as a whole. When they asked how they might go about that, he shot back, "That's your job. If you can't figure it out, I'll find someone who can."

Jack Murrah, now Lyndhurst's president, worked with his colleague Rick Montague to figure it out. "We discovered ways to put visionary experts together with ordinary citizens to create pictures of the future that people were able to agree about, willing to work for, willing to invest in. Rick's pioneering work, together with the toughness and optimism of Jack Lupton, created a disposition and a set of skills that this community continues to draw upon years later."

Many in Chattanooga give Jack Murrah a sizeable share of the credit for sustaining the legacy of Lupton and Montague in the past fifteen years, as the scope of work has extended further into depressed public schools, distressed neighborhoods, and threatened environmental assets. It is a role for which Jack says he was not prepared by nature or nurture. He arrived in Chattanooga in 1971 out of a working-class background (born in rural Alabama, he shocked his family by going "up north" to Vanderbilt), with a degree in philosophy and teaching experience in a boys' reform school, a military academy, and a prestigious prep school. Years later, that curious mix of shaping influences can be heard in his description of the neighborhood into which the foundation moved its offices in 1995.

"On the broadest, highest hill in downtown Chattanooga, rounded by the Tennessee River and bordered by the university, lies a neighborhood that was once a dense and intricate weave of private buildings and public streets. Visually connected to both city and river, grand homes shared common ground with more modest family dwellings and apartment houses. There were pharmacies and grocers, churches and schools, all of which thrived through a long period of the community's history, perhaps as long as seventy-five years before beginning to yield to the great American move to the suburbs.

"Brabson Hill quickly deteriorated after World War II, and by 1980 had become a scene of dereliction. Among the empty lots and parking lots clung a few survivors—here a modestly refurbished apartment, there a finely restored home for an architect's business. A couple of newer developments intruded gracelessly—a massive windowless sports arena, and a squat, windowless brick law office, its back to the street. The other end to that same street was anchored by three large butterscotch houses, all chopped and larded with formless additions to serve as weekly rentals. Together they projected the fearful message of the late twentieth century: 'city equals poverty equals danger.'

"What we wanted to do was to revive an old urban model of neighborhood where a variety of institutions and families live together in a compact and walkable area where there is a more satisfying communal life than if they were to live apart in sprawling residential and commercial pods segregated by class and function."

Under Jack's leadership, Lyndhurst has made a series of investments in the Brabson Hill community and others that are slowly but definitively turning things around. As Jack sees it, "Those who would be leaders must first be citizens. Those who would act wisely must know more than theory and do more than talk. Those who would make a difference must put much at risk."

The harmonizing of eclectic elements in Brabson Hill is but one example of Chattanooga's need to rise above differences—racial, economic, and class—that are often exaggerated in our society.

"You can see it in our national cultural divide. We treat the other side as the devil incarnate, even though the degree of separation is not that great. We all yearn for similar things, there is common ground, and the political majority is only the majority by the barest of margins, yet we turn extremism into the social metaphor, an abstraction to live by or to fear."

This became Lyndhurst's point of departure in its communal endeavor. "Communities are most healthy when they are whole, when they are a unity incorporating diversity. It is not about the exploitation of our differences, or a clichéd celebration of diversity, shallowly conceived and hardly meaningful beyond a festival mentality. It is closer to the paradox of the loaves and fishes, where everyone is challenged to bring forth whatever they have, because only then does there seem to be enough."

Jack learned this lesson in the mid-1980s from the successful community-wide planning process that grew out of Jack Lupton's challenge, Vision 2000, and the Chattanooga Venture. "We learned from a consultant we hired, who knew a lot about cities, that we should avoid being overly analytical. 'See what you and your fellow citizens would like the city to be in twenty years. Don't ask them what the problems are because they'll go to quarreling and blaming,' he told us."

There was no organization in town that people would trust to facilitate such a process, so Lyndhurst created one, Chattanooga Venture, and it paid for the first three years' operations. It had a board with sixty people drawn from all the sectors, labor, business owners, neighborhood leaders, police, school people, and others.

"Over time, we have learned a great deal. To be opportunistic is one lesson, especially to support leaders who emerge, and who have the drive and commitment to get things done. We learned, early on, to speak to people's feelings. A foundation has to tread softly while acting decisively. There is always someone ready to say, rightly, of course, 'Who elected you?' This was especially the case with my being associated with Lyndhurst Foundation. Here I was, a gay man, representing the wealthiest family in a conservative town, engaging in public issues usually reserved for public officials."

Part of the Lyndhurst story has been plain old persistence. You have to be in the game for a very long time to build trust, to form collaborations that work, and that is what Jack has done over twenty-five years. One important lesson has been around the incremental nature of social change. A big failing of many foundations, including the large national players, is that they expect to make a difference and after two or three years walk away. Even a five-year commitment is often insufficient. You cannot begin to think about meaningful change in the short term. Awareness of this fact is finally sinking in, and more and more thoughtful donors are making longer-term investments.

The Lyndhurst Foundation has the advantage of being "of the place." Its roots are in Chattanooga and Jack understands the politics. His ability to avoid the ever-present tendency toward in-fighting, the kiss of death for collaborative action, has made a huge difference. That might not have been the case had a national foundation come in, expecting results, without having the local knowledge.

"To put it in the context of working to engage a school system, you may have to watch a great superintendent come and go, but it is important that you keep holding up the vision and staying faithful to the work even through the setbacks. And, oh, yes—plan on twenty years."

The product of Chattanooga's visioning process, in which more that 1,500 citizens participated, was a set of forty goals that covered a wide span of projects, none prioritized. Whenever there were resources, energy, and leadership willing to go to work on any one of the forty goals, Chattanooga Venture was there to help set up meetings, find consultants, and raise money. Over the next ten years, the community saw the construction of the world's largest freshwater aquarium, the first two miles of the Riverwalk, a new city/county courts building, a new airport, and a safe place for victims of family violence. It saw the restoration of two downtown performing arts centers and the oldest bridge over the Tennessee River. It saw a neighborhood rebuilt on the river across from downtown.

But Chattanooga is a story of rare success. "When the consultant who helped in the visioning process, architect Gianni Longo, came up with the idea of writing a book about cities of vision a few years ago, we thought, 'Great idea,' and gave him a planning grant. A year later his conclusion was there was no book to be written, maybe a long article, so I realize now more than ever how fortunate we have been in Chattanooga."

While Lyndhurst played a key role in the whole story, the city turned around based on a combination of timing and circumstances. Many factions in the city felt a pent-up desire to deal with its decline. Unemployment was high; the future was bleak; the city had hit the wall. Even so, there are always forces that can work against you.

"Some people don't want a better world, as implausible as that sounds. They either are perfectly happy with the way things are or are temperamentally disaffected no matter what the circumstances. Some people will discredit good intentions and even good results. You have to learn to listen carefully to the voices of resistance and figure out where they are coming from. When we got serious about reviving the inner city, we ran into opposition from the newer suburbs, people who couldn't understand why revival was important. Some members of the county government saw themselves as agents of the 'manifest destiny' that cities would decline and suburbs would grow. Another countervailing force has been the private schools, which educate a full 20 percent of the population. The community is very proud of these elite schools, and of course I had taught at one of them. When I spoke out publicly and said the private schools had a segregating effect and that excellence isn't achieved though segregation, I got a chilly reception from some old friends. But one must, at a certain point, stand up and be counted.

"It seems that 90 percent of the time, things can be pretty temperate, and one can find common ground, but there are those other times when you have to struggle. When the Boy Scouts established a national policy against gays becoming scouts, I was on the United Way strategic planning committee. I argued that the very principles we had just developed around inclusion and access were being challenged. What started as a group discussion of the risks to the United Way became a very public debate when a right wing internet news source turned it into an attack against the Boy Scouts by the foundation. There were months of being dragged through the mud. It was personally painful, but I believe that if you do not know what line you will not cross, then guiding principles are meaningless. I guess you cannot work for twenty-five years in the public arena and never get in trouble."

One big bet these days that is pulling the community together in Chattanooga in quite wonderful ways is a riverfront project that began in 1982 with an idea for a six-hundred-acre piece of riverfront property jointly owned by the city and county governments. An urban land analysis and task force study—paid for by the Lyndhurst Foundation, the city, and county—led to a much broader mandate, breathtaking in its scope: a community riverfront plan for all twenty miles of the Tennessee River as it flowed below the Chickamauga Dam through Chattanooga.

Much of that dream has been realized, but the mayor recently led the community to invest $120 million in a bigger and more refined development of the area where the downtown meets the riverfront. "When the mayor invited people to come talk about what kind of public art should be incorporated into the plan, more than five hundred came. It was amazing. There were times in this community when you couldn't get twenty people out for anything. In less than six months, the community raised $50 million in private money toward the goal. That could not have happened fifteen years ago. Interestingly, all of this is being done through partnerships linking every imaginable category and class of authority, power and resources, not just the individual organizations and institutions in the redevelopment area." Now that is a true collaboration.

There is more than the river flowing in Chattanooga. There is a broader flow here. It's openness is striking. So here we have open sourcing without technology. How interesting.

The accomplishments of the Lyndhurst Foundation stand as a record of communal endeavor. "To me, it is a reminder that the word *philanthropy* is rooted in the idea of love not of an individual but of mankind, of the whole embracing all its parts, even the unlovely and unknown. It goes beyond abstraction and becomes a life practice; it is a humbling and exhilarating force that reveals the enchantment in the most plain facts and figures, most ordinary people and places in our world. It moves us, in other words, to make our communities more beautiful, more wholesome and robust, by loving them. The great sixteenth-century English poet Spenser wrote, 'Entire affection hateth nicer hands,' and former Yale president Bart Giamatti translated that line into this more contemporary form: 'If you truly love, you must truly touch.'"

To touch and be touched. To serve and be served. What a good stopover Chattanooga has been for us. And a good launch to someone who works in the same way in faraway places. Meet Dr. Jonathan Quick.

Reader's Guide Questions

1. Which are your "street scenes"—the ones that have influenced who and what you are?
2. Have you, like Jim O'Connell, had the experience of thinking you "knew next to everything" only to learn you did not?
3. Closing the big state mental institutions in the 1980s was done for what was believed to be good reasons. Should those involved have known more, done more? How does accountability, after the fact, fit into a situation like this?
4. Is it beyond the responsibility, and capacity, of any society to provide for someone like Greg? Or is that exactly what a society must do?
5. Which view do you believe prevails—human capacity to betray or to transform for the better?
6. Is philanthropy too often a "tacit commitment to keep in place the conditions that demand it"? If so, what must change? What other examples come to mind?
7. The notion of voice and agency and philanthropy as a promissory act is an interesting and original way to think about the process. Where does it lead?
8. Do you believe, as Stephen Melville does, that the U.S. society is "near the breaking point" on the resolution of social dilemmas? Why or why not?
9. Does the story of Elyse Cherry and Boston Community Capital suggest other ways the market economy intersects with social issues? What are they?

10. Elyse purposely has built a life around crossing diverse boundaries. How good are you at crossing boundaries, and how do you go about doing so?

11. Would you like to learn how to have a more diverse life? If so, what steps might be useful to do so?

12. Jack Murrah is drawn to the richness of urban life. He also worries about "pods separated by class and function." How can community be made more vital in cities, suburbs, and rural areas, and what are the different challenges of each?

13. If in our society the differences between us are truly not so great, what kinds of things would help heal the divide?

14. The Lyndhurst Foundation has learned "to tread softly while acting decisively" and to be opportunistic. Can this kind of behavior be taught?

15. What does Jack mean by "you cannot love without dissent" and "those who lead must first be citizens"? What are some of the challenges of being a "long-distance runner"?

Notes

1. Steven A. Schroeder, "When Execution Trumps Strategy," in *Just Money—A Critique of Contemporary American Philanthropy,* ed. H. Peter Karoff (Boston: TPI Editions, 2004), 179–203.

2. Dr. Joseph Cohen, who was for many years chief of medicine at the Lemuel Shattuck Hospital, took what was then an unusual step to open a homeless shelter at a state hospital in the late 1980s. He was an early champion of Jim O'Connell's work.

3. Connecticut's Supportive Housing Pilots Initiative grew out of the partnership. In 2006, it received the Innovations in American Government Award from the Ash Institute for Democratic Governance and Innovation at Harvard University's John F. Kennedy School of Government. It comes with a $100,000 prize so winning programs' models may be shared with other communities.

4. The partnership includes the Conrad N. Hilton Foundation, the Rockefeller Foundation, Fannie Mae, the Robert Wood Johnson Foundation, the Melville Charitable Trust, Fannie Mae Foundation, and Deutsche Bank—each of which have committed $1 million or more to the effort. It also includes the Corporation for Supportive Housing and the National Alliance to End Homelessness, which will be responsible for implementing the partnership's strategy to end long-term homelessness by raising public awareness and creating 150,000 supportive housing units across the nation within ten years.

THE GLOBAL CHALLENGE

Go to the people
Live among them
Learn from them
Start with what they know
Build on what they have
But for the best leaders
When their task is accomplished
Their work is done
The people will all remark
We have done it ourselves.[1]
—THE TAO OF LEADERSHIP

I
T IS FEBRUARY 2005, and I am on the phone for an emergency board meeting of Management Sciences for Health (MSH). Jono Quick, the president of MSH, is devastated. The ever-present risk of international development work has been brought home in the tragic deaths of three young and dedicated MSH colleagues who have been killed in a plane crash in Afghanistan.

MSH is a highly respected NGO that for thirty-five years has been working around the globe providing expert management and leadership advice and training on public health policy systems and issues for government health ministries, as well as international and indigenous NGOs. With staff from more than sixty nationalities, MSH works in thirty of the world's poorest countries. This tragedy has shaken those at its Cambridge, Massachusetts, headquarters to the core.

At the memorial service a month later honoring Amy Lyn Niebling, Cristin Gadue, and Carmen Urdaneta, Dr. Jonathan Quick spoke about his former colleagues:

> In a world where too many people rush through life self-absorbed and burdened by life, Amy, Cristi, and Carmen each left a trail of joy and energy wherever they lived and worked.
>
> In a world increasingly filled with division among people and hateful schisms, Amy, Cristi, and Carmen treated each person with dignity and respect.
>
> In a world in which most people stay close to home and have never confronted firsthand their fears and misconceptions about people who are different, Amy, Cristi, and Carmen set out to work among people from places very different from their own homes in Kansas, Nebraska, Vermont, and Venezuela.
>
> In a world where too many young people grow up with a me-first mentality and entitlement mind-set, Amy, Cristi, and Carmen cared deeply about other people, and especially about the welfare of women, children, and those less fortunate than they.
>
> And in a world where many of us have too much to live with, too little to live for, Amy, Cristi, and Carmen each had discovered exactly what they were living for. When they found their passion and meaning, they embraced it.
>
> They knew why they got out of bed every morning. And they knew that each night they could look in the mirror and say to themselves, "I did something to make the world a little better place."

This is Jono Quick's world of commitment. His sensitive comments helped the 1,200-person MSH family deal with their grief and also offered a kind of renewal of vows for the organization.

MSH helps organizations around the world manage the people, money, medicines, and information to transform public health information into action and better outcomes. MSH's mission is to "close the gap between knowledge and action in public health."

Jono defines that gap as "the ten million people who die every year in the world, not because we do not know what to do, and not because we do not have the medicine needed to prevent those deaths, but because we do not have the management capacity to deliver."

From where does this sense of purpose come to fight killers such as AIDS, tuberculosis, and malaria in fragile states like Angola, Haiti, Mozambique, and Afghanistan despite security issues, civil unrest, and natural disasters? "It takes courage to explore the world and find your own meaning, and it takes strength of character to pursue that purpose once you have found it. And it is work that generates a surge of adrenaline for those who participate."

There is a fascination with those who choose to spend so much of their lives away from home to work abroad on seemingly intractable problems, often in very difficult circumstances. They are not missionaries, but they are on a mission.

Personal risk, however, is not an academic issue. In October 1989, a time leading up to the first Gulf War, Jono and his family were living in Peshawar, Pakistan, close to the Khyber Pass and Afghan border. One evening, there was a sharp knock on the door. When Jono answered it, no one was in the dark street, but an envelope had been left on the doorstep. Inside was a single sheet of paper that simply said, "If Bush takes action against Iraq, you are dead."

The death threat had nothing to do directly with Jono's MSH work, which was related to a project providing cross-border support to Afghan health committees working in various parts of Afghanistan in the aftermath of a decade of Soviet occupation.[2] A similar threat was received by six other American families that same night who were living in Peshawar. A few weeks later the Quicks did leave Peshawar, but Jono in telling this story, death threat notwithstanding, makes it clear that his wife Tina was planning to return to the United States for the delivery of their third child, and he for a scheduled assignment on essential drugs in Kenya. The U.S. government ultimately did evacuate the entire MSH team shortly before the Gulf War as part of a region-wide effort to keep U.S.-related staff and families out of harm's way. Jono and his family were subsequently reassigned by MSH to Kenya, where they lived for the next four years.

Jono's perspective comes out of his unique career experience. "There is intense excitement and curiosity in the diversity of the people and the places combined with a propensity to believe that you're truly doing good despite the risk. In fact, that propensity to 'believe' is powerful even when progress is slow. It helps to drive you.

"People do this kind of work because it's in our wiring, knowing we are here for others rather than simply for ourselves. There can be some conflict with other selfish parts of our makeup, but there is a fundamental human reflex to help others and a surge of satisfaction when we do. It becomes a positive addiction."

Jono feels deeply the responsibility for results. "Monitoring ourselves and determining how effective we are is extremely important even though evaluation is not always easy. This is especially true since the real test of MSH's work is very long term, five or ten years out. That puts a lot of pressure on the work. It must be done carefully and well, without arrogance and with humility. For us, *The Tao of Leadership* is more than a creed."

"It is extremely important to be clear up-front on what the purpose of the effort is, and then to focus on what is achievable. There are many examples. The Eastern Caribbean Drug Service, for example, was established through an MSH project to provide essential medicines to seven of the poorest islands and it has now been self-sufficient for over a decade. Haiti is another where 30 to 40 percent of health care is delivered by NGOs that have continued to provide services through all of that country's civil unrest. In fact, there is a misperception in the press about Haiti. The truth is the network of NGOs and government providers that MSH supports in Haiti has continued to be effective even in the midst of chaos in the rest of society. It demonstrates the centrality of health care in the lives of people everywhere."

Over more than twenty-five years in this field, Jono has held senior positions at the World Health Organization (WHO) and led project management work in many countries. Progress in health care over that time has been stunning. Twenty-five years ago, half of the four billion people on Earth did not have access to the simplest and most essential medicines. Today two-thirds of the world has access. "And successes tend to multiply themselves. With multiple interventions there is synergy.

"There are six million people on earth with AIDS who would benefit from treatment. Three years ago, only 350 thousand of these were being treated and today that number has risen to over 1.3 million. Those statistics may seem discouraging, but they represent a tremendous increase in a three-year period, and there is every reason to think it can and will continue to improve. Even the reduction in cost of AIDS treatment has been remarkable, moving from $10,000 per treatment to $200 per treatment in a five-year period."

This is a critical moment in time. The pressure is on for global actors, which include organizations like MSH, to deliver increased results. There is a tremendous amount of money on the table, more than ever before. New sources of funding like the Global Fund for AIDS, the International Finance Fund for Immunizations, and the Bill and Melinda Gates Foundation are now available. Advocacy efforts to continue that upward trend have begun to pay off.

"Overall, international health is an even higher priority, and health will remain a strong element in international development, both internationally and in the U.S. There is, however, a pragmatic paradox. Even as health has appeared to be subsumed under democracy and governance in context of U.S. foreign policy emphasis on transformational development, the U.S. has simultaneously launched and participated in the largest international disease-specific initiatives in its history.[3] As a result, there are now complementary sources of U.S. funding that have been added to USAID (United States Agency for International Development), which has long been the primary funder of U.S. development efforts."

Jono sees inroads being made on several major global health issues including the elimination of diseases like polio from the Earth. Third World development needs, however, are not only a matter of money.

It has been a strange fact of global economics that the flow of resources from the poorest countries of the South to the wealthy countries of the North has historically gone in the wrong direction. According to Jono, there is a near silent conspiracy around a related issue, the reverse flow of human resources from the South to the North. Through this diaspora, increasing numbers of highly trained professionals are leaving their poor countries of origin for the higher incomes and standards of living in the North.

"The North may be subsidizing the South in the cost of medicine, but the South is subsidizing the North in terms of people," Jono says. In countries like the United Kingdom, more than 30 percent of nurses are imported professionals from the developing world. Of the 600 doctors trained in Zambia since independence forty years ago, 550 have taken jobs abroad. There are more Malawian doctors in the British city of Manchester than in Malawi. Some programs, like the Joint Learning Program sponsored by the Rockefeller Foundation and WHO, are working to provide incentives to reverse those trends, but the problem has not been solved. It is true that diaspora remittances and philanthropy are increasingly important sources of income back into poor countries, but in the long term, it is the professional development and training of qualified leaders, managers, and professionals that will determine the pace of economic and social development.

MSH believes that the science of management, leadership, and organizational capacity building produces results. "Without it," Jono says, "human, financial and material resources go underutilized at best. The enormous health challenges facing lesser developed countries require good systems that are managed and led well. The Millennium Development Goals will not be met at the current pace in many developing countries. We have the knowledge and technology to reach many of the goals by 2015. Financial resources are now available in many countries through new global funding initiatives.

Aid is increasing, especially for Africa. The limiting factor, in effectively using the knowledge, technologies, and resources available, is a lack of sound leadership and management systems to scale up and sustain the delivery of proven practices."

In 2000, MSH's Management and Leadership Program—Developing Managers Who Lead (M&L)—was awarded a USAID five-year cooperative agreement designed to improve the performance of leaders and managers, organizational management systems, and the ability to anticipate and respond to changes in the external environment. M&L became a very successful USAID program. Not only was the original funding ceiling increased from $58 million to $76 million in 2004, but the Management and Leadership Program received expanded long-term funding from USAID in 2005.

Some examples of the Management and Leadership Program's results include the following: In Egypt, the average number of postpartum care visits per client doubled in a Dawar district health center. In Guinea, the coverage of fully immunized children went from 0 to 62 percent in one year in the Boké region. In Guatemala, APROFAM (an affiliate of the International Planned Parenthood Federation) increased sustainability of clinic services to achieve the highest level of clinic self-financing in the hemisphere. In Bolivia, improved organizational capacity of the faith-based organization COMBASE enabled four out of five of its clinics serving 1,500,000 people to recover over 100 percent of their costs.

Jono Quick has lived and worked on global health issues outside the United States for many years, and he has come to some conclusions about what works, and where. One of those conclusions is that our government has it right in the promotion of democracy. Analysis shows that it is within democratic regimes that progress around health and other issues can be made and sustained. Senegal and Guinea provide an example. Both achieved independence about the same time. Senegal is a democracy with an elected president, and it has made real progress in improving its health system, while Guinea, run by a series of despots, lags far behind in basic health services for its population. Indonesia and the Philippines are another example. Indonesia had great public health systems that were dissipated over a fifteen-year period under a dictatorship, while the Philippines' support for local democracy has helped make a decentralized health delivery system more accountable to the people it serves. Indeed, there appears to be a connection between democratic society and the likelihood of successful development efforts.

In Jono's view, development aid should be influenced much less by political considerations, and much more by which countries have the will and the capacity to change. The criticism that huge amounts of money have been wasted by postdevelopment efforts, which in many cases is justified, is directly linked to the politicizing of decisions. If funding decisions were based on competence and capacity to deliver results, the scorecard would be very different. What is needed is much more rigorous evidence-based analysis of what works and what doesn't work. If that was the criterion and expectation the international development dynamic would change for the better.

MSH's annual budget, which in 2005 was in excess of $150 million, comes primarily from USAID and other government sources. MSH views itself as a technical organization, yet the organization is nonetheless subject to shifts in government policy. Accommodating change is always challenging. For MSH, it comes down to a question of core values, as in *The Tao of Leadership*, and from those it does not deviate.

The real test of MSH's work is what remains five or ten years after the project has been completed: are local health care leaders and health workers still applying the lessons learned and the systems developed with their MSH colleagues? Jono believes that an attitude of humility is vital. Ignorance and arrogance is not self-correcting while ignorance and humility are.

What has struck me in learning more about the impressive work of organizations like MSH is what a well-kept secret they are. MSH defies the stereotypes that global social investments are rampant with corruption and inefficiency. Few Americans know how much real progress is being made on so many major health issues and the degree of professionalism and commitment demonstrated by MSH and others.

In the TPI experience, there is too little connection between development efforts and private philanthropy, which continues to think in terms of relief efforts, really charity, as opposed to long-term systemic solutions. There are more foundations and individual donors with an interest in global issues than actually contribute. One of the reasons is the belief that there are not effective intermediaries that can deliver results. MSH is certainly one that can deliver.

In an e-mail to the MSH Board, Jono noted, with cautious enthusiasm, that in a recent speech Secretary of State Condoleezza Rice defined transformational diplomacy in a manner that seems notably resonant with *The Tao of Leadership*. Secretary Rice said:

> I would define the objective of transformational diplomacy this way: To work with our many partners around the world to build and sustain democratic, well-governed states that will respond to the needs of their people.

Transformational diplomacy is rooted in partnerships, not pater-
nalism in doing things with people, not for them.

We seek to use America's diplomatic power to help foreign citizens
to better their own lives, and to build their own nations, and to transform their own futures.

These are dictums that MSH can embrace. They portray an American perspective that would make most Americans proud. We can only wish this secretary of state well in her efforts to integrate the *Tao* into American foreign policy.

On the Ground in South America

The voices thus far on this journey have been U.S.-centric, even when the
work has been global. MSH works in thirty countries around the world, the
1,600 Ashoka fellows are all from less developed countries, and the Synergos
Institute is in the business of connecting grassroots leaders from those countries to business, and philanthropic resources, yet, those organizations, and
their leaders, Bill Drayton, Peggy Dulany, and Jono Quick, are all American.
What about indigenous voices—is their perspective of "policy" different? Is
there progress in America's southern hemisphere, and in Asia where democracy can be a moving target? What is the view on the responsibility of the individual to the collective? How big an issue is corruption for those working on
the ground? Is there a private social sector developing? Are the trends and
themes the same or different?

I know some of these answers through TPI's increasing international
work. More and more U.S. foundations and donors are venturing abroad, and
at the same time, there is growing interest in the potential of promoting philanthropy worldwide. TPI is part of the International Network for Strategic
Philanthropy (INSP), which provides a forum for dialogue and a decentralized think tank on the role of philanthropy and its impact on societies around
the world. INSP is one of a number of efforts to understand and support these
emerging trends. Another is a Brazilian organization, the Institute for the
Development of Social Investment (IDIS), which was established in 1999 by
Marcos Kisil. I talked with Marcos, who tells quite a story.

Marcos Kisil is yet another physician, and his perspective has been influenced by living in a rapidly developing country with an all-too-recent totalitarian past. Marcos became radicalized during the period that led to the
overthrow of Brazil's dictatorship. To this day, he sees too little equity in Brazil,
and he talked to me about a civil society that is struggling.

"My father's family was Austro-Hungarian, and during World War I, they lost everything and moved to Yugoslavia, what is now Bosnia. My father immigrated to Brazil and here met my mother, an Italian. I grew up in a middle-class home and went to university and was in medical school during the years of resistance. It was then I became aware of the inequities in the Brazilian society and became part of the team that was organizing the ideas for the new democratic government in 1985. I had the amazing experience of looking firsthand at other countries that were in the same situation. It was a tremendous break for me to observe the democratization process in seven countries of the region.

"I was working as a doctor to very poor people, and my heart was drawn to those who were at the bottom of the social scale. It is certainly when I became focused on the critical importance of fostering economic growth.

"After thirty years of working in the nonprofit sector, I no longer see the world the way I once did. In particular, I see better policy ideas and implementation coming out of the private sector rather than from government and NGOs; that is not the view I once had."

It is, however, a view that we on this journey have been hearing from others.

"I want a world that is equitable, where social justice and economic opportunity is for everyone. I want a society that is *values-based* and draws upon our Christian heritage. The sad part is that the society I live in is very egocentric with people looking out for themselves. As a consequence, we have lost a lot of the basic values held in the past.

"The destruction of the rainforest is one example, but you see the patterns of self-destruction everywhere. Multiple spouses are common along with broken families and early pregnancies. Children are taking care of children. The schools and other institutions have taken over the role the family used to play.

"There is a tremendous gap between the rights given to Brazilian citizens under the constitution and the reality. Government is not enforcing those rights, and the truth is the problems are too complex for government to solve. What is more, the government is dysfunctional and corrupt. To make matters worse, the civil society, which during the 1990s grew enormously to more than 250,000 organizations today, has been co-opted. It is ironic, but after the 2002 election, a significant number of NGO leaders, especially in the environmental field, took positions in the new administration. We lost our best people. Many are now mired down in bureaucracy, or worse. As a result, the civil society is struggling.

"We badly need to raise the fundamental question of what responsibility does the individual bear to the collective. Brazil became a democracy in 1985, the constitution was signed in 1988, and thus we are still a very new country. The trend over these years has been to decentralize and shift the tax burden to the states and the ongoing power struggle over resources has exacerbated the lack of equity.

"My work with the W. K. Kellogg Foundation as their Latin America and the Caribbean representative for almost fifteen years led to the establishment of IDIS, 'to promote and organize private social investment as an instrument to develop a fair and sustainable society' in Brazil.

"In Brazil, there is a closer link between family and corporate wealth than in the U.S. as we have many family businesses. In that way, we are more like Europe. IDIS has had some success over the past nine years. This experience has only reaffirmed my belief that it is the corporate sector that really gets things done when leading a partnership with civil society and government.

"In my own thinking, the barrier between nonprofit and profit has been removed. One exciting example is in the state of Pernambuco. Fifty of the largest corporations in the state have taken the responsibility of running eight hundred public schools with promising results. It is unprecedented in Brazil or anywhere. Businesspeople here are entering into contracts and agreements involving the governor of the state, the department of education, plus a nonprofit organization created specifically for this work of gathering together those with influence and funds, and another nonprofit organization as a technical group to support the education system. The point is they are doing this as a voluntary decision—it's not an obligation. This is very interesting to see, especially in Brazil, where the tax benefits are minimal.

"I believe we are looking for social justice and some sense that everyone has a chance. I don't have any doubt that we want a society in which ethics and ethical behavior in human transactions are the norm, which is not the case today. In essence, what I am talking about is a values-based equitable society where social justice and economic opportunity is the reality.

"To get there the name of the game is institutional building, leadership, training, and education. Institution building on every level is helping to create an infrastructure that Brazil has never had before, and it is here that the civil society is critical. We also have lots of traction around leadership development, especially with young people who are poor. These are amazing developments, and despite my despair over many aspects of our society, I remain optimistic. To be otherwise is simply not an option."

Marcos Kisil is not alone in that regard, and he is joined by Rory Francisco-Tolentino.

An Outlook from Asia

Rory is the executive director of the Asia Pacific Philanthropy Consortium, which works to increase the quantity and quality of philanthropy in Asia by strengthening the institutional infrastructure, supporting donors, and improving the operating environment for the nonprofit sector. Rory has a dream that, to me, sounds anything but radical. She spoke to me about it from the Philippines.

"Despite this being overused, I am not ashamed to admit that I continue to dream of a world where every child is born with a positive future—one that provides that child the means and the opportunities to be whatever he wants to be when he grows up—where that child feels safe and secure, knowing that health and education are things that she is entitled and has access to, where that child feels loved and cared for because parents have the time and resources to help shape their children into caring citizens of the world."

These same aspirations, these basic "commodities" of a decent life are at the center of what we all want, so why does Rory, a Philippine national, feel compelled to say she is not ashamed of that dream? People are sometimes cautious about stating the "simple" truths, not wanting to sound naive. But Rory has no illusions, and she has thought carefully about what conditions might lead to her dream's realization.

"To be able to achieve this vision, it seems to me that there is a very real need to change the way we look at ourselves and the world—to see ourselves as integral but interrelated parts of the whole, whether it is of our families, our communities, our societies, our regions, and the world. When we see ourselves this way and accept that what happens to one happens to all, we then look at ourselves and the world in a way that honors both.

What does that mean in practical terms? "It means we shun violence as a way to resolve issues; we shun poverty because it causes suffering for others, and therefore for ourselves; it means we see ourselves as stewards of the world's natural resources, so we care for it in a way that preserves it for ourselves and future generations. This attitude means moving away from a competitive framework into a collaborative framework. It means giving up widely held beliefs that the only way to succeed is to be ahead of everyone else. It means moving to a different definition of success, one based on our ability to lift up ourselves, and all others along with us."

Different words and a different culture, but echoes of other voices.[4]

"The biggest obstacle is our own fear of the unknown, our reluctance to give up ineffective ways of doing things simply because it is easier to keep doing what we know than to risk other ways. Our lack of willingness to own up to our individual contribution to making the world fragmented, individualistic, and uncompassionate is another obstacle. There is a real resistance to reflecting on that from the groups in our societies that have the opportunities, the resources, and the ability to make a difference. When so much has been given to us, so much more is expected of us. But often the feeling that we are the sole ones responsible for our own good fortune makes it difficult for us to have empathy for others, especially those who are poor and who have not had as many blessings. And that is what they are—blessings.

"I continue to dream because I have seen the impact of collaboration and working collectively for a greater good. In the Philippines, where one out of every three people lives below the poverty line, business corporations, civil society organizations, and government have worked together to bridge the digital divide to bring computer and Internet access to public schools, where the poor go. In this case, government prioritizes the schools to be given computer laboratories, and corporations either pay for new labs or donate used computers they no longer need. Nonprofit organizations work with the schools to train teachers and parent–teacher associations to manage the computer laboratories and to use software to prepare teaching materials. The telecommunications industry, where competition is some of the fiercest in the country, banded together, put competition aside, and committed to provide free Internet access to these schools as well."

Why do companies do it? "They don't want to be seen as being uncooperative or get left behind. They do it, too, because they realize that their businesses cannot thrive in an economy whose human resources do not keep up. In the process of striving to be successful, they want to bring the rest of society with them.

"Consensus building and collaborative action among sectors are in our best interest because we know, as a developing country, there are not enough resources to go around. It is not always possible, but where it happens, it has a huge impact. Recently, a corporate-led foundation, the Philippine Business for Social Progress, convened discussions around the business response to the Millennium Development Goals—convening not just its member corporations but representatives of other business associations, the church sector, government, and the nongovernment sector around what they call 'square tables.' All four sectors sit together and look at how businesses can help our society meet the Millennium Development Goals through their core business operations, in social investments, and in advocacy. Because the process is convened by business, they 'own' the recommendations, so they have published them and are advocating for companies to look at these recommendations and implement them as much as they can.

"Business, nongovernment organizations, church, and reformist government organizations are also working together in a Coalition against Corruption, where the different organizations undertake a corruption monitoring project or work with selected government agencies to simplify and make more transparent or accountable their processes. In this case, because governance and corruption are major problems that are obstacles to economic growth and poverty reduction, there was felt to be a need to do something about it. Various sectors have made contributions and lent skills—this includes training volunteers (sometimes retired business executives) and fielding them as observers to Bids and Awards Committees of various government agencies. Citizen organizations such as the Boy Scouts and the Girl Scouts are taught how to inspect textbooks (both quality and quantity) as they are delivered to schools in rural and urban areas. In this case, the Education Ministry has committed not to pay suppliers who have provided inferior textbooks or who have not provided the adequate number of textbooks. These are just some examples of positive impact when people, and sectors, begin to think in terms of 'we.'

"We are finding that by working together, we bring great resources, human and material, to bear on problems—and as we continue to work together, we also find that our own suspicions, and skepticism about others, are minimized, because in the end, we do share common values and common goals—to make a difference—and the result, we find, is often so much greater than we had thought. I think it is where the most hope lies to see my dream become reality."

We are hearing from Marcos and Rory that among the sectors in their countries, there is an advanced shared ownership of social issues that include improving public education and eliminating the digital divide. In Brazil, a new attitude about corporate citizenship and private social investing makes Marcos optimistic about the future. Along with that, in Brazil and in the Philippines there is an increasing focus on institution building and developing leaders from all strata of society including the poorest. In many ways, these collaborations are more mature than those in the United States. As Rory and Marcos see it, each of us as individuals has an ethical and practical responsibility to the rest of society.

So here's a Brazilian and a Philippine, and the moral aspirations and visions for a better world are little different from what we have thus far heard.

The commonalities are not a surprise but what is different is a more natural flow of intersector collaboration, with much more taking of responsibility by corporations in areas like education. We have even gained a sector, the church, and learned a new term—*the square table!*

Be the Change You Want to See

Priya Viswanath calls India "the land of paradoxes, a challenging, energetic, entrepreneurial, and fascinating place."

As CEO of Charities Aid Foundation (CAF) India, Priya grapples with the complexity of a country that supports more than a sixth of the world's population, about 1.2 billion people. Religion, caste, and language continue to play a major role in the social and political organization of India; of the eighteen official languages, Hindi is the most widely spoken. It is a vast and varied country where most of the population still live in villages (70 percent in more than 550,000 villages), yet when North Americans visualize India, they think of cities teeming with people and crippling poverty.

"Every individual can do something to make this world a better place. There are many in my generation who practice organized giving, donating generously to social causes, and yet there is a large majority among the growing and wealthy middle class in India that have no empathy or thought for the less privileged.

"My family was not philanthropic, but my grandfather was a landlord, and there was a degree of largesse. I grew up seeing both my maternal and paternal grandmothers ensuring that no one went hungry if they could help it. In my household, now, we set aside 10 to 15 percent of our annual income for social causes and issues we care about, often in areas that do not receive much popular support. I am passionate about justice for the marginalized and encouraging social entrepreneurship, but very few people give to social justice causes in India. It is not very high on the radar screen here. People see it merely as a buzzword of the West."

Among the efforts Priya supports is an NGO that provides legal literacy and legal counsel for poor illiterate "undertrials" of Tihar Jail who have no means to adequate legal recourse or justice. She also supports charities working in the area of mental health; entrepreneurship development for the disabled, the blind, and destitute women; and a soccer league for street kids through the Salaam Balak Trust. "There is so much that one person can do if we can just communicate that message to the middle class."

Priya joined CAF in 2003 after having worked a decade on projects to increase philanthropy in India. CAF's mission to increase the flow of resources from corporations and high-net-worth individuals to the nonprofit sector made it a perfect fit. She had been part of several pioneering diaspora[5] initiatives, including working with the Asia Foundation and Give2Asia in the United States to reach out to the Indian community in the United States for support for development projects in India.

"Working toward equity and justice through philanthropy is a living passion for me. I am not an activist, but I have always been driven to be creative and to exploit new opportunities. In my own small way, I am trying to make the world a better place and I refuse to give up amidst challenges posed by inequities."

Education is a critical issue, as is child nutrition, since almost 40 percent of Indians are younger than fifteen years of age. Like other countries that have adopted the UN Millennium Development Goals (MDGs) and stand to benefit from them, India is working to address the vast inequities among its rich and poor through global social investing and government intervention.

"One of our great challenges in growing philanthropy is to develop qualified human resources. The structure of our system of education is such that a large portion of people are unemployable. The goal of universal primary education I agree with completely, though I am skeptical of achieving some of the other MDGs. Empowering women is too complex an issue to quantify, and this goal is too ambitious. Traveling north to south, some Indian states are far ahead and others are behind, but certainly, making sure that every child goes to school and has the basics, shelter and food to eat—those are the real priorities."

But the biggest challenge, perhaps, is to change the mind-set of the middle class.

"To engage the public in what we do and to move them into more organized philanthropy is most important. India has the largest-growing middle class in the world. Most giving goes to religion, and some of it ultimately goes to social programs of religious organizations, so this adds to the general well-being. But I believe it is important to get people to involve themselves in a social development agenda and to take ownership of the issues that are critical for development. People here can be suspicious of each other's motives. The government could help by creating an environment that enables people to invest more easily in the NGO sector. And it needs to remove archaic legislation to help us to do our work."

Government will always be the primary player and it needs to increase public spending in specific areas. But Priya agrees completely with Peggy Dulany, of Synergos, that a huge amount of money is available in some areas, and getting programs to work is more an issue of infrastructure and coordination than the availability of resources.

"We are, indeed, building our capacity. India, you will recall, after the tsunami was hesitant to accept foreign aid, but we very much welcome support such as the Ford Foundation's investment in growing philanthropy through skills development and training. We can handle large investments, we have the capacity, but as is the case everywhere, it is important to choose partners wisely.

"To make more progress, we must decide what we want philanthropy to look like in India in twenty-five years, so we can design programs. However, there is a real lack of quantitative data to show us where people are giving and how much they are giving today. We know there are a great many individuals of high net worth and a great deal of wealth to be put to good use. I am talking about families and also companies—old, established ones where there has always been a history of giving, as well as new wealth in the technology and finance sectors.

"There is also a huge potential in the diaspora community in the United States, UK, the Far East, and the Middle East. But in order to encourage the large Indian diaspora to invest in sustainable development, and to tap into that wealth of human and financial resources, it is necessary to demystify the workings of the social sector in India and to encourage an understanding of development issues and needs.

"Thanks to a large grant from the Rockefeller Foundation, we have been able to look at the whole area of venture capital, though we are still in the learning and networking stage, exploring innovative ideas and seeing where investment would be most useful and welcome. We are seeing how we might attract it to the areas of education, health, information technology, microfinance, and faith-based giving for social development."

Through a host of offerings and products, CAF India raises substantial resources from the corporate sector, primarily in Delhi and Bangalore, and Priya believes the sector could do even more. "Still, there are always problems of miscommunication and suspicion in the Indian mind when it comes to charity from corporations.

"Year 2005 was a watershed year for me. I spent much of it evaluating projects and partners for our Tsunami Rebuilding Lives Fund. I reconnected with communities at the grassroots and reviewed with others the enormous potential for microcredit and women's empowerment through self-help groups. Going forward, serious investment in social entrepreneurship is perhaps a way to ensure economic growth with social balance and conscience.

"India can and will change if we believe in ourselves and our resilience, and we recognize our own enormous potential. As Mahatma Gandhi said, *'You have to be the change you want to see in the world.'*"

Reader's Guide Questions

1. Have you experienced what Jono Quick calls the "adrenaline" and surge of satisfaction that comes from this work? If so, describe it.
2. Which challenge to meet global health and poverty issues seems greater: not enough resources, or not enough management and infrastructure? Do these challenges apply to other issues?
3. Political considerations have an impact on U.S aid. Is this immoral, pragmatic, or something in between?
4. Should "high" competence be the criteria for U.S. aid? What else?
5. Are you a global donor? Does the MSH story encourage you to become one? If not, what is missing?
6. In what ways is Brazil's society similar to U.S. society, and how is it different, according to Marcos Kisil's description?
7. Both Marcos and Rory Francisco-Tolentino provide examples of remarkable corporate social engagement. How does it compare to what we have in the United States?
8. Should/could religious organizations, broadly defined, become more of a participant/player in the U.S. social arena? Do you see benefits, obstacles, or drawbacks in such activity?
9. Marcos aspires to social justice and economic opportunity for everyone, and Rory looks to a future where a child has opportunity and means and is safe, educated, healthy, and loved. Are our goals universal? Are they any different from the ones you aspire to?
10. Are you being the change you want to see?

Notes

1. See John Heider, *Lao Tzu's Tao Te Ching Adapted for a New Age* (San Francisco: Jossey-Bass, 2006).
2. MSH has worked in Afghanistan for more than twenty years and in 2006 had two hundred staff in the country as part of a major effort to help rebuild its medical infrastructure.

3. Examples include the Global Alliance for Vaccines and Immunization (GAVI), the Global Drug Facility (GDF, for tuberculosis), the Global Fund to Fight AIDS, Tuberculosis, and Malaria (the Global Fund), the President's Emergency Fund for AIDS (PEPFAR), the President's Malaria Initiative (PMI), and the International Partnership on Avian and Pandemic Influenza.

4. Alan Broadbent, Lucy Bernholz, and Elyse Cherry all express these sentiments.

5. Individuals residing outside their home country are an increasingly significant philanthropic resource in many countries.

THE CONSCIENCE OF A PLACE
Being of a Community

M AHATMA GANDHI's advice about individual responsibility is to "be the change you want to see." Gandhi lived those words with passion and dignity and his voice became the moral conscience of a whole society.

Where does the moral conscience of a community lie? Who keeps the legacy of a community? Who welcomes those who are newly arrived? Who are the storytellers, the historians who transmit the social and cultural mores? Who are the gifted givers who contribute to making a community healthy and vibrant? Who takes responsibility to help those in need to help themselves? Who are the arbiters of wrongs? Who determines what is just and what is unjust?

To some, and I am one, these questions may be the most important for the world we want. Every community is distinct in responding to them and along the way invents a range of mediums and intermediaries—civic, social, nonprofit, and religious organizations and institutions, associations, and networks that in the aggregate shape the moral conscience of a community. These are the schools, chambers of commerce, Rotary Clubs, teams, museums, churches, temples, and mosques where we hash it all out.

One increasingly important American invention has been the community foundation. The first community foundation was formed in Cleveland, Ohio, almost a hundred years ago, and today there are more than 1,200 of them around the world, with over half in the United States. These are public charities dedicated to serving the long-term social needs of a community.

Community foundations solicit donations from a broad base of private sources and manage them under community control for charitable purposes that are usually local or regional. They also provide services and support for donors. Many believe the community foundation movement has great potential to be a conscience of a community. But like every other movement, it needs to be renewed, and the morale of a society needs to be continually stirred.

We now meet some of those doing the renewing and the stirring and look at the impacts on the world we want.

Cash and Cache

Emmett Carson remembers growing up on the violent side of Chicago. His road changed the night someone got shot on his doorstep and his father dragged the young man inside bleeding, in the middle of a gang fight, bullets still flying. His family moved across town and enrolled Emmett in a public school. He remembers that all of a sudden he could leave his bike in the grass outside his friend's house and not have it stolen. All of a sudden, the world changed. "But I was the same person," says Emmett, president of the new Silicon Valley Community Foundation and former president of the $640 million Minneapolis Community Foundation.

His history may have something to do with why he wants community foundations to support and represent a positive social movement, not a better business plan.

Part of his passion and commitment for social justice comes from the knowledge of where he grew up. But his experience also contributes to his frustration. Emmett, who is chair of the Council on Foundations board, is a highly unlikely critic of organized philanthropy. Yet, in a steady stream of news articles, interviews, and speeches, he berates donors and foundations for their timidity and their failure to address the critical issues of poverty and inequity in the United States.

"Genetic markers—birth, race, gender, sexual orientation, weight—and parental wealth have too much influence on how an individual will prosper. I lived in the middle of hell, and then a few things changed, and I live in the middle of plenty. I feel an obligation to make society work for everyone, to get for others that basic right, a right of life that is everyone's due, as true for the kid in Rio or Johannesburg as it is for the kid in Chicago."

Emmett is a man on message, one he shares with people like activist and U2 star Bono, who has taken on the tragedy of hunger in Africa under the emblem "Where you are born should not determine whether you will live."

He believes we have not faced up to our obligation to do something about these inequities. "Philanthropy has lost its way." Something went missing in the field—the internal knowledge of what philanthropy is and why it exists.

Ted Leavitt's article "Marketing Myopia: What Business Are You In?" in the *Harvard Business Review* back in the 1970s described the U.S. railroads' fatal failure to understand they were in the transportation business, not the "railroad" business. The article transformed the way corporations from Exxon to Microsoft to the latest high-tech start-up today think about who they are and what they do.

Similarly, at the 2005 Technology, Education, and Design (TED) conference in Monterey, where people from around the world come to stretch the boundaries, the animating question for the technology leaders in the room was "What does technology want to be?" Viewing technology simply as the technology business or as applied technical knowledge or as the latest breakthrough, instead of what it could mean for the world, is a vision cut off at the knees.

Emmett is asking the same questions of philanthropy and community foundations in particular: "What business are you in? What does philanthropy want to be?"

The dilemma is fundamentally a question of vision, mission, and meaning. It is felt personally and organizationally. But for Emmett, one choice is quite clear: "Community foundations have to decide if they are charitable banks or if they are change agents. If they are just charitable banks, they are nothing!"

Community foundations are the fastest-growing part of American philanthropy. They represent a vehicle for donors to give back to their community as part of a pool of long-term assets that are invested in systemic social issues. Community foundations are both a financial and knowledge resource to a community. There is increasing interest in adapting the community foundation model in other countries around the world.

"There was a time when community foundations were in effect a social movement. But in the drive to increase assets, and be more business-like, too many have lost the sense of their reason to be, their purpose. I'm not saying don't be a good fund-raiser; just don't lose sight of why you are raising the money—it is the means, not the end. Individually and collectively, community foundations need to focus on how they can address equity and social justice issues in their communities."

Emmett has been delivering this message for a long time in many forums, with mixed reactions.

"Here I am, a member in good standing of organized philanthropy, telling everyone who will listen that we have to be in the social justice business, or we are in no business. In the United States, the response I get is often surprise or disagreement. But the reaction in other countries is positive. E-mails and letters from people around the world, who have these issues in their face every day, talk about the importance of confronting social injustice, and those letters resonate with my argument. Do we not see it here, or are we are just too polite to mention it?

"To be fair, there has been some progress. More often now, the ambition to act as a true change agent is out there. At the same time, there are inherent conflicts between a donor-advised approach to increasing assets under management, which has become the norm in the community foundation world, and the idea of collectively raising and directing resources to address common community problems. But I also believe you can move money once it is in place, and you can educate those who have established donor-advised funds toward strategic investments in the community. Every donor ought to be exposed to that opportunity. When they see what is being done for the community, when we demonstrate that, they often respond.

"That is the difference between being a movement and being a bank. People in this field who spoke about being a movement were made to feel ridiculous and naive, particularly as the rhetoric increased around being more business-like. A bank seeks increased assets to build market share and grow profits; a movement raises money to achieve a larger purpose. Without that, what are we?

"We have to be intentional about community change. Every donor has two assets, cash and cache. It is in the intentional design and execution of plans on these two parallel tracks that you can really get something important done. In philanthropy, cash is usually the focus. Cache—which includes giving voice to the public, the capacity to convene, to access, and to advocate—is underrepresented. Our biggest leadership asset is our cache; people do see community foundations as having a broader and more reasoned view of things. Cache gives us an opportunity to exercise our public voice and say our work is not just about making grants—it is about what all of us want for our community. It's a form of leadership.

"Being a leader means saying the difficult things. A doctor sometimes has to say, 'Given the science we have today, the success of this procedure is kind of slim but worth attempting.' Good grant making comes with a measure of risk, but we have gone overboard on measurement as an objective. Too much focus on risk reward makes us risk-averse."

At the Minneapolis Foundation's second major conference on immigration, more than six hundred people came together for several meetings to wrestle with the problems and see the opportunities for new immigrants. Minneapolis has had a rich flow of new people. In the public schools, students speak more than eighty different languages. The educational, job training, and citizenship orientation challenge is huge, but the human resource potential for the region is equally large.

"We had tremendous representation and inclusion at these meetings. We broadcast them on public TV and radio and got the ideas out into the community, started a dialogue, and I think we woke a lot of people up. There is a raging debate over immigration in Minnesota and nationally, but people don't know what it means for their communities."

It wasn't just the formal program; the conversations among advocates, nonprofit and religious leaders, corporate and government agency representatives, and policymakers were just as valuable. They talked about the implications for the pubic schools and exchanged business cards and learned the language of the bigger picture.

"We have former child soldiers in our classrooms dealing with the trauma of war, and we have Mexican migrants' kids, just off the truck, whose families are working off the books. The great thing about the convening was the learning, in every corner, that nobody's gumbo tastes the same."

A foundation using its cache can create communities of interest and networks that give everyone a taste of what's happening and a chance to show off their own best recipe. "There's no way to quantify or give a metric for what that is worth."

Speaking out against injustice is the first step. The Community Foundations of Canada are ahead of the U.S. curve and have made a formal commitment to social justice. They understand that issues of social justice acquire legitimacy and value when respected institutions like foundations focus on them and speak out.

"The issues that trouble me the most are: the wealth disparity between the rich and the poor, the big cuts in the social safety net, and the debate about the elimination of the estate tax. I find it unconscionable that agents of philanthropy, especially community foundations, do not feel the obligation to speak out and to use their influence. We live in a society in which the wealth disparity is one of the largest in the world, and the greed is very noticeable. We debate whether or not it's fair for the richest one percent to pay an estate tax. We debate whether or not all kids should have access to health insurance. Foundations don't get to decide, but they can inform and influence."

But to suggest Emmett's mission is focused only on public policy would be wrong.

"One reason we are so divided as a society is that ideology has trumped purpose. Take the conservative movement's success that was funded by a small number of conservative foundations. The effort by a group of liberal donors to counterattack on the basis of ideology is the wrong idea. We need to ask the question 'What is best for society?' instead of dogmatically stating a position or funding only things that pass an ideological litmus test, and then spending all our time trying to prove it's right. Liberal or conservative should not be the fundamental question; instead, it should be what are the problems and what are the best ways to solve them. After that, we can argue about the tactical approaches. It might be free market sometimes; other times it might be subsidy and regulation.

"I want philanthropy to be a movement. A movement focuses on the absolute necessity for the work. That is everything. Then we can figure out what can be achieved and how. For community foundations, that means a financial model that over time primarily relies on the accumulation of assets directed for the common good rather than individual donor interests. And we may have to leave behind those who are wedded to the path of being charitable bankers rather than social change agents."

The Small Are Many

In this poorest rural region of Ohio, part of Appalachia, there is a history of dependence on the exploitation of natural resources, from coal to timber, along with some manufacturing and a small number of family farms. Changes in the economy, however, have caused huge displacements and the migration of people and resources. It was far more than coal that was stripped from the land.

While a great deal of wealth was generated from these natural resources, it seldom got to institutions that reinvested it in this region. In this part of the country there are no large foundations, big corporate grant makers, or Fortune 500 companies, even though in many instances, the genesis of the assets that built such entities elsewhere came from this region.

In many cases the wealth went to urban communities like Columbus, Cleveland, Cincinnati, and New York, which ironically swelled with the relocation of Appalachian communities. The captains of Appalachia's mining and timber industries rarely resided where their fortunes were made and traditionally directed their philanthropy to areas close to home.

In many instances, the poor of the one place followed the trail of money to where it came to reside. Lost to Appalachia were both financial and human resources, and it suffers from those losses still.

When Leslie Lilly, president of the Foundation for Appalachian Ohio, thinks about a vision for the future, it is based on those realities.

"My vision begins with what it means to be part of a commonwealth where your investment as an individual is in a community where resources and assets are jointly shared, and where an individual can play a role in contributing but not be limited by what they can contribute."

She envisions community institutions, particularly those hard-strapped in rural areas, that are healthy and prosperous and that play a central role in encouraging civic participation, providing leadership, and demonstrating responsibility on its behalf. This vision reflects the work she has been involved in for more than twenty-five years.

Leslie comes out of a background in not-for-profit work in rural communities in the South and Appalachian regions of the country. In local grassroots organizations, she has struggled to raise dollars for ideas and programs where there was no prospect for either public or private investment. The search was always most difficult in trying to identify financial resources that were home grown and locally available to do community development work.

"I knew we had assets in our communities, yet every time I needed to raise money for a local initiative, I had to leave the community to find the dollars to do it. It made no sense to me.

"Twenty-five years ago it was fairly common to plan on a trip or two to New York, because that was where the money was; there were few centers of organized philanthropy, even in many urban areas of the South, unlike today."

One reason that the situation has improved is because of Leslie, and others, who have proven the case that in rural communities across the country almost any increase in assets can make an enormous difference. "My institution has been joined by a proliferation of small community foundations and hundreds of efforts to build institutional infrastructure in places where philanthropy once meant posting a thermometer on the outskirts of town to keep score of the annual United Way fund-raising.[1]

"We have a strong tradition of neighbor helping neighbor, but not the mechanisms to leverage the more sophisticated forms of giving. That is what we are trying to create."

Large institutions from outside the region could be of assistance, but stereotypes and misconceptions about rural living often get in the way.

"We value the uniqueness of what they have. But, from the outside looking in, people tend to romanticize rural communities as pristine country
where people live in quaint circumstances and reject change. They see problems in rural areas as less serious than urban problems. These perceptions are
compounded by the false assumption that folks have the choice to move it if
they don't like it.[2]

She believes that larger national institutions and foundations should take
more of a leadership role to steward and grow the capacity of smaller community foundations and community-based organizations. "Not only would
that ensure the quality of work but would provide assets to communities that
are unlikely ever to have their own version of the Cleveland Foundation
(which at more than $1 billion is the second-largest community foundation
in the country). Some of the major national foundations have adopted this
role and it has been immensely helpful.

"One example is the ongoing project to promote philanthropy in the region
led by the Foundation for Appalachian Ohio and funded by the New Ventures
in Philanthropy Fund.[3] Grant makers in the region are coming together to talk
about how they can grow the pie. With the involvement of Ohio State University
Extension, this coalition of funders has gained additional leverage. There were
many intersections. We are creating more awareness about the 'options for giving' part of the conversation in doing estate-planning workshops, for example, and in working with farm families around financial planning."

A Philanthropy Index project designed to help community leaders assess
the potential for philanthropic giving in their communities has also been
promising in helping them figure out how to build a fund and get the community organized around that discussion.

"We've piloted that effort in four counties, and in each case, a community
fund has been created. There have been local partnerships where a grassroots
group has married up with a local community foundation or private foundation so there's a home to seed and grow the fund. These were small grants of
$3,000 to be matched on a one-to-one basis. All have mustered that match,
and some have gone beyond. Modest, but this is the first time there has been
a focused discussion of philanthropy in some of these areas.

"I just came back from a community meeting where we announced four
new funds that will become part of the family funds that we are managing and
it created great excitement among the fifty to sixty people in that room. The
more visible these efforts become the more they attract others who have not
acted on their values. I see things really starting to ignite in counties on feelings that have been latent for twenty-five years.

"One of the things we struggle with is a high level of balkanization where the competition for public funding has bred a very tough competitive spirit. You don't have a strong history of village working with village or foundations working with other foundations toward a common goal. So, the vision for promoting philanthropy has to get beyond the idea that you're in it to build a chest of gold. It has to be about what you are building a chest of gold to create and support. If you can get people focused on the conversation of 'philanthropy for what?' it helps to transform the conversation."

Leslie is challenged to make the community foundation economic model work, and it is not easy. The field is changing dramatically, partly because of the public policy climate but also because internal expectations are transforming this field.

"Larger community foundations are adopting affiliate fund strategies, where the larger foundation becomes the umbrella under which smaller community funds are developed. The 'mother ship' provides the support services and manages and stewards the assets. That business model for community foundations is simply not sustainable for most small community foundations. Our capital base isn't large enough to create a revenue stream sufficient to support operating costs. We have to build sources of operating capital. We definitely have more work to do to figure out a model that is sustainable, and we will."

In the last four to five years, the Foundation For Appalachian Ohio has played a part in supporting entrepreneurship focused on heritage and culture as unique assets out of which opportunities can grow that will improve the social and economic well being of people living there. "Being Appalachian has not always been a source of pride and respect, and people have hidden from or denied their heritage because it is mired in stereotypes about hillbillies, backwardness, and ignorance."

But there has been a revival in traditional art being expressed in new forms and contemporary art. "We have a thriving artist colony and marvelous art institutions. It is really about finding those things in your own backyard, respecting them and using them as building blocks upon which to think about what the future could look like for the region and to decipher the values that will be important in guiding that conversation.

"The old saw about collaborating—the willingness to give up a little of yourself for something that can be accomplished by the whole—is very true. Once you experience what it feels like when those values are reflected in how people are living and working together, you really do not want to go back to living without them.

"There's a lot of noise and contradiction in our society about the cultivation of the individual versus the cultivation and support of community. I sometimes feel that our culture sends a message that you only deserve it if you can buy it. Education is a pretty good example. No institution is more important or meaningful in a community than our public schools in raising young people to understand and embrace the responsibilities of citizenship. Showing them how their acts of selflessness help to build a better community helps ensure that they will become involved. Yet the debate about education often misses how fundamentally important that institution has been to the quality of life both for local communities and to the country as a whole.

"In an area like this, you see remarkable things unfold. You get to work with all kinds of people committed to a vision and you see that you really can make a difference. I look back over the years and all the people I've worked with and see many are still out working in the community, perhaps with different jobs, but the commitment has remained constant through the years."

Whether we are doing a good enough job in creating pipelines to attract talented young people into community service and philanthropy, particularly those who may not come out of a traditional academic setting, is a question that bothers Leslie. "It is extremely important that we take time to affirm, celebrate, and reflect on the good work that people are doing."

"I was living in Mississippi when Oseola McCarty, an African American woman who did everyone's ironing for years, died and left a gift of over $150,000 to establish a scholarship program at the University of Southern Mississippi. People were stunned. Here was this woman, for all intents and purposes without wealth, leaving a testament to the future greater than a lot of other people in much easier circumstances. I can't think of the number of times the story of Ms. McCarty has been told. It trumps all these issues that people have about getting to the point where they are ready to become philanthropic at whatever scale is appropriate for them. I think there are a lot more stories out there of personal sacrifice. You needn't be a donor with a capital D to make a difference.

"But the climate in our society is neither tolerant nor forgiving and people need to be reminded of their better selves. Leadership is needed to provide a better vision. The destruction of institutions and erosion of values that have helped form the tenets of citizenship are troubling trends. What does it mean to be a citizen of this country today? The call of the commonwealth needs to be as clear as the recognition that government is not bad but neutral. The distinction comes in what we make of it ourselves."

Listening to Leslie Lilly talk is to be reminded how community, even the poorest, can be renewed and made vibrant, and how bereft we are without that renewal. These lines from Nadine Gordimer's novel *The Burger's Daughter* express beautifully that sentiment: "For us . . . , that was the real definition of loneliness: to live without social responsibility."

The Stirring of Conscience

"The absolute starting point for the world I want to live in has got to be the presence of economic justice—something I would simplistically define as equipping everyone who is able to work to find employment that pays no less than a living wage."

The tendency for some people of wealth to ignore the fact that their comfortable-to-lavish lifestyles are at least partially subsidized by the labors of the underpaid poor troubles Martin Lehfeldt, president of the Southeastern Council of Foundations.

"Empathy instilled at an early age may be why some people are moved by compassion to address economic injustice while others appear unconcerned; why some people are sensitive to human need and others remain oblivious. It may be in large part a matter of the right kind of education and instilling a conscience."

The Georgia state legislature mandated "character education" several years ago, but Martin questions what that means. Should children read the autobiography of Ben Franklin or the speeches of Martin Luther King Jr.? Should they study the writings of Andrew Carnegie or Jane Addams? Could they perhaps be exposed to the kind of education that he received at Moorestown Friends School in New Jersey—one that fanned the spark of social justice?

It taught him to see something of the divine in every human being and to feel an abiding respect for every person. "We took seriously the notion that all of us are citizens of the world, literally celebrating United Nations Day every October 24. We learned also that everyone has the right to challenge the decisions of his or her government and to stand in opposition to those that require a violation of conscience.

"Weaving a framework of values—similar to the one that was transmitted to me gently but without apology—into what we teach our kids is what I mean by character education. I have great faith in the essential sense of fairness that young people have. Exposing them at an early age to examples of social injustice and giving them opportunities to learn how to practice personal generosity and voluntarism and engage in political action is tremendously important. People are not born with charitable or philanthropic genes; they learn generosity from parents and teachers and mentors."

Spiritual Yearning Falls Short without Service to Others

Martin was raised in a strong faith tradition and completed a master of divinity degree at Union Theological Seminary in New York. He recognizes and appreciates the spiritual yearning that seems so palpable in this country, but he is wary of it. "It has driven too many people into the arms of religious groups that serve up simplistic theologies and focus on personal salvation. Eventually they run into a dead end. I believe we find ultimate meaning not in religious self-improvement or an intensely personal relationship with a Divine Being but in human community and service to others.

"Religious fundamentalism and the fear of change it represents around the globe are dangerously natural extensions of any faith that is self-centered; they therefore are great obstacles to achieving a vision of a more socially just world."

Martin has worked both sides of the nonprofit street, starting out as a program officer for an operating foundation in New Jersey, and then serving as a college development officer and a consultant to nonprofits. The opportunity in 1969 to become the vice president for development at Clark College (now Clark Atlanta University), a historically black college, was "transformational." As the only white member of the administration, he acquired a unique lens to look at the South and indeed the world. "Seeing life through the prism of fellow Americans who have been ignored and deprived changes your entire perspective."

What began as a search for a brief cultural experience stretched into seven years, followed by three years with the Atlanta University Center, a consortium of African American institutions that also includes Morehouse College and Spellman College. Drawing on those experiences, he began working with other historically black colleges and many nonprofits and community foundations around the country.

Like many other people, Martin believes the fundamental way to achieve economic justice is through changes in public policy. "The problem is that we lack the political will. Instead, we build poverty into our public policy. Most poor people want to work and sustain themselves, but they can't figure out how to do it on minimum wage rates that have less purchasing power each year. Meanwhile, we have corporate welfare programs that are depleting tax dollars that once provided a critical safety net for things like children's health insurance.

"Part of the problem is that we accept poverty as a necessary reality. Our favorite proof-text on the subject is 'the poor you will always have with you'— never really pondering the fact that it is in a lot of people's interest to keep folks poor.

"Even the most well-meaning individuals continue to institutionalize poverty. The Atlanta Community Foundation Food Bank started in a church basement twenty-six years ago. It's a great organization that does wonderful work and has a remarkable director. Because of the support of many generous foundations and individuals, it recently was able to dedicate a new $11 million state-of-the-art facility that will serve it well for many years. However, few people seem to appreciate the implied irony in this achievement. In effect, generous and compassionate people are conceding that we're going to continue to have widespread hunger in a booming metropolitan area in the wealthiest country in the world."

This all touches on the way philanthropy in general too often operates. "Top-down" approaches cannot work. As it is, organized philanthropy is too much of an oligarchy, dominated by a relatively small number of foundations— and they still haven't come up with the answer to building a perfect world. In part that's because there is no single way to get the world we want; it's going to require a lot of people and institutions rethinking their philosophies and restructuring their methodologies and then linking their efforts.

"Hurricane Katrina's greatest contribution to the strengthening of our moral fiber *may* have been the way it surfaced the economic disparities of American life. Poverty in places like New Orleans and Atlanta and many cities around the United States has always been a badly kept dirty secret. We all have known about it and either ignored it or became frustrated by our inability to change the situation. Now, at least temporarily, the subject is back on the table again. And philanthropy has the opportunity to ask itself whether it will accept the responsibility to use its resources to promote greater equity."

Here's a column that Martin recently composed for his organization's newsletter:

> Sun sparkled on the surface of the 11-mile stretch of water that was part of the Mississippi River before it changed its course hundreds of years ago. Now it's a beautiful lake, ringed by increasingly expensive homes along the shore.

I was in New Rivers, Louisiana, the jurisdictional center of Pointe Coupee Parish—a small town that still has a few lovely old plantation houses, some very nice neighborhoods, one truly great restaurant (Ma Mama's), and a handful of antique shops. It would be a nice place to retire, or, if you're still part of the workforce in Baton Rouge, the state capital is only 30 miles away.

Ernest Gaines, the noted author, is a native son of the area, and he has built a home here. However, he is one of only a handful of African-Americas who live in this part of town. The rest of the black community is a mile or so away, literally on the other side of the tracks where living conditions are much bleaker. They're even worse outside of town in the more rural sections of the parish, where shacks sit on the edge of vast tracks of sugar cane growing under the hot sun.

In the early Sixties, I read Michael Harrington's *The Other America*. If I remember correctly, it opened with a description of how well the beauty of the blossoming giant rhododendron, West Virginia's state flower, masked the utter destitution of people who lived in the "hollers" of that part of Appalachia.

We're not the only ones who do it, but we're especially good at hiding the poverty of our region behind both natural beauty and artistic artifice. If you confine your travels to the interstate highways that links our gleaming urban centers and sleek suburbs around them and route your metropolitan excursions away from the other sides of the tracks, it's all too easy to ignore or forget the fact that we still have the highest poverty rate (more than 14%) of any region in the United States. It is the bane of our existence, and its offspring of bad education and bad health continue to cripple all of us.

Clearly, we have made some important progress. It's instructive to remember that as late as 1959, one-third of the South's citizens lived in poverty. Foundation giving has contributed to the improvements. However, our region's ability to realize its full potential will continue to be determined in great measure by our shared determination to keep the issue of poverty squarely before us and to be guided by a common vision of its ultimate eradication. That is a most worthy goal for all of organized philanthropy.

"If foundations were courageous enough to use not just their financial resources but their leadership positions, they could play a major role in changing the public policies that maintain the status quo. Greater support of nonprofit organizations that advocate for change would be a wonderful starting point." A great believer in the not-for-profit sector, which he describes as the "glue" that holds society together, Martin is also a strong proponent of grants that help strengthen the management of nonprofit organizations and thereby their ability to serve their communities.

He also would declare a moratorium on any more studies or needs assessments and focus instead on what we already know works. "We know, for instance, that infants who are cuddled three times a day are more likely to succeed in later life than those who don't receive that early expression of love.

"We know that what happens to kids before they are two years old has an enormous impact on what kind of adults they become. We know that high school dropouts are much more likely to end up in prison than those who stay in school. And we know that adult mentoring is one of the most positive experiences some young people can have.

"What if our nation's foundations were to provide collective leadership to citywide, long-term commitments to give all poor children a guaranteed regimen of cuddling and preschool nurturing and a series of adult mentors until they finish high school? Sure, it would take a lot of coordination—and advocacy—and it would mean that some other things might not get funded, but I guarantee you it would begin to change the culture of poverty that's crippling all of us."

Asked to summarize his thoughts, he notes, "The essential question—and it's a tough one—for our society as a whole is simply this: do you slap bandages on admittedly very real problems, or do you work to change the structures that contribute to those problems?"

For many, including me, Martin's essential question is the essential question, but he raises another critical question. How does a society teach the next generation the lessons of civic responsibility? Put directly, how do we go about the business of making a citizen?

Let's meet some people who, so to speak, are in the business.

Reader's Guide Questions

1. What do we mean by "the moral conscience" of a community?
2. Where does community conscience lie in your community? Does it lie with you, and if so, how?
3. If a foundation is about giving, what is wrong with thinking about it as a bank?
4. Do you believe, as Emmett Carson does, that philanthropy must be in the social justice business?

5. Do you use your cache? Could you use it tomorrow?
6. Leslie Lilly believes the role an individual plays should not be limited by how much he or she can contribute. Do we undervalue some kinds of individual initiative?
7. How big is the opportunity to promote citizen involvement and philanthropy in your community? Where are the hidden assets?
8. Leslie tells how a community, irrespective of resources, can build pride. What could you do to build pride in your community?
9. Martin Lehfeldt was taught his values "gently but without apology." How did you learn yours? How are you teaching values to your children?
10. Martin had a "transformational" experience as a white person working for a historically black college. Have you ever been part of a minority, in terms of gender, race, privilege, impairment, or principle? How did it affect you?
11. Is the Food Bank story another example of philanthropy institutionalizing services? Is it possible to provide food and plan for "going out of business" at the same time?
12. How do you answer Martin's tough and essential question—Band-Aids or structural change?

Notes

1. The Southern Rural Development Initiative is a collaborative of rural and community-based stakeholders, led in part by Funders Who Fund in the South, an affinity group of the National Network of Grantmakers.
2. Research by the W. K. Kellogg Foundation has described both the patterns of giving in the South and the sociological assumptions that have affected it.
3. The New Ventures Fund is a project of the Forum of Regional Grantmakers and represents to date an investment of $14 million in more than thirty innovative efforts to promote philanthropy around the country. Funding has come from a number of progressive national foundations.

CITIZEN LIGHTS
Citizenship and Education

H OW DO YOU make a citizen?

Martin Lehfeldt suggests that empathy and values are best instilled at an early age, as they were in him, "gently but without apology." How is that actually done? How do you educate and motivate young people so that they understand and value their role to be an active citizen?

How do you objectively inform an entire society? What is objectivity in a divided and polarized society?

As it turns out, there are citizen makers hard at work on those very questions.

Citizen Makers

Alan Khazei is on the boat that goes from South Boston to the Thompson Island Outward Bound dock, and he's got stage fright. It is 1988 and casting off with him is the very first City Year cohort of young people who have signed on for a bold new experiment, a full summer of learning and service in Boston's inner city. This is before City Year will get its own distinctive bright red jackets, before the organization will grow into a national program, and long before the organization will serve as a model and inspiration for the Clinton administration legislation creating the national service program AmeriCorps.

On this beautiful July day, the harbor is deep blue, and the islands are silhouettes on the horizon. This day is the culmination of a dream that began several years before when Alan and his college roommate, Michael Brown, conceived the City Year concept while both were attending Harvard College and Law School. Rather than joining the ranks of highly paid corporate lawyers, they chose to start from scratch a high-impact nonprofit organization with the ambitious goal of transforming the notion of service learning in American society.

All of the talk and plans were about to become real, and it was daunting. As Alan puts it, "I thought, 'Holy cow! What am I going to do and say that will be meaningful to these young people?' It wasn't that we hadn't thought about it. I had a script, but I didn't know if it was the right one." It was then that Alan did what he does so naturally and brilliantly. He started telling stories, stories about growing up in America as the son of an Iranian father and an Italian mother, of why he was drawn to do something for this country, for society, stories of his heroes, among them Robert Kennedy and Martin Luther King, and how their passion for social justice had become his. Alan was mesmerizing. The first City Year corps members no doubt remember that day, as so many who have followed remember their first taste of becoming part of a movement that is engaging young people in an ever expanding network for good.

City Year's *Founding Stories* has become part of the organization's rich lore and the basis for skits and role plays that are the first step in the immersion of corps members in their intensive year of personal and social exploration. For Alan, it is always about the stories, the passion and power of young idealists. We are in City Year's national headquarters in Boston, a warren of workspaces in an older building, and outside Alan's office is a wailing baby whose mom is his assistant. Alan is oblivious to the background noise. He is, naturally, telling us a story.

It is of the around-the-world, year-long trip that he and his wife, Vanessa Kirsch, took in 1995–1996. As a plan for a honeymoon, it had to be a first. It was a high-energy year of meeting and connecting with social entrepreneurs around the globe, and coming face-to-face with the pain and the glory of an astounding number of social activists from many different cultures. That trip, eight years into the City Year experience, was inspirational. It not only renewed Alan's energy for the social entrepreneurial work that City Year does, but it also reaffirmed his belief in the Tao and the concept of the servant leader. (Jono Quick and Alan Khazei have met, but only spiritually.) The trip also led Vanessa Kirsch to create New Profit Inc., an innovative organization that invests in and supports high-impact social entrepreneurs in achieving their missions.

Vanessa has a talent for seeing spatially and thinking differently from others. She was recognized by both *Newsweek* and *U.S. News & World Report* as a leader of her generation and by *Forbes* as one of fifteen innovators who will reinvent the future. Alan's respect for her sets a pattern for our conversation. He is generous in his praise of others, and constantly acknowledges the value and contributions of those around him. It is part of his gift and part of what makes him so appealing.

An article in 1994 by Lester Salamon[1] in *Foreign Affairs* mapped out the growing potential of the civil society and the decline in the capacity of government alone to solve social dilemmas. In that piece, which had a great influence on Alan, were the seeds of what has become the social entrepreneur movement.

He traces his motivation to great events—Mandela and the overthrow of apartheid in South Africa, the fall of the Berlin Wall with the reawakening of democracy in Eastern Europe, and the memorable images from Tiananmen Square of courageous young people standing up for what they believed was right. These stunning and world-changing events served as a powerful magnetic force for Alan and his colleagues. A special kind of drive infuses City Year with an energy and commitment that enables it year after year to inspire young people.

For Alan, national service for every young American is more than a nice idea—it is one of the key elements to making a democracy work. City Year is citizenship making in action.

City Year is an immersion experience that fulfills the yearning that so many have for connection, for community, for values, and for personal growth. Serving with and meeting others who are different from oneself, often in the way of opportunity and resources, is a powerful learning experience. "Everyone wants a better life for their kids, and that may mean increasing their awareness. City Year brings diverse individuals from a wide spectrum of backgrounds who find far more common ground than they had ever imagined possible. Service learning is experiential on the front line. Participants work in teams to improve local communities and become witnesses to injustice, to prejudice, to people in great need who aspire to a better life, but are held back through no fault of their own. It is a program that is as much about personal growth, which includes spiritual growth, as about learning critically needed community-building and leadership skills."

But do those kinds of experiences have the potential to bring our divided society together?

Alan's reaction was counterintuitive. While the American society is polarized by huge cultural and ideological divides and finding common ground is difficult, the deep feeling of community and bonding that develops among those with partisan interests can be positive. What gives him hope is in those unique moments when all the divisiveness is put aside, and the country comes together as it did in response to 9/11, the tsunami in Southeast Asia, and Hurricane Katrina. Alan believes that inspirational leadership can lead us to common ground. He sees that leadership emerging every day in the work that AmeriCorps and City Year does.

The theory of positive deviance argues for the resolution of social dilemmas through investment in those who get it, those who produce, and those who are motivated to be excellent in their work. It's a theory Alan embraces. For example, to improve child nutrition, it is more productive to study the 20 percent who are healthier and use the knowledge gained from that to meet the needs of the 80 percent who are malnourished. With or without a City Year bright red jacket, he believes in analyzing what is working to fix what is broken.

Alan credits Hubie Jones, a longtime activist, leader of the Boston community, and an adviser to City Year, for urging the organization to kick into high gear and actively share its message and vision with government, community, and business leaders. An invitation to then governor Bill Clinton to visit City Year Boston, which he accepted, at which he expressed his strong vision for a national service program, gave City Year a whole new platform on which to operate.

Jim Collins's books *Built to Last* and *Good to Great* have been important guides for City Year's organizational development, but Alan has no illusions about the remarkable series of events that led to the creation of AmeriCorps. It is rare for a privately funded nonprofit organization to be able to convince government that it should step in and take a modeled concept to scale. A relationship with the new administration helped. City Year invested in its organizational and fund-raising capacity, and was able to present to Congress a successful working model of what service learning could accomplish. If City Year had not existed, reached a certain scale, and been able to prove its results, AmeriCorps might never have come into being.

Philanthropy has played a large part in the City Year story, especially Atlantic Philanthropies, which in Alan's experience offers support "just right." Atlantic came to City Year when the organization was young, and asked three questions: What is your biggest vision? What is holding you back? What is your biggest need? Atlantic not only funded City Year in the early days but steadily increased annual funding and in 2002 made a $10 million challenge grant based on a two-to-one match. The goal was to raise $30 million for core capitalization. City Year successfully met that challenge.

Today City Year has a $40 million budget, but it is heavy lifting to maintain that revenue. Much of it comes through small grants that range from $1,000 to $100,000. Too many support programs for only one or two years, but corporate funding is often more solid; City Year has had a great relationship with Timberland for sixteen years.

City Year was caught in a political cross-fire in 2003 when AmeriCorps had its budget radically reduced. The organization took a big hit, and in Alan's assessment, it is an example of the difficulty in sustaining a nonprofit economic model.

As we have learned, unlike the well-developed infrastructure that exists for capital formation in the for-profit world, there is no counterpart in the nonprofit world. One is needed. If Alan were making the decisions on, let's say, a $1 billion foundation, he would do the following: Find twenty high-performing organizations led by talented social entrepreneurs, and make some big bets—$50 million in each of them, with the goal of enabling them to get to scale and become economically sustainable.

Now there is an idea whose time has come!

Two decades after Alan and Michael Brown founded City Year, with about nine thousand young people in sixteen cities having served in the program, the accolades keep coming in. The *Boston Globe* in April 2006 designated Alan and Michael as "Bostonians Changing the World." "We as a society underestimate our young people," said Alan. "We always have to label our young generation negatively, when they've actually always been at the forefront of change."[2]

True, Alan Khazei, especially when there are people like you and Michael Brown to show the way!

Practical Visionaries—Educating the Next Generation

"It's time to reclaim the public service mission of the university. Teaching values and skills of civic leadership used to be a core priority of institutions of higher education, but many of them have retreated from that commitment. Education for private gain is just not OK; we should be emphasizing education for active citizenship—developing practical visionaries in all fields of study and all walks of life. This isn't a radical idea—it's both an institutional responsibility and a route to higher-quality teaching and research."

Not exactly an academic conclusion from a respected academic, but that's what we got from Rob Hollister, dean of the Tisch College of Citizenship and Public Service at Tufts.[3]

Rob, it should be said, grew up on the Antioch College campus, a creative place committed to innovation and experimentation. His parents, both Quakers, instilled in him a strong set of values about the basic goodness and equality of everyone. His father taught political science.

"I had no intention of being an academic. My dream as a college student was to be an urban planner. What I cherished most about college was the co-op experience; working as a coordinator of volunteers in a southeast Washington, D.C., neighborhood house, as a project assistant for the U.S. Conference of Mayors and then as a teacher's assistant at a Waldorf School. I was immersed in community building by the time I went to graduate school at Harvard and at MIT. Making those connections, between the academic world and the real world, became very important to me. This work, and the experience I carried with me from Antioch, fed whatever innovation I've been able to accomplish in institutions where I later worked. But organizations resist change, and organizational culture is powerful."

In contrast, the Tisch College is a marvelous example of organization change. It is a bold and ambitious experiment that has the goal of integrating the themes of public service and citizenship throughout the entire under-graduate experience at Tufts. Its goal is to provide students with an intensive experiential community and volunteer experience. Another major objective, one that is truly transformational and has never been done before on any university campus, is to integrate the themes of citizenship and service into the entire academic curriculum, from literature to biology.

Hollister explains: "I've always had a love-hate relationship with universities. I love the collegiality, the quest for truth and knowledge, the commitment to personal development and education, and the belief in using knowledge to improve society. On the other hand, universities are places of immense privilege and innate conservatism. Like other groups, professors can be very protective of their own interests. Sometimes I wish their mind-set had a stronger commitment to making the world a better place. You often find intellectual commitment to social change that doesn't carry over into how people define and carry out their jobs. They say yes to being an agent of social change, but only within the strictures of the academic culture and the tenure system, and that of course can be terribly limiting."

There are, naturally, exceptions. "A number of my colleagues in the Education Department formed an urban teacher training collaborative in partnership with the Boston Arts Academy and Fenway High School to train future teachers in the same way physicians train, with a heavy emphasis on clinical experience. This group of faculty gets their hands dirty, and they work a much longer week than if they were spending all their time teaching in classrooms at Tufts.

"The program, the Urban Teaching Training Collaborative, would not work without this kind of involvement. It is a very successful model, a residency approach to providing a master's education to future K–12 schoolteachers. Instead of coming to the university and taking education courses and then doing some practice teaching, master's students are teaching in the partner schools from day one. A remarkable 95 percent of those who have gone through the program are now teaching in urban schools.

"It was initiated by people who had some depth of experience as practitioners but were frustrated with what they were accomplishing with established programs, so they worked in real partnership with public school administrators and teachers to develop an immersion model. This effort is a marvelous example of how the university can simultaneously elevate the academic quality of its programs *and* provide greater benefits to the community in which it is located.

"Yet most faculty who run professional degree programs are not fully embracing field-based education—even though we have evidence that it can better prepare future teachers, urban planners, and others. It's a missed opportunity."

What Rob loves to do is push on those kinds of intersections, even though it is not always comfortable.

"Tufts president Larry Bacow wants to make Tufts need-blind in admissions, which is very tough and has huge financial implications. There was a lot of skepticism that it could be done, but Bacow believes that all students should have a fully equal shot at a liberal arts education. I admire that very much, and to me it is another aspect of a university wanting to be in the social change business. There is no bigger tipping point in social change than an educated citizenry that is more diverse.

"There are other intersections as well, especially between the university and the community. Universities have huge resources, and local communities have huge needs. The town-grown problems have existed forever, but the work we are doing with a collaboration of Boston area colleges and universities has shown there is enormous potential. That we are doing this work under the auspices of the Boston Foundation, which is a community foundation, is another reason for optimism.

"The Tufts–Boston Foundation partnership has been enormously effective. Twenty-five years ago, Carol Goldberg, a Boston philanthropist and Tufts alumna, established the Goldberg Seminars, in partnership with the Boston Foundation. One of the most successful of these community dialogues was around Boston's green space issues. The developed plan became the blueprint for a complete revitalization of Boston's magnificent parks.

"It is this kind of public/private process of planning and dreaming that is really pulling together people from different walks of life, leaders from different sectors. It is the first step in developing the practical discoveries that lead to change. The seminars have been a form of social education for the community. I think that this kind of agenda setting is one of the most powerful uses of private philanthropy. The Goldberg Seminars are a powerful way to link university resources to community needs."

I am intrigued with Rob's idea of educating a new generation of practical visionaries, and that is what Tisch College aims to do. The uphill battle is against the traditional tropism that is neither visionary nor practical enough. While that behavior is hardly restricted to institutions of higher education, Rob thinks that the raw potential for social gain when a college or university embraces an expanded civic role is greater than in any other domain.

"To answer the question for what it means to be an educated citizen, one who combines family, career, and civic obligations, is one of the most important things we as a society need to do. My adrenaline really gets going, and maybe I push too hard, but how to strategize, sell, and encourage others into believing in this is so important."

What is encouraging is that Tisch College, which is only in its sixth year, has begun to get real traction, and the energy level on campus around citizenship themes has intensified. But Rob still thinks we are too comfortable and that we have only begun to realize the potential. "After all, we haven't even talked about the eighty thousand Tufts alumni. What they are starting to contribute to this university-wide effort is tremendous."

Do you get the sense that Rob Hollister is a subversive, an undercover agent for citizenship, credentialed as he is, working diligently the hallowed halls of academia in pursuit of physicists, biologists, psychologists, and English professors crying, "Citizen! Citizen!" I do, and as a Senior Fellow at the school, I have even seen him in action. I forgive Rob's excess and love his passion. The motivations are good, and the product, newly minted and enthusiastic citizens, is great. He is also not alone in his passion. There are whole communities that have the same goal and are having terrific experiences working with school-age young people.

Santa Barbara, California, is one such place. Under the leadership of Charles Slosser, the long-term CEO of the Santa Barbara Foundation, every high school student in the city now has a community service requirement for graduation. "Yes, it is seen by some students as an imposition, but for many others it is an opportunity to experience the personal joy of giving. I never had that as child, but I think this kind of experience is the best way to educate the next generation about citizenship and philanthropy," he says.

The Santa Barbara Foundation designed the Care and Share Philanthropy Grants program. Adapted from models elsewhere, the program funds small grants of up to $1,000 to K–12 public school teachers and classrooms in Santa Barbara County. The program is run by the Teachers Network of the county to help students develop an appreciation of philanthropy and public service, cultivate an ethic of giving, and engage in a learning experience that enables them to realize their own power to make a difference. One grant supports fifth- and sixth-grade Adam School students researching the needs of children at a local homeless shelter and preparing backpacks full of needed items for home and school. Another helps Book Buddies, first- and second-grade students of the Santa Barbara Charter School, to present books to children at a state preschool and serve as reading role models to the children in the program. The grant to the Kids on the Block of Nightingale School enables fifth- and sixth-grade students to give a presentation on disabilities using life-size puppets so students, with and without disabilities, learn to be more accepting, tolerant, and understanding.

A small amount of money can do a great deal in the hands of smart teachers, and these kinds of simple but direct learning experiences are quite powerful. But learning has only begun for these students, and the "love of learning" in the U.S. society, for many reasons, needs renewal. Cora Marrett is one who believes scholarship is one of the key foundations for a caring and responsible world.

On Liberal Education

Cora Marrett is first and foremost a scholar, and she is not persuaded that our society is as divided as is commonly perceived. In fact, she finds more that binds us than separates us. As senior vice president for academic affairs at the University of Wisconsin, Cora thinks of learning, education, and scholarship as strong communities of interest that can bring us all together.

She is the youngest of twelve children, so it is no surprise that early in life she learned getting her own way required a fair amount of persuasion and negotiation. She grew up in a family where *conflict resolution* was not an abstract term, so her insight is from a very practical standpoint.

"You have to have passion, and for me that comes through the love of learning. In fact, my vision for a better world is one where humankind is guided by the love of learning. I think of scholarship as the best way to cross lines not crossed before. Through scholarship, data are developed and analyzed, and new ideas are formulated that might ultimately lead to individual and collective social action. In this we add to the common good.

"Among the many things that unite us is a common appreciation of beauty. The arts, for instance, are an area of common ground, even if we differ in our tastes and appreciation. We also agree, pretty much universally, in wanting a better future for our youth. That is the reason I am so attracted to higher education. The interconnections and the places of common ground are what make the argument for an education based on the liberal arts so strong, and why I am so excited about the efforts under way at Wisconsin and elsewhere to renew the liberal arts curriculum for today's world.

"The challenge is that the relevance of liberal education is not always well understood or appreciated. We have not done a good job of making that case, or even trying to understand what the broader community is thinking. There is no better example than a state university system like ours where the legislature that controls our funding answers to constituents who have very specific concerns. Today those concerns primarily revolve around the cost of living and high taxes. We need to do a better job of presenting the case for education within that context.

"The research world, which should be more of a bridge, is instead just one of the many divisions in the society. The truth is we scholars do live, if not in an ivory tower, in a silo of our own making. It is the direct opposite of the kind of open society that the academy and scholarship should represent. I would love to see scholarship and learning used as a bridging force. It is the right role for us to play in bringing value to society.

"What I have tried to do is ask some fundamental questions, beginning with the internal silos in the university between administrators at the various campuses, between the professors and the administration, and between the academic disciplines. It is in the facilitation of those dialogues that you can make real progress."

Cora Marrett makes these comments in the context of the University of Wisconsin System's participation in the LEAP (Liberal Education and America's Promise) Campaign. LEAP is a ten-year initiative sponsored by the Association of American Colleges and Universities (AAC&U) to engage the American public around the kinds of learning every student needs for productive citizenship in twenty-first-century democratic society. Wisconsin is the pilot state and the university system is partner to AAC&U in implementing the campaign. Wisconsin's lieutenant governor, Barbara Lawton, has signed on as one of its most passionate advocates. As she expresses it: "The price of admission to this twenty-first-century economy is a liberal education—intellectual agility and ethical competence. A state and a nation's commitment to higher education will determine our success in developing America's next generation of economic producers. How we prepare and support our young people will drive our ability to compete and adapt to economic challenges both within and beyond our borders."[4]

The Liberal Education and America's Promise Campaign is designed to

- spark public debate about the kinds of knowledge, skills, and values needed to prepare today's students—from school through college—for an era of greater expectations in every sphere of life;
- challenge the widespread belief that students must choose either a practical education or a liberal education, by building widespread support for educational changes that already are producing a new synthesis of liberal and practical education;
- make visible the inherent inequities in current practices that steer low-income students to college programs that teach narrow job skills, while more advantaged students reap the full benefits of a first-rate liberal education;
- document national and state progress in providing every student with access to a high-quality education that develops intellectual and ethical capacities; expands cultural, societal, and scientific horizons; cultivates democratic and global knowledge and engagement; and prepares graduates for successful participation in a dynamic and rapidly evolving economy.

Working with postsecondary schools throughout the country, the goal of the campaign is to ensure that by college graduation, all students achieve

- strong analytic, communication, quantitative, and information skills;
- deep understanding of the disciplines that explore the natural, social, and cultural realms;
- intercultural knowledge and collaborative problem-solving skills;
- civic, social, and personal responsibility;
- the ability to transfer knowledge from one setting to another.

Cora makes the case from the perspective of scholarship, and the lieutenant governor makes the case from the perspective of economic competitiveness.

Both arguments are compelling. It is encouraging that Wisconsin, one of the leading state university systems in the United States, is seriously looking at ways to deepen the connections that Cora references. What is discouraging is that the goals and outcomes of a liberal education, of which scholarship is an important qualitative aspect, are not viewed—as they once were—as central to building and maintaining the vibrancy of an open society. The value is acknowledged, but within the mainstream culture, it is no longer embraced. Other than a small number of wealthy, elite colleges and universities, the liberal arts are increasingly being diminished within university curricula.

Budget constraints are the surface culprits, but the bigger issue is the face-off between values and value. For parents and students, the cost of higher education is so high that a cost-benefit analysis can make the idea of liberal arts courses appear to be a luxury. State legislators, who struggle within our anti-tax culture, may not have the necessary data, and as Cora mentioned, the academic world has not learned to make a compelling case.

Business employers send mixed signals. The prevailing rhetoric is that the most important ingredients in the workplace are critical thinking and collaborative skills, which can only be taught within a wide-ranging educational experience. Those who graduate with strong liberal arts backgrounds become the highly coveted employees, successful professionals, and entrepreneurs, but businesses also often demand very specific skills that preempt a student's options.

So where in this domain is "the body of Gods" that needs to be confronted. It seems legion, and in the words of Pogo, my onetime favorite comic strip character, "the enemy is us." Today, narrow interests and insularity is the norm and holding on to a parallel track is liberal education, which in my view is still deeply relevant to our societal roots, historical and democratic. The challenge is significant, but LEAP is exciting because it puts in practice Cora Marrett's and Rob Hollister's beliefs in the power of education in promoting active citizenship. It is also why I have enthusiastically joined the LEAP National Leadership Council.

Let's turn now to another institution that offers a wide-ranging educational experience to the public through dialogue, creativity, and imagination.

Toward a Higher Affection

The way you get change is to win people over by appealing to what Bill Moyers calls "a higher affection," the yearning that lies within for self-improvement and for giving back to society. For thirty years Henry Becton, president of WGBH Boston's Public Broadcasting Service (PBS) has been at the very axis of public broadcasting and, through creative television and radio, he has been doing just that. WGBH has developed and produced more than a third of total PBS programming, and its influence and experience in winning people over through education, not confrontation, has been impressive. But navigating toward tolerance and openness through the tumultuous waters of America's cultural divides, something public broadcasting must do every day, is not simple, and sometimes you have to take a stand. The reality is that the definition of what constitutes "higher affection" is in the eyes of the beholder.

PBS meets all the criteria of a parallel track that John Abele describes, and in the process it generates its fair share of disruption.

Here is an example. One of WGBH's big winners has been the animated children's series *Arthur*. Producers at GBH came up with the idea of taking one of the most beloved characters from *Arthur*, a lively rabbit named Buster, and building a new program around this cool make-believe character making house calls on real live children living in diverse American families. The goal of the program was to introduce to more children the extraordinary range of subcultures that make up the American society. The concept behind *Buster* is that all kids share common dreams and feelings, no matter what color, religion, income levels, or family background. WGBH believed in the project and produced a great product that combines lively animation with real people, and by attracting large audiences gradually won over its network of local stations and the television critics.

Well and good, but in the course of Buster's travels, he visits in Vermont a multiracial family where a same-sex couple adopted some great kids. While PBS at first had no objection, the program came to the attention of the Bush administration's secretary of education, who strongly objected to there being two mommies—and did so publicly. Pressure mounted to withdraw the program, and PBS eventually refused to include it in its schedule. Henry Becton and his colleagues believed this was not only an overreaction but an error. The episode focused on the children, and the parent's alternative lifestyle was in the background. At the end WGBH held its ground, distributed the program itself, and more than half of the PBS stations broadcast it. As predicted, viewers had no issue with the material.

That public broadcasting is caught in the increasingly contentious culture wars is hardly a surprise. But that it is able to push back, hold its ground, and win some battles proves one of Henry's main conclusions taken from thirty years of experience. "Program vehicles that people trust can lead and successfully present tough and complicated themes. At the end of the day, trust is the most important thing we have, and surveys show that public broadcasting is one of the most trusted institutions in America. We have worked hard to be open and fair, and not ideological or doctrinaire. I think that the way out of social dilemmas, all those issues where the desires and fears of the individual confront the broader needs of the public, is by building trust. Trust begins by helping people experience how others think and feel, and by connecting people who are actually doing things with others. That is a big part of our job.

"One of the great things about public television and radio is that they are free and available to everyone. People get introduced to things they would otherwise know nothing about. Our audience is more diverse than you might think. It is not just 'wine and brie' elitists. It pretty much mirrors the demographic breakdown of the nation overall, covering all income levels and ethnic groups. Public television's marketing problem is attracting busy adults in their middle years. We have good coverage with young audiences and with older audiences and we need to learn how to better serve those in between. Nonetheless, public radio does succeed with this group, and the reach of public broadcasting overall expands horizons, expands access to education and information, and as a result is deeply democratic."

Democracy is a key word to Henry and underlies WGBH's educational mission. "In a society where the reach of mass media has eroded, and thousands of media choices are available on cable and the Internet, there is a tendency for people to go narrow. Some aspects of this are positive, as recent immigrants can now tune in their home country radio stations. If you want to watch golf all day, then you can. But it can also prevent people from learning about others, from happening upon new cultural or educational experiences. It is part of what erodes the trust and understanding needed to build a healthy civil society."

With the rise of niche media, the ability of commercial TV and radio to tackle the big important issues has all but vanished. It is only public media that can present programming that is not commercially economic. At WGBH, they can do programs around teaching second graders to read, or a serious analysis of public health issues, or explaining the physics of String Theory. "We cover the whole panoply of fascinating, sometimes beautiful and sometimes troubling, aspects of the human experience that you do not get anywhere else. Our only limitation is our funding and our own creativity. WGBH has been built on high intellectual standards where taking risks, and sometimes failing, is an important part of the dynamic."

Building trust is one way out of some of our social dilemmas. WGBH builds trust by informing, connecting, and familiarizing audiences through its programs. It is one of the reasons I am glad to be on its board of overseers.

"If the Human Genome Project taught us anything, it is how intrinsically, how completely, we are biologically connected to each other. Science now shows us that there is a 99.9 percent commonality to all humanity if you can get past the many cultural barriers we learn growing up. It is profound to realize how close our DNA is to most of life on the planet. How can we not believe in life's connectedness?"

When I asked where that kind of belief gets him, Henry responded, "I suppose I find comfort in believing. I am not a religious person, but I do believe in the human connection to one another and to all life. To the extent I believe in a higher being, it is in the intersections between our humanity and the natural order of the world.

"We took our family to the Galápagos Islands a few years ago, and it was quite wonderful. Seeing firsthand these amazing living creatures up close and without fear, and knowing even a little of how they connect to our own biology, was a life-changing and spiritual experience.

"And out of the natural order come powerful analogues. Look how Google, eBay, and the Internet generally are reordering human intersections in ways that we could not even conceive of ten years ago. It is all part of the flow that has so much potential. Public broadcasting has an incredible opportunity to take our technological infrastructure and our creative capacities and help make those connections aspirational for millions of people. That is why we are excited about the WGBH Forum Network,[5] where viewers can watch a range of live and archived webcasts and public lectures from key cultural and educational organizations, including those that TPI has produced on philanthropy. We are only beginning to learn how to use these new information mediums."

I think of Henry as a glass-half-full kind of person, someone who sees the positive aspects of things. He went to law school instead of business school because he felt it was more intellectually rigorous, but after his second year, it was clear that being a lawyer was not what interested him. He backed into broadcasting in the early days, when public television and radio were new and exciting. But his legal training has helped him in the long run.

"It brings a rigor to solving problems, and that's especially useful when I am told we can't do something. I have little tolerance for being told what to do, and I like others around me who feel the same way. If nothing else, being a lawyer has helped me work with lawyers so they find solutions rather than roadblocks.

Like others we have spoken with, Henry is attracted to the rule of the law.

"To me, the rule of law is all about common sense, which is another variation on the notion of the commons. It is part of why I am so convinced that information and knowledge flowing freely from diverse perspectives is critically important to a democratic society. It helps us all find the commonsensical common ground."

I wonder how Henry, a man of big themes and major productions, faces the big questions that seem so daunting, some of the issues and challenges behind this book, like the fragile environment, weapons of mass destruction, population, and global issues of poverty and equity? His answer resonates with what we have heard from so many others.

"You do what you can do. I think of the great novel *Middlemarch* by George Eliot. The principal character, Dorothea, is a passionate and good-hearted person whose whole life is dedicated to her big 'projects of improvement' for the less fortunate. At the end of the book, Dorothea realizes that often it is not the big projects that make a difference. There is not any one great answer to poverty or the other issues in her community. Instead, it is by a succession of small things that one makes a difference. I think that is true. Big things are less daunting if you take them one step at a time, gaining more understanding as you go. I remember a quote from Saul Bellow that Bill Moyers introduced me to. I think it was his character Herzog who said about people, 'Their great need, their hunger is for good sense, clarity, truth—even an atom of it—when day is done.' And of course, that is what we try to do at WGBH for our audience, each day."

It seems to me that having Henry Becton around has been a good thing for those of us interested in the making of citizens, in the making of a better world. The legendary Massachusetts congressman, Speaker of the House Tip O'Neill, once said, "Never underestimate the intelligence of the average American voter"—or viewer, as the case may be. Old truths are subject to new interpretation, but the success of public broadcasting in a commercially dominated society is reassuring. How to nurture the quest for new ideas and strengthen the courage to pursue them is one of the central aspects of this journey.

But there are other aspects of insight that go beyond the linear or intellectual. There is emotional intelligence. There is spiritual intelligence. And there is passion and commitment. There is will. There is the knowing of yourself.

Welcome to the Beloved Community.

Reader's Guide Questions

1. Alan Khazei talks about his heroes. Who are yours, and why did you choose them?

2. Alan believes the seeds for consensus in the American society are there, and what is needed is inspirational leadership. Do you agree?

3. Building on the strength and talent of the best sounds like a good idea, but why do you think it is called the theory of "positive deviance"? Do you agree with the notion?

4. Do you think community service should be part of every young person's experience?

5. Rob Hollister believes "It's just not OK to be comfortable." Is our society in general too concerned with comfort? Are you?

6. Universities and faculty are not alone in representing privilege and conservation. What else comes to mind?

7. What can be done to encourage people in the comfort zone to do the tough and difficult things?

8. The Santa Barbara County Care and Share program is just one example of a program that does a great deal (creative hands-on experience for the students) with a very modest grant. If you were to adapt the program for your community, what would it look like?

9. Cora Marrett believes that love of learning and scholarship are "the best ways to cross lines not crossed before." If so, what would promote that idea?

10. The LEAP Campaign is ambitious and faces many tough challenges. If you were to join Cora and the author as advocates, what would you propose?

11. Who else, other than scholars, would benefit from getting out of their silos and making bridges?

12. Henry Becton makes the case that the Public Broadcasting Service is trusted as an authentic and reliable source. What are the key elements that make that so?

13. PBS presents the "tough" issues. If government is providing the resources, should it have a say in what is presented?

14. What other strategies or mediums could increase the level of learning and discourse across our society?

Notes

1. Lester Solomon is the director of the Center for Civil Society Studies at Johns Hopkins University.

2. From Michael Blanding and Monica Hellstrom, "One-Year Wonders" in "Bostonians Changing the World," *Boston Globe Magazine*, April 30, 2006.

3. In 2006, Jonathan Tisch made a $40 million gift to endow the College of Citizenship and Public Service at Tufts University.

4. In her remarks opening the Association of American Colleges and Universities ninety-second annual meeting.
5. The Tuesdays@TPI conference held on May 17, 2005, that is part of The World We Want project featured Peggy Dulany and Peter Karoff on the subject of poverty. It was recorded by WGBH and is one of several accessible on the Web Forum site www.wgbh.org/forum.

BUILDING BELOVED COMMUNITY
Spirit and Activism

THERE ARE MANY dimensions and surprises in seeking what Henry Becton calls a "higher affection." One surprise is the realization of how powerful the unexpressed feelings we batten down in ourselves can be. Typically, we are circumspect and polite, conditioned to approach issues in a rational and linear way. Passionate outbursts we resist, and passion itself may be elusive. If we were to say out loud what we really believe, would it lead to a more loving community? Can we even talk about love openly? Chad Wick is someone who believes we can and should.

Chad Wick's Gift

Chad was the last to speak. When he choked up and then began to weep, everyone in the room was taken aback. The emotion was palpable, right out on the conference table for all of us to see and feel.

"Take your time, Chad," one of the board members said. There was a murmur of support, "Yes, certainly, it's OK," and then silence for a long minute or two. It had been a good day, and the KnowledgeWorks board retreat . . . a success, with more harmony and a greater sense of common purpose than we had ever achieved before.

KnowledgeWorks Foundation came out of the sale of a student loan organization and its conversion into a charitable foundation. The ultimate size, some $200 million in assets, would be a surprise to the original board members. No one quite realized its value. It is the only statewide foundation in

Ohio dedicated to education, an operating foundation that runs programs and brings expert staff and technical assistance directly to schools, in addition to making grants. Chad Wick is and has been its gifted leader, his vision and drive key to everything from its ambitious vision and mission, to selection of nationally prominent board members, development of its sound strategic plan, and the all-important recruitment of the right staff.

Its growth of assets and influence was significant, and when the Bill and Melinda Gates Foundation chose it as an intermediary on a national small high school initiative, the ante went up. The Gates money, along with national foundation support from Ford and Carnegie foundations, gave KnowledgeWorks the annual spending capacity of a foundation five times its size.

This was heady stuff and a challenge for the board and the staff to manage. I was in the room to facilitate this retreat, because even though the vision was still about improving schools in Ohio, the board also saw KnowledgeWorks as a national model, a template that could be replicated or adapted in other regions of the country. A lot was at stake.

Since the foundation began operating, the economics for public schools in Ohio and nationally have only become more strained as state and local support has diminished. The political situation is especially difficult, and support in Ohio for the charter school and voucher movements has dramatically increased. KnowledgeWorks is up at bat facing one of the most important and complex issues of our society.

That board retreat was rich and full. The COO of the Henry J. Kaiser Foundation shared his experience in leveraging the influence of media outlets like Viacom for gains against the global AIDS pandemic. Tom Vander Ark, director of the Gates Foundation education initiative, gave a candid account of the conundrum of making high schools work better. Tough minded and intense, he expressed his unabashed admiration for Chad, the team, and the potential of KnowledgeWorks. We all beamed.

Chad took a deep breath—we waited, wondering what had troubled him. He apologized for having "lost it" and then spoke words still stuck in his throat. "It simply is not right that a full one-half the kids who should be graduating from big-city high schools in Ohio will not graduate. It is so unfair, so distressing, so unnecessary. We have no choice but to do this work and we really must succeed!"

"Amen" and "Right on" echoed around the room as the board burst into applause. Exposure and gratitude competed amiably for hearts at the KnowledgeWorks Foundation retreat.

From deep within, Chad found what he wanted to say, reminding us all that the work was not about us, our brilliant analysis and ideas, but about the students, especially those who should not be left behind.

Tears in a conference room or an emotional response are rare. Passion behind one's work is so central, yet we cloak our feelings in euphemisms. We become subsumed by the "busy-ness" of process, by data, in all of its linear iterations, and by the difficulty of execution and measurement. If we allow it, process can remove us from the very reason we are in the room in the first place, the meaning of it all. We need to continually touch that base and renew it.

Chad's gift of tears helped renew and reinforce our commitment. In his observations that follow, we see how integral he has made the emotional connection in the work of the foundation he leads.

Doable Utopia

"When Sir Thomas More's *Utopia* emerged in 1516, the reactions were the perfect reflection of the human condition at the time, as they always are when ideals are articulated. Many critics, of course, thought such a society would never work, so no one should even try. Others thought it must be the reason humanity exists, and the only work to do on this planet, while still others thought that More must be making a 176-page joke. How could humanity possibly aspire to such heights?

"And to think, More's utopian vision was simply a book of fiction.

"Imagine the reaction had there been money involved, and had More been attempting not to reform European society but, perhaps even more ambitiously, to reform the public education system. Let's say, for instance, More invested over $50 million in Ohio's high schools because he thought that kids who were already doing poorly in high school courses would do much better if they were given more rigorous courses, even college-level courses.

"The reaction might sound something like this: 'It's like trying to build a bridge without a clear blueprint. . . . I applaud the people trying to do it, but frankly, I have no idea what will come of it.'

"In our seven-year history, our foundation has invested in thousands of kids in Ohio's public school system. We've supported both small school and Early College reform in Ohio's high schools, and a restructuring of both the state's public education systems through grand, sweeping, systemic changes.

"In response, we've heard many reactions like the one above, contributed by a professor of education at Stanford University, as quoted in the *Chronicle of Higher Education.* In a profile of one of our Early College high schools, Dayton Early College Academy (DECA), ours was painted as a venture of 'high hopes,' 'good intentions,' and 'challenges.' Already, these high schools have shown great promise. After only two years, DECA is supporting forty-nine formerly struggling high school students in taking college courses.

"Ohio is in the midst of an aggressive school improvement effort that is transforming the state's large, low-performing urban high schools into fifty-eight smaller, more successful high schools where students are able to learn in innovative ways and form personal relationships. Thirty years of research suggests that these schools will succeed by improving student performance, reducing violence, and increasing graduation rates."

Chad could go on forever listing the statistics and evidence that support the work. But while the numbers are important to him, there is a quality more inchoate and less quantifiable that transcends the statistical "evidence." This is the immeasurable, endless nature of human potential.

"On the campus of Ohio's Youngstown University, science teacher Holly DiBernardo of Youngstown Early College takes her class to the college chemistry lab for a simple experiment. Considered 'at-risk' students, these kids like to get rowdy. They enjoy rebelling against the system, but today they're strangely quiet. Listening with rapt attention, the students gaze in wonder. Asked to don a lab coat, one student remarks, 'I feel important.'

"At the schools supported by our foundation, it's recognized that even the most simple act of faith in people, such as asking them to wear a lab coat or attend classes on a college campus, can make them believe that such dreams are possible, even if every person in their lives has told them that they're not."

At these schools, human potential is paramount. Chad does not need evidence from prior test scores. The belief is in the power of the educational process. The idea is to empower students to visualize success, engage them in real, relevant, and interactive education experiences, and thereby awaken the curiosity and brilliance in every child.

"In our current education system, brilliance is not assumed. Rather, a mechanistic system substitutes for the real life of the mind. Rote memorization, adherence to rigid structure, productivity, and only one type of output—perfect test scores—are expected. A bell goes off, students work silently for forty-five minutes, and then they're ushered on to the next task, as if they were products on a conveyor belt. There's little talking, little thinking, and constant input. Like digital intelligence, they're expected to process, analyze, and deliver the output their teacher is seeking. Where is the life of the mind?"

In the current system, quantifiable, marketable skills are valued over emotional intelligence, or creative ability. Children are praised for the skills that will earn them "good jobs" so they can make "good money." In this system, answering your soul's calling to be an artist, a clergy member, a social worker, or someone who wants to just help the human condition is not highly honored. The message is that it may not be wise to listen to your own voice.

To reform the failing public education system, KnowledgeWorks believes that the mechanistic system in place must be replaced with a growing network of students, educators, administrators, and community members who are forming amazing connections and thinking of education in new ways.

"Relying on human relationships takes some work and even some loss of efficiency. Human interactions are messy and sometimes we wish we could just hand the problem over to a giant supercomputer, without fussing over human input, and simply have our answer a half-hour later, as we sit back and eat our lunch.

"But somewhere inside of us, we know we must do justice to our basic human capacity for caring and our remarkable ability to create. To bring to life the most beautiful parts of humanity, we are driven by the heart, whether we're philanthropists or educators or parents. Do we help to educate humanity so it operates at optimal efficiency, or because we believe that humanity is wholly worthy?

"I tell people I meet who are deeply involved in this initiative, 'We have to be on fire for this.' Being on fire means that we may burn clear through the existing structure, but in the process, we will transform, purify, and spark creative brilliance.

"We have only to look at some of the most creative inventors, scientists, and artists in the world to realize that brilliance is not activated by a lever. In fact, most moments of genius do not begin with a goal, a result, or occur in the 'right places,' such as the office or classroom. Generally, intelligence is much less well behaved.

"Consider, for instance, Nobel Prize–winning physicist Richard Feynman, who says he discovered the beginnings of his comprehensive theory of quantum electrodynamics accidentally, while watching a boy in the college cafeteria spin plates into the air, on a day he decided he'd probably never do anything great again.

"In such humble places are discoveries made. It is these spontaneous moments of interaction, when people are relating directly to other people, places, and things, that brilliance is ignited. The energy must be moving to ignite the flame; it cannot be at rest, sitting in neat little lines, in a fluorescent-lit high school classroom."

In Columbus, Ohio, on the sprawling high school campus of Brookhaven, students at the Leadership Institute for Student Development speak loudly, exchanging ideas at a rapid-fire pace. Not even one year into the new small school, seventeen of these students, some of whom are labeled "special education," raise their hands excitedly when asked by a member of the foundation if they are planning to attend college.

A great transformation occurred here, at this school that is part of the foundation's Ohio High School Transformation Initiative, an aggressive school improvement effort. Infused with enthusiasm, these kids who were formerly 'at risk' are getting to know their teachers for the first time, studying what they love, and not being asked nicely, but expected to, perform to high standards. This is the foundation's philosophy in action: The 3 R's of education, 'Rigor, Relevance, and Relationships.'[1]

"Inspired by college classrooms, this type of learning sparks kids' desire to learn through team projects and dialogue, not 'stand and deliver' lecturing; through group activities, not silent listening; and through dissolving the walls between learning inside and outside the classroom, as schools form relationships with colleges, local businesses, and community organizations that provide students with provocative learning experiences.

"We're all familiar with the analogy 'It takes a village.' The student walks through the African village, and meets the blacksmith, who declares, 'I'm a teacher,' as every other profession declares the same. In Ohio, a hair salon owner has declared herself a teacher. Ella May Edwards Settles is so interested in the lives of her community's children that she turned her hair salon into a safe, after-school retreat for kids."

Some of the small schools are transforming their systems so rapidly that they alternate between "feeling like they're flying to feeling like they're losing ground," Chad says. But this is the nature of transformation.

"In this new world of education, teachers need a different set of credentials than they had before. Teachers still need to know their subject areas and know how to teach, but educators must also be highly engaging, skilled in human connections, and able to form a deep and loving relationship with their students. If we value this critical role of educator, we should provide them with as much training as it takes.

"Practically, we are helping educators visualize the results of their hard work, providing professional development, coaches, and opportunities to see successful small schools, and early colleges, in action. Because our strongest non-negotiable is autonomy, we're giving educators, students, parents, and community members the freedom they need to create and succeed by putting the power of education back into the hands of those to whom it belongs."

The foundation has no blueprint for this work, which is probably just as well considering the vision. "Our goal is to convene amazing, passionate, intelligent, and driven people and both guide and lead them through an authentic process that reflects the minds of many, not one. I'm fond of saying to my colleagues that the heart has no agenda. I believe that authentic human interactions will never come from preconceived ideas, or analysis, or rigid structure but from the honest, altruistic intention to help humanity in every human interaction."

Thank you, Chad Wick, for what you do, the way you do it, and the way KnowledgeWorks is renewing liberal education in Ohio. As to Chad's comment that the "heart has no agenda," there are some who call that arguable. One of those is Shirley Strong, who introduced me to the Beloved Community.

Beloved Communities—What Will It Take for Their Realization?

Shirley Strong learned that "head work" is important, but "heart work" (which can leave you exposed, vulnerable, and feeling rather scared) is more important than anything else in building a real movement of "beloved communities." Listen to her voice.

"Early on in my Project Change[2] work, I came to realize that I was not as well equipped as I thought for the task that lay ahead, and I had no idea how difficult the task would be.

"When I first came to Project Change as a volunteer, I thought I could just 'do the work.' Many of us did. The missing ingredient was money, but given that, and committed people, and some organizational development thrown in, we would have everything we needed. Fourteen years later, having experienced incremental positive changes, Project Change—along with many other organizations—is still trying to figure out the right combination in order to ignite a new social movement.

"The challenges I faced in 1993 when I became staff to this national anti-racism initiative were both internal and external. I asked myself, 'How will I grow my own soul in order to respond to the opportunities at hand, and how will I support others in doing this as well?' I also knew I would need to deepen and broaden my understanding of the complex issues we faced such as racism, sexism, classism, heterosexism, Christian hegemony, not to mention rapidly changing demographics within the U.S. and worldwide globalization on an unprecedented scale. At the same time, I would have to help open a space for others (project leaders and task force members) to broaden their worldview while maintaining the focus on anti-racist community change. This was no small task.

"It felt as if that old Negro spiritual, 'It's not my brother, nor my sister, but it's me, oh Lord, standing in the need of prayer,' had my name written on it.

"After much trial and error, blame and drama, I finally admitted that this work—like everything in life—required a great deal more humility, and much less ego than I was feeling or exercising. There were numerous training opportunities for Project Change leaders, but what we neglected, especially early on, was our own 'inner work.'

"It sometimes seems that we are only able to progress in direct proportion to our ability to speak the unspoken. Unless we are willing to talk openly and candidly with people different from ourselves racially, ethnically, religiously, and culturally, we aren't able to address what Martin Luther King Jr. in his 1967 Riverside Church speech ('A Time to Break the Silence') called the triple evils: racism, materialism, and militarism. Today, we are still having a hard time being open and honest about these."

It can be just as difficult to be honest and open about oneself. A big for instance . . . .

"Project Change leaders in one southern community refer to the socialization process they, well, many of us, internalized in childhood—to be polite no matter what and never hurt other people's feelings—as just 'being southern.' This socialization taught us we could avoid mental discomfort by not discussing or putting out for discussion any topics perceived to anger, hurt, or otherwise elicit negative feelings in others. Our own internalized oppression of all kinds from racial to gender to class becomes a stumbling block to our own growth and therefore to substantive change.

"Out of this socializing can also grow a kind of internalized racism. An oppressed group may actually support the supremacy of the dominating group by maintaining and participating in the attitudes, behaviors, social structures, and ideologies that undergird the dominating group's power.[3] Addressing our own internalized racism required a great deal of courage. We thought we could maybe get by with what Dietrich Bonhoeffer called 'cheap grace.' If we could take the easy way out, we did. It took a while for us to realize that we either pay up front or we pay later, but we do pay. I thought my insight was limited to paying attention to group process issues and interpersonal dynamics. Little did I know that was only the tip of the iceberg! I had to learn the hard way by seeing my own internalized oppression manifest itself in me and prevent me from being my most effective self.

"Initially, I thought another training session could get me over my stumbling blocks. But doing more of the same 'head work' only produced more of the same. What I needed was heart work, really scary stuff that left me feeling vulnerable and exposed. Open to attack, powerless, and out of control. More than anything, I needed to be in control, or so I thought. Not being in control meant I wasn't doing my job. Little did I know that this job—indeed, this calling—required me to give up my reliance on hierarchical structures and linear thinking and to let go of my need to be right, look good, feel important, and gain acknowledgment. This job required me to let go of pretenses and assumptions and seek a new way of understanding. Nothing that I had done up to then prepared me for this new way of being.

"I had a colleague who often said this work is not rocket science, and we would all agree and smile, thinking, 'Yeah, but it sure seems like it.' I now suspect that it might be even harder than rocket science. This work calls on us to use a part of our anatomy that most of us have forgotten. Martin Luther King Jr. often pointed to the contradiction between our technological overdevelopment and our human underdevelopment by saying 'we have guided missiles and misguided men.'

"It's important to see internalized oppression as systemic in the same way we have come to understand that oppression is systemic. It's not just a matter of personal inferiority or self-hate; internalized oppression occurs in an oppressive system. It's the air we breathe, and we are so accustomed to breathing it that we can't imagine that the air is harming us while supporting our life. Therein lies the complexity of the challenge, especially with the current racial and cultural climate in our country.

"Therefore, if we hope to experience success in this very complex twenty-first-century world, one of the very first questions that must be asked of leaders and participants in any movement-building effort is, Does everybody understand that we are coming to the table to work on our own stuff? This is usually not the case when groups of progressive thinker-leaders come together. We assume that we are gathered to solve community problems only, and we become impatient, even hostile, with any attempts to broaden the focus to include attention to our own way of being in community with each other. This realization of having to do our own work more intentionally as part of the cost of doing business becomes a basic requirement for everyone gathered at the table if we want to increase our chances for success and reduce both the intraracial and interracial tension.

"Until recently, we have been reluctant to become immersed in interpersonal and group dynamics because we feared it would draw attention away from what we collectively have considered the 'real' problems (e.g., Dr. King's triple evils). Activists often think this inner work is disorganizing, and they discourage people from paying attention to these inner, personal issues. The concerns in some ways are valid. Focusing on interpersonal dynamics has been used as a tactic to avoid the difficult and painful aspects of institutional racism and white skin color privilege in particular. If we could solve our problems without doing our own work, I would be all for it, but I do not believe that we can. It has become clear over the last forty years that we have no choice but to turn and face our own shadows.

"In collaboration with the Claremont Graduate University's Institute for Democratic Renewal, Project Change recently brought together a group of twenty-four people to explore the connection between spirit and activism through a concept articulated by Dr. King and referred to by the civil rights movement as 'Beloved Community.' This is an inclusive, interrelated space based on love, justice, compassion, responsibility, shared power, and a respect for the dignity of all people, places, and things. Out of it individuals may be radically transformed and institutions radically restructured.

"At various points in the conversation participants were asked to imagine and envision together some of the central elements of such community, looking specifically at how Beloved Community might be nurtured and manifested in internal, interpersonal, institutional, and cultural interactions using a model developed by the Women's Theological Center. The group identified the following:

- Honoring hospitality and traditions of welcoming
- Encouraging dynamic, respectful intergenerational engagement
- Engaging in storytelling
- Acknowledging fear and encouraging awareness of personal and collective power
- Accepting change and vicissitudes
- Addressing concerns for physical and emotional safety
- Committing to work for the well-being of youth and elders
- Recognizing and adapting to complexity
- Developing structural responses to address Dr. King's critique of racism, materialism, and militarism
- Promoting radical inclusiveness.

"After almost fifteen years, we have learned the importance of articulating a vision that includes the kind of world we want, not just what we don't want.

We must be prepared to address all the issues—racism remains a primary focus, but we cannot ignore other '-isms' when they rear their ugly heads. We must be strong allies to others who are fighting oppression. We must be willing to engage our heads and our hearts. Personal growth and transformation is essential in building and sustaining a movement to reshape our values and reorder our priorities. In so doing, we need to create a new prototype for twenty-first-century movement builders. Here is a good description of those who build authentic movements, inspired by Grace Lee Boggs (a ninety-year-old activist who has spent over sixty years in the movement). I hope others will add to this understanding in our effort to create the Beloved Communities we seek:

- Movement builders understand that suffering and oppression are not enough to create a movement. A movement begins when the oppressed begin seeing themselves not just as victims but also as pioneers in creating a new, more humane society.
- Movement builders are able to recognize the humanity in others, including their opponents, and therefore are able to see within them the possibility of change.
- Movement builders are conscious of the need to go beyond slogans and to create programs that transform and empower participants.
- Movement builders believe in the concept of two-sided transformation, of both our institutions and ourselves.
- Movement builders are intergenerational, involving children, youth, and adults.
- Movement builders can accept contradictions that develop in the course of a struggle. Great movements create great hopes, but they can also lead to great disappointments.
- Movement builders choose boldness over timidity.
- Movement builders call forth a vision that is larger than the issue at hand—distinguishing between social reform and social transformation.
- Movement builders strike a balance between control and autonomy—recognizing the importance of allowing people to make mistakes.
- Movement builders recognize the possibility for historical moments in the convergence of time and events.

"The last fifteen years has been a long journey. It has called for growing our souls while we seek to transform society. One thing has become clear—there can be no sustained institutional transformation without individual transformation. They are inseparable."

Howard Thurman, twentieth-century mystic, offers the following cautious optimism:

> We are never under any obligation to achieve results. Results are important and may be the reason the effort is put forth. But results are not mandatory. There are many forces over which the individual can exercise no control whatsoever. A man or woman plants a seed in the ground and the seed sprouts and grows. The weather, the winds, the elements, cannot be controlled by the farmer. The result is never a sure thing. So what does the farmer do? He plants. Always he plants. Again and again he works at it—the ultimate confidence and assurance that even though his seed does not grow to fruition, seeds do grow and they do come to fruition.[4]

When I heard Shirley Strong share these wise and moving sentiments at a conference sponsored by the Santa Barbara Foundation Roundtable in February 2005, her honesty and authenticity took my breath away. It reminded me of some of my own unfinished business.

When FUND (Fund for Urban Negro Development) was formed in 1968 following the death of Martin Luther King, those of us involved had to confront a similar set of questions that included the mixed agenda of what had brought us to the table. FUND was a white organization that had made an alliance with the newly formed Black United Front, a coalition of many of the organizations and communities in Boston's black community.

FUND's first big meeting was the first such event I had ever run, so I remember it well. We took over the ballroom of a Boston hotel on a Saturday morning, and more than seven hundred people showed up. Turning over $75,000 to Chuck Turner, the organization's Dashiki-clad organizer, someone asked him how he wanted it (as in what form), and he said, "In my hand," which I thought was quite good, but he got even better. After a series of speeches and calls to action, a speaker asked, "So, Chuck, who is in and who is out?" implying there was opposition and heads would roll. Turner's response was "Everybody's in. Understand, everybody. Nobody is out; everybody is in!" Somehow these responses set the tone for FUND's relationship with the Front for years to come. It was to be a partnership and not based on paternalism or dependency. It was just right.

Not all of what motivated those involved in FUND was noble. For some it was the excitement of the game, hanging out with our black brothers and sisters on dangerous city street corners (when that was far from the reality). For some it was a kind of liberal credentialing, the "look how wonderful I am" that juiced up one's cocktail party chatter. For some it was guilt, unadorned and unflattering. For some it was fear, and for many it was outrage at inequity and unfairness. For me it was all of the above, and it became very clear that my colleagues and I had a big need to work, in Shirley Strong's words, "on our own stuff." And we did. Led by a talented psychotherapist experienced in group dynamics and psychodrama, the board of FUND met weekly for more than a year to specifically confront our preconceptions about race and prejudice, and our reasons for why we were there. The goal was both inner and outer, and they were hard sessions. We began to understand that if we could work through those feelings, then we would be far better able to address those very same issues within the broader community, and in the process be more successful advocates. We did not finish, some things are never finished, but we did learn a lot about how to listen and how to enable others to express themselves. Even more important, we got better at differentiating between honesty and posturing, *in ourselves* as well as others. I don't know if I would go so far as to say we grew our souls, but I still look for those same elements, those ambiguities of purpose, in every meeting, every proposal, and every vision and visionary, because that is what it takes to make it real.

You can see why I deeply admire Shirley Strong.

Battling Bigotry

Ask Allen Bildner why he got involved in fighting bigotry and racism in this country, and he will tell you the story of Bess Myerson, the first Jewish Miss America. "She said, 'You don't have to be Jewish, black, Hispanic, or any other minority to fully understand how inhuman prejudice and bigotry are, but it sure helps.'"

He remembers, too, his own first encounter with bigotry in the 1950s, after moving from Long Island to an affluent New Jersey suburb, mainly white and Protestant. "Within the first week of school, two classmates beat me up and taunted, 'Go home, Rabbi! Go home, Jew boy!' I ran off crying, not really understanding what happened—it was my first experience with anti-Semitism."

He eventually became president of the student body in high school, was successful in athletics, and went on to Dartmouth College and then to build the Kings Supermarket chain into a major company in New Jersey. But along with the good experiences, he will never forget how his sister and he were banned from ballroom dance classes in those early days because they were Jews. It's a tender spot.

Things are better today for Jews and other minorities, but bigotry and prejudice have not disappeared. "Later in life, when Joan and I were married, we would be in a business or social setting and sometimes hear people making anti-Semitic jokes or comments because Bildner is not a typical Jewish name. Joan always interjected quickly, 'You may not be aware that we are Jewish.' Perhaps our response was enlightening."

In the world Bildner wants, those kinds of experiences would be unconscionable. To make it so, and to do their part in eliminating racism and discrimination, he and Joan have created and supported a range of initiatives that have addressed these complicated issues in the American society.

When I met Allen in the late 1980s, he had survived a fight with cancer and had decided that it was time to become more strategic in his giving. He spoke passionately about the problem of bigotry in this country and how he wanted to make a difference.

"In the year 2050 or earlier, one of every two Americans will be African American, Asian, Hispanic, or some other ethnic description, if the labels even apply then. The white population will no longer exist as a majority. For all of us, our kids and grandchildren, the quality of our lives and our economic well-being will depend on our ability to live and work together. That is why Joan and I focus on issues of intergroup relations.

"Yet, even with the speed of demographic change, intolerance is still alive, and the evidence of bigotry, discrimination, and hate crimes persists. As the population becomes more diverse, the potential for conflict grows as different groups begin to interact in new ways. We are regularly confronted with all kinds of bigotry in the media, and there are thousands of hate sites on the Internet.

"But discrimination against people with disabilities or those of a different gender, race, age, ethnicity, or religion has changed and is changing. There is a deepening awareness of the complexity of our society. I remember when the Hudson Institute first issued its Workforce 2000 report back in the 1980s predicting huge demographic change—few people believed it. Now, we're there."

Consider, for example, the hundreds of thousands of legal and illegal immigrants, residents, and citizens of all hues—more than half a million in Los Angeles alone—who marched recently in cities coast to coast under the banner "Day without an Immigrant," intending to influence the debate over granting legal status to America's eleven million illegal immigrants. Their work stoppage did not bring the nation to a halt, but the protests did reflect America's diverse face and continuing tensions as a wide range of ethnicities and minority groups took to the streets, though support was not uniform, even among different immigrant groups. Meanwhile, meatpacking plants in the Midwest that employ more than twenty thousand people were closed, produce and flower markets in some cities were empty, and truckers who move 70 percent of the goods in Los Angeles ports were absent.[5]

"Our own business experience is a big part of the reason Joan and I have such passion for this issue. When we sold Kings Supermarkets to Marks and Spencer in 1988, we had more than fifty different racial, ethnic, and national groups among our 3,500 employees. We all worked hard to learn about each other. We led and managed diversity very effectively, beginning with recruitment and orientation. We found that the culture we built led to fantastic teamwork and communication; it was a competitive advantage. Respect for one another contributed dramatically to our productivity, but it also gave us much of the satisfaction and joy that we had from that business."

I talked with Allen at those early meetings about the difference between charity, which is about giving money, and philanthropy, which is about effecting change. Joanne Duhl, a colleague at TPI, helped him explore ways to address issues of intolerance and bigotry and found that promoting constructive dialogue and interaction offered an opportunity to move members of different cultural groups to greater understanding and respect.

Over the years, the Bildners have supported a number of organizations, including the National Conference of Christians and Jews and the Anti-Defamation League. In 1991, Allen and Joan established an Endowment for Human and Intergroup Relations at Dartmouth College. That experience showed there was enormous opportunity within colleges and universities to reduce prejudice in the next generation.

In 2002, the Bildners created the New Jersey Campus Diversity Initiative, which awarded eight New Jersey colleges and universities multiyear grants that ranged from $75,000 to $225,000 to encourage cultural interaction inside and outside the classroom.

"In colleges," Allen says, "you will find multicultural studies, but there are still huge barriers between the different races and cultures on and off campuses. Students from all-white suburbs just outside Philadelphia do not see how they have much in common with black students growing up in the urban center, in West Philadelphia for instance. They are worlds apart."

The Association of American Colleges and Universities (AAC&U), which has years of leadership in diversity working with hundreds of its member institutions, provided the expert resources to design, manage, and evaluate the program. Every college and university in New Jersey was invited to submit a proposal, more than half (twenty-seven) did, and from these, eight finalists were selected. "We laid out our expectations under which the funding would proceed during each year of the grants. Galvanizing top leaders proved critical, which in my experience is always the case."

Rutgers University used its grant to develop several programs, including an English composition class that coordinates letter writing between Rutgers students and freshmen at West Philadelphia High School. "The exchanges are amazing," Allen says. Another program, Introduction to Music, celebrates not only Bach, Schubert, Vivaldi, and the music of the West but also Trinidadian pan steel orchestras, the pelog and slendro music scales of Indonesia, and the gagaku court music of Japan. The programs extend beyond the classroom and bring the different groups involved together through cocurricular activities.

Allen introduces another aspect of what constitutes a liberal education.

"We need to foster understanding using education to empower our future leaders, the young people in our colleges who will be the leaders in their families and businesses, in the nonprofit area, education, and government. If we can begin to effect significant change in higher education, then we stand a chance of creating a society where people can live and work together and truly respect their differences.

"To bring about real systemic change, schools need to take a fresh look at their recruiting, at the literature and materials that go out to prospective students. They need to look at curriculum and at how administrators, faculty, and students work together in this effort.

"Getting teachers to look at their own classes to see whether they measure up to what's happening inside and outside their classrooms can be difficult. This has to do, in part, with the insularity and preoccupation with individual disciplines. The grants we have made are based on the level of faculty involvement, because it is a critical factor.

The New Jersey Campus Diversity Initiative is a great example of how philanthropy can express the values of a donor and make a real difference, but Allen is still disturbed by what he sees.

"I've lived three-quarters of the twentieth century. After World War II, with the establishment the United Nations in 1948, I thought people would one day be free of disease, hunger, poverty, homelessness, and have governance that protected human rights and individual freedoms. But the last few decades have made me feel that my earlier hopes and expectations were unrealistic.

"The political and governing leadership in America and abroad lacks the vision, political integrity, selflessness, and responsibility to bring about the social justice we need. We could use Franklin D. Roosevelt reincarnated for his political courage and vision. We could use Ronald Reagan because he, as much as any president, understood the importance of separation of church and state, even as a devout Christian. President George W. Bush may be a genuinely religious and moral person—I think he is—but he has contributed to the divisiveness in our country.

"It troubles me that so few donors have a passion for justice and tolerance. Many political, and corporate, and even educational leaders do not seem to understand the fundamental importance of social justice. The demeaning and dehumanizing impact of bigotry and prejudice seems to be a nonissue, despite the overwhelming evidence in front of our eyes.

"I do believe that the majority of Americans want more out of life on these terms. They do want to reach common ground regardless of their racial and ideological differences. But many are silent when they should speak up. They're what you, Peter, have called 'sleepwalkers.'"

Allen Bildner received the Charles Evan Hughes Award from the National Conference of Community and Justice, in 2005. In his remarks, he gave this little history lesson: "In 1927, the nomination by the Democratic Party of Governor Al Smith, a Catholic, for the presidency, unleashed a horrific campaign of hatred and abuse. The Ku Klux Klan added Catholics and Jews to their mob-spirited lynching of blacks. An estimated five million Americans at that time belonged to the KKK, which was active in all but three states. Outraged by this sickness in America, a few enlightened men, including Chief Justice Charles Evan Hughes, organized to convince fellow Americans: 'Brotherhood is vital to our nation's unity and strength. Without it our future is in jeopardy.' It was true then, it is true today."

Allen leaves us with these two questions:

"How is it possible for us to interact without understanding our differences?

"Without such interaction, are we not in for a world of conflict?"

Penguins and Our Common Future

Human beings could learn a lot from the documentary *The March of the Penguins*,[6] at least in the view of Deepak Bhargava, executive director of the Washington-based Center for Community Change. He presents the all-species viewpoint for an agenda that well could come to bear on the world of challenges many have voiced.

"Living in the unforgiving climate of Antarctica, the Emperor penguins in the film understand that their individual survival depends on collective effort. They brace themselves against the fierce winters by huddling together for warmth, and they waddle for months from the sea to their breeding grounds in giant migrations. While individual effort is obviously important, it's hard to imagine a penguin boasting that she 'pulled herself up by her bootstraps.'

"We humans, by contrast, like to separate ourselves from each other. Whether it is an economy that provides fabulous wealth to a few at the expense of many, or an aggressive foreign policy that seeks to control others around the world through military force, or environmental policies that show no sense of connection or obligation to future inhabitants of the planet Earth, we're behaving more like sharks than penguins. Were they able to speak, penguins might tell us that even though they live about as distant from humans as any creatures in the world; their destiny is utterly linked to our collective behavior. (Given the chance, penguins would certainly waddle in protest against the threat of global warming!)

"At the core of our problems is the illusion that we live and die alone. We construct a desperate struggle of 'us' against 'them,' when in fact we are bound together in what Martin Luther King called a 'garment of destiny' that links our individual aspirations to the well-being of others. This 'independence illusion' is a defining characteristic of the culture of the developed nations in the early twenty-first century, and, increasingly, of the developing nations as well.

"But changing conditions are making the independence illusion more and more untenable. Public health conditions in other parts of the world are very much the concern of residents of the developed world, since new diseases easily cross national borders. Persistent poverty and military conflicts in remote corners of the world generate viral political instability and waves of mass migration that are felt everywhere on the globe. The more we hoard, isolate, and go to war, the less secure, safe, and prosperous we will become. Paradoxically, though, the growing reality of interdependence is being met by a fierce instinct to pull up the drawbridge—through restrictive immigration policies, more unilateral and militaristic foreign policies, and more unequal economic systems.

"So how might one apply the notion of 'shared fate' to the question of what a just world would look like? There are two central questions that will likely determine the prospects of humans and penguins alike on planet Earth. First, how can we create shared, sustainable prosperity within countries and globally? Second, how can we create a set of democratic institutions and practices that draw everyone into developing a program for the common good?

"Income inequality is on the rise throughout the world, both within nations and between the global North and South. Although the middle and upper classes in the West are the chief beneficiaries of this trend, these benefits have come at a high price: declining leisure time, greater insecurity, and a pervasive lack of connection and meaning that results in profound social pathologies. A new national and international regime would have to simultaneously address the problems of drastic inequality within nations, the deep poverty in much of the developing world, and the ecological crisis that affects all of us. For many residents of the developed West, this might involve lower consumption of goods, but in return they would get more economic security, more leisure time, less inequality, and a less violent, materialistic culture. Some of the potential components of a solution include

- "an international 'floor' on income, pensions, health care, and working standards and a 'ceiling' on income disparities and wealth accumulation;
- new forms of corporate ownership or chartering that encourage firms to be responsive to issues now treated as 'externalities,' in part by giving workers and communities a greater role in governance;
- explicit limits on resource consumption and pollution creation that are consistent with the carrying capacity of the Earth;
- policies to reduce work hours and increase family and leisure time for workers in developed countries;
- fair compensation for caregiving—the indispensable but largely invisible work that women do for low or no wages throughout the world;
- a titanic investment by the developed nations to insure that basic social goods—clean water, public education, primary health care—are available to everyone on the globe."

Deepak insists, as others have, that the democracy agenda relates closely to the economic program. Only a robust democratic system and culture can achieve just economic outcomes, and, conversely, radical economic inequality and concentrated wealth inevitably undermine democratic culture and practice. Possible reforms would include

- an increase in the authority of international institutions, including the creation of enforceable minimum economic and democratic standards, while at the same time devolving power on important questions like regional planning and economic development from nation-states to cities, counties, and states;
- broad expansion of the franchise, including full citizenship for immigrants, voting rights for ex-felons, standardized and accessible voting and election financing, and an extension of the notion of universal suffrage to include obligatory voting;

- greater support for civil society, which provides the foundation for any healthy democracy, including civil liberties, the right to organize, and the rights of minorities;
- a requirement that all children attend public schools and be served by the same health care system, to create common experience and shared interests;
- one-year sabbaticals that allow everyone to travel the world, in order to foster a greater sense of global interdependence.

On paper, this agenda looks improbable, even utopian. In a culture that is increasingly hostile to the very idea of common enterprise, it's hard to imagine a just world that embraces the shared fate of humanity as a guiding principle. How might we make even incremental progress toward such a vision?

"I find it implausible to believe that the world's elites will generate the ideas or will for such radical changes, though it is arguably in their self-interest to do so. A raft of expertly written reports explaining the scope of the problems won't save us either. And, sadly, even charity on a massive scale can't overcome these deep structural trends.

"The history of the past two hundred years suggests that changes of this order are only achieved by broad-based social movements. Universal suffrage, the abolition of slavery, the eight-hour workday, the liberation of women were all dismissed as utopian dreams at one time. What made these dreams a reality were movements that engaged millions of people in self-help, public education, political action, cultural renewal, and the creation of new social institutions.

"While the problems and dilemmas of our age are different, and the techniques of public engagement are always evolving, we know what it will take to make change. Our great hope lies with organizations of ordinary people that are working to create real democracy around the world. Although these forces seem weak at present, there are signs of renewal. In the West, successful efforts by community organizations to expand health insurance, extend immigrant rights, secure living wages, create affordable housing trust funds, and reform the criminal justice system are not only winning policy changes in a difficult time; they are developing the leadership skills of ordinary people and, in small ways, showing that another world is possible. The international movements for global justice and debt relief, and the work of mass organizations in the developing world to combat discrimination and promote economic justice are accessible to the whole world through global media and the Internet.

"Whatever our role—organizer, philanthropist, NGO, advocate, academic, elected official, or citizen—the central question we face is how to create, support, and connect organizations that can build a real constituency, power, and agenda for change.

"Any objective analysis of our predicament wouldn't be hopeful about where our world is headed. The 'I've got mine' worldview is clearly ascendant, and I fear we do not have the luxury of time to reverse it. But penguins, for all the rigors of a cold, dark winter, keep marching together, and as long as there are creative and dynamic movements for change there is abundant opportunity for a different future."

Reader's Guide Questions

1. Chad Wick's gift of tears was powerful for the KnowledgeWorks Foundation Board. Why are emotion and passion so often subsumed by process? Could that change?
2. *Utopia*, as well as a world "imagined as the ultimate good," is on one level unattainable. What is possible?
3. When does one decide to go ahead without "blueprints"?
4. Chad's counsel to teachers and his colleagues is "We have to be on fire for this!" Do you bring fire into your citizen work?
5. Shirley Strong speaks of growing her soul. What does that mean to you? Have you had that kind of experience?
6. If you were to introduce the idea of doing "inner work, heart work," in an organization you are part of, what would be the reaction? Should you?
7. Shirley believes that what Martin Luther King called the triple evils of racism, materialism, and militarism are all connected. Do you agree?
8. What does building a movement entail? Can you characterize movement builders?
9. Allen Bildner has been ahead of the curve in understanding diversity. What do you think the implications are for all of us in a nonwhite, non-majority America?
10. Do you believe Allen is correct in believing there is not enough passion for social justice and tolerance among donors and in the society as a whole?
11. Are we getting any better at understanding our personal differences? Or (if we cannot live and work together) are we in for a world and life of increasing conflict?
12. What is the difference between prejudice and preference?
13. What can we do to counter the "us against them" mentality, the "independence illusion," and begin to move toward the notion of "shared fate"?

14. How compelling are Deepak Bhargava's solutions and reforms? What is the difference between something that is "realistic" as opposed to "aspirational"?

15. Where and how do human beings fit in as a species on the planet? Would there be "meaning" on the planet if humans were not here to agree/disagree about it?

Notes

1. The Gates Foundation coined this term in its work to reinvent the nation's high schools.

2. Project Change (PC), based in Oakland, California, was created in 1991 by the Levi Strauss Foundation. Headed by Shirley Strong, executive director, PC's original mission is to combat racism through locally driven community-based initiatives. See www.projectchange.org.

3. Women's Theological Center, Boston, 1995.

4. *For the Inward Journey* (Richmond, Indiana: Friends United Press, 1961), 64.

5. "Immigrants Take to U.S. Street in Show of Strength," *New York Times*, May 2, 2006, A1.

6. *March of the Penguins* was awarded the 2005 Academy Award for best documentary.

TIME STOPPED

Time stopped at 4 A.M., I continue to breathe.
Sheer white curtains move in a slight breeze,
Nothing else the same when time stood
Suspended, disturbingly, unnervingly, still.

It happened once before sailing east all night.
We had made good time just past Matinicus,
Rock guardian to the great Bay of Maine,
Muscongus, Penobscot, and Scoodic beyond.

I was at the tiller as this glorious sun
Rose huge, shining gold, then incredibly stops,
Vibrates the horizon, unsure whether to lift
Into the clear morning sky or roll along

The lip of the earth into the void of another
Universe or just slip back down, leave the world
Bereft, lit by pale moonlight or forever dark.
Terrifying, but the sun slowly began to climb,

And the clock moved finally after what seemed
Eternity past 4 A.M., but what if time did stop
For white cells, red cells, children who stay young
Forever we hold on to them, as to life itself.

GENEROSITY AND SACRED SEARCH
Motivation

WHAT MOTIVATES us to be generous?

Much, as we have seen, is experiential. The motivation flows from who we are, how we were brought up, and what we have witnessed that moves us.

There are other factors, like our biology, the idea that we are somehow wired, as Steve Case says, to be generous. Are the Emperor penguins equipped with a special kind of survival gene that in humans gets translated into generosity?

Another factor is cultural. Many domains—philosophy, sociology, psychology, and especially religion—explain and rationalize generous behavior and provide motivation and incentive for it as well.

Some cultures much older than our own have understood that the self is most realized through creative altruism. In the *potlach* of the North American Indians or the *Kula* of the Melanesians, gifts are made without any expectation of a personal reward or gain. The assumption is that "the return is guaranteed by the virtue of the things passed on."[1] In these cultures, the act of giving is a group process where interdependence is an assumption. There is a "pervasiveness of the social obligation"[2] that is an example of shared community. It acknowledges that we are all in this together and answers one of the central questions—Who is my stranger?

EARTH ON ITS AXIS

We are travelers
We are connected
We are caretakers

My daughter, son-in-law, and grandchildren live in Madison, Wisconsin. Next door is an elderly woman in failing health. Despite very busy lives of their own, my kids have assumed a caretaker role, mowing her lawn, shoveling her walk, and just keeping an eye on things every day. There is always a "Verna" story. They are neighbors, not kin. What do you call that? Kind, certainly, but not big purposeful humanitarianism. There is no rhetoric, but my two grandchildren, age ten and fourteen, have absorbed into their precious selves the fact this is simply what one does.

In his remarkable book *The Gift Relationship*,³ Richard Titmuss asks, "Who is my stranger?" Different cultures answer the question in different ways. The "gift" in *The Gift Relationship* is blood. The book looks at how societies, the United Kingdom and the United States primarily, have chosen to collect and distribute blood. The universal "stranger" is the unknown recipient who the blood donor will never meet or know.

The Gift Relationship documents the difference in social policy between the UK system of voluntary giving of blood and the U.S. system where blood has become a commodity. Turning blood into a market transaction, and privatizing its distribution, creates a set of dilemmas.

One is a practical issue. To use Titmuss's term from the 1970s, the paid (professional) donor is often down and out, "right off Skid Row," which, as it relates to blood, raises questions of quality, including the increased risk of hepatitis. The book was written long before the AIDS pandemic vastly complicated the difficulty in maintaining quality in blood.

A commoditized blood market, however, also raises issues of equity. It increases the separation between rich and poor. When blood is sold, donors are often poor, and the recipients have means enough at least to have secured care. This regressive economic policy creates an inequitable flow of the resource—in this case, a most vital resource. But what has this to do with generosity?

How we organize our social structures greatly affects behavior in other spheres, for good or bad. Titmuss's conclusion is that the "commercialization of blood represses the expression of altruism, and erodes the sense of community." Taking away the opportunity of the individual to make a gift of blood—a gift of life itself—is a restriction of freedom and contributes to the retreat of the individual from public life. Titmuss writes that "altruism is both morally sound and economically efficient" and, even more important, essential to the human experience, essential to becoming "whole."

"A competitive, materialistic, acquisitive society based on hierarchies of power and privilege ignores at its peril the life-giving impulse toward altruism which is needed for welfare in the most fundamental sense" is how he sums it up. In other words, it is because we are materialistic and acquisitive that we need the counterbalance of generosity, without which we are at risk of losing our humanity.

Perhaps Walt Whitman was being more than metaphorical when he wrote in *Song of Myself*:

> I celebrate myself, and sing myself.
> And what I assume you shall assume
> For every atom belonging to me as good belongs to you

Biology teaches us that every species, including our own, has certain built-in things that are essential to living together well and flourishing.

The Selfish Gene by Richard Dawkins was first published in 1976,[4] and it immediately created a stir. The title suggests the subject is selfishness, but as the author makes clear in the introduction to the thirtieth anniversary edition of this classic book of Darwinian thought, it is really more about altruism.

The central question is which entity survives and which perishes, the unit in question being the gene, which simply pursues its manifest destiny. Dawkins's famous and famously misunderstood metaphor is that genes— and by extension, mankind—are "born selfish." This in no way, however, prevents organisms (or individuals) from behaving altruistically for the good of all. Dawkins speculates that his message might have been better served if the book had been named *The Immortal Gene* or *The Altruistic Vehicle* or *The Cooperative Gene*.

It would seem we should not put too much faith in our genes if we aspire to a world where "individuals cooperate generously and unselfishly towards a common good."[5] Or should we? It's a bit like relying on the market economy— another inherently "selfish" organism—to solve society's problems.

Dawkins helps us out somewhat by introducing another central Darwinian concept, reciprocity. Here self-interest requires certain behavior that looks and smells a lot like generosity and altruism. "You scratch my back, and I will scratch yours."

Watch out, however, for motives that complicate what is and what is not a generous act. In eBay, which is fast becoming for us a poster child of business as community, do we care whether the business acts primarily from the profit perspective or the community perspective? The answer may be that we don't, so long as the net community and public value is positive.

The more interesting redemption for those of us who get completely discouraged by the view that genes/humans are mere survival machines, is Dawkins's introduction of memes, which he calls the "new replicators." These are new in the sense that genes were here first. Memes are defined as the cultural aspects of human behavior, and in the end they outlast genes, which over time are diluted; that is, after twenty generations, original genes have been transformed many times and may be hardly recognizable. An example of a persevering memes, for starters, is the work of Socrates, or Aristotle, Copernicus, and Chaucer. (Things like the wave or the Macarena might only make it to the next millennium.) These cultural influences are the ingredients of the human soup that override the selfishness of our gene-directed basic nature. When it is good, it is the stuff of our better selves.

Another redemption is our capacity for foresight and our ability to determine our own destiny. As Dawkins summarizes it, "We alone on earth, can rebel against the tyranny of the selfish replicators." Whether we have the wisdom to do so is another matter, but that is why we are on this journey.

We could go on to make the case that *nice guys finish first*. Dawkins does, armed with data from the extensive computer modeling done by game theorists. The Prisoner's Dilemma, the game, was first developed by the Rand Corporation in 1950. It pits one prisoner's self-interest against another. If both prisoners rat on each other, they both go to jail. If only one rats, the other goes to jail. If neither tells, they both go free—all in all a tough existential situation.

Of the many strategies tested, the one that prevailed, was called *Tit for Tat*,[6] based on the concept of reciprocal altruism. In the Tit for Tat strategy, the player begins by cooperating with and trusting the other player but thereafter simply follows and copies what the other player does. If the other player cooperates, the first player does as well and if the other player defects, the first player follows suit. The Tit for Tat strategy scored more points and won out over all the others, including many that were based on deception and cheating. It is, of course, exactly what makes eBay work. The players, buyers and sellers, will only play, buy or sell, if the other players act appropriately.

Does this reinforce the belief that people are basically good, or that there is a truth force out there? Perhaps, but at the very least it certainly provides lots of incentive for being good and true, especially if one wants to win the game.

Game theorists make the distinction between zero-sum games in which the win for one player results in a loss for the other player—as in chess—and a non-zero-sum game in which both players can win if they act in certain ways. In Tit for Tat, both players can win but they must, among other things, be able to forgive the other player. Not unlike the way businesses in technology seem to be operating. And not unlike the argument for increased cooperation in every sphere. In this sense, generous behavior is a "non-zero-sum" process. Dawkins adds that it helps to understand that we are in the game, for our purposes the game of life, for a very long time. It is for him "the shadow of the future"[7] that hangs over so many of the social dilemmas we face as individuals and as a race.

Mutually beneficial replicators will in the end prevail in his view. But what does that mean for us? I believe it means there will be more investors like Steve Case, more social entrepreneurs like Bill Drayton, more philanthropists like Stephen Melville, more world-class citizen actors like Peggy Dulany, and more people in touch with their feelings, like Chad Wick and Shirley Strong.

Have we made the case for a generosity gene? I think so. Do you?

The Gift

There was a strange, almost surrealistic, article in the *New Yorker* entitled "The Gift."[8] It was a story about Zell Kasvinsky, a successful real estate investor who first gave away his $45 million fortune to charity, and he followed that with a gift of one of his kidneys to a complete "stranger." One got the sense that this man would give away his second kidney or even his heart, if allowed. Kasvinsky's extraordinary acts were driven by an acute, painful sense of his individual responsibility to others, in the case of his kidney, to someone who would have died without it. This man has taken a dramatic and poignant stand against the notion of impotence. He is shouting to the rooftops!

Kasvinsky's extremes are extreme, and the price he, his wife, and friends paid is evident in the article. The man could be called crazy, he may even be crazy, but his moral instincts are stunning. His struggle between "I" and "we" may be over the top, but it lies at the center of the prima facie source of common good.

There are many ways to make a gift, and there are many ways to come to this work. Meet Tom Tierney, who brings his own very unique skills to the giving.

How We Come to the Work

Among the interesting people this work attracts are many willful and powerful folks who you might expect would never be drawn to a nonprofit. Tom Tierney is the cofounder and chair of the Bridgespan Group, a nonprofit organization that works "to build a better world by strengthening the ability of nonprofit organizations to achieve "breakthrough results" in addressing society's most important challenges and opportunities." He has thought a great deal of how one comes to this work and why some people are more generous than others. And Tom knows a great deal about how to think at a very high level, having served as CEO of Bain & Company, the global management consulting firm.

"This seems to be how life works. My metaphor is to imagine you are a piece of steel, and magnets surround you. One magnet is your personal and spiritual life, and one is your family. There is your community magnet and the organizations you belong to, one magnet is your job, and all are of varying intensity, depending on their size and relationships to you. In demanding professions, a person might be pulled inexorably toward the job. In some cases, the other magnets exert no pull at all. Family is ignored, friendships atrophy, and community involvement postponed. The word *balance* doesn't quite capture this dynamic. I think it is more about equilibrium. If all of these forces are exerting positive influence in a wonderful way—if you love your job and you love your spouse and care about your community, you can do a great many things over time."

When Tom Tierney was twenty-two and had just graduated from University of California–Davis, he went to work for Bechtel. He was sent to Algeria, and he started a journal. As he put it, there wasn't a lot to do in Algeria besides work. He is now in about volume 20. They are all handwritten.

"I write regularly. Over the years I purposely never read my journal entries because I didn't want to be influenced by past perspectives. But in my midforties, I stepped down as CEO from Bain & Company (early 2000), and I took a three-month sabbatical. Among other things, I read all my journals for the first time. What I found in my written history was an underlying tension during all those years between a desire for public service and the desire for a business career. This was not a complete surprise. I had always taken a few days at the end of the year to reflect on how the elements of my life were ordered—personal, professional, spiritual. These reflections often surfaced a desire to more directly contribute to the common good.

"Coming to this work, I think, starts with family and how you are raised, or at least it did with me. Youth is the time of development, for setting priorities and forming ideas about the world. Mine was a middle-class, close-knit family and I had an exceptionally happy childhood. My family was certainly not oriented around material stuff. For example, we always owned old cars, older than the cars other people drove. At some point I must have said something, because I recall vividly my father proclaiming, 'It's not the car you own that matters; it's the person you are.'

"The people we knew were by and large working-class people, contractors and such. My dad worked at Colgate-Palmolive, starting out as a night foreman producing toothpaste on the manufacturing line. He always told stories about the regular people he worked with, blue-collar people. The principle that everybody matters and no one is more important than anyone else became deeply ingrained in me. I honestly didn't know what 'CEO' stood for until my first week at Harvard Business School. I had no idea how to tie a tie, didn't own a suit, and had been on an airplane only once. Flying from San Francisco to Algeria was my second time."

When Tom graduated from UC–Davis, he wanted to escape California and see the world, but he found himself driving a bus, which is how he put himself through college. His friend's father worked at Bechtel, he applied and they offered him a job as a field engineer, assigned to a project in Algeria. "My expression must have given me away because the interviewer said, 'You don't exactly know where Algeria is, do you?' I didn't but I was positive it was not in California."

Two weeks later, Tom arrived in Oran, Algeria, with a two-year contract. It was the right place at the right time.

"I am always asking myself, 'Is this the right spot for me at this phase of my life? Am I in equilibrium'? If you fail to ask these questions, you can end up years later with regrets. Still, every day you come to work committed to do your very best that day. When you are on the field suited up, you play the sport as hard as you can, but that doesn't necessarily mean that you should play that sport for the duration.

"When I attended Harvard Business School, I was a pretty confident guy, having seen a lot in North Africa working with over fifty nationalities in demanding circumstances. The Business School was filled with prep school graduates, and there was a lot of posturing, but the classroom experience and the professors were truly extraordinary. I had assumed leadership roles all of my life and been promoted several times in Algeria, so Harvard's leadership learning was especially exciting to me.

"HBS catapulted me into Bain & Company. I was attracted to Bain because it was diverse, demanding, and highly entrepreneurial. I knew that I would learn an enormous amount, though I did not plan to stay long, and would not have if I had not become a partner and moved into management. I wanted to keep achieving, but the tension between being in business versus public service always lurked in the background.

"At Bain, I felt I was adding value to people's lives and to the organization. I could help people succeed and I loved that. Bain was, and still is, an effective platform for developing extraordinary talent. At the same time, my roles at Bain led to all kinds of community-oriented opportunities. For example, I became involved in a number of pro bono projects while running Bain's San Francisco office. This was a novel approach at the time, yet I felt that it was essential for us to contribute to our community."

Where did this pull to public service come from? Is it your "generosity gene" in play?

"It depends on what you mean by generosity. There are perhaps various forms of generosity. One person donates financial assets. Another gives time, which is far more precious than money. Someone else serves a cause through their professional career. But there is also what might be called day-to-day generosity. I remember in college giving a talk arguing that there are fundamentally two kinds of people in the world, givers and takers. Givers care about the welfare of others and demonstrate that caring in their daily lives. Takers approach life with a 'What's in it for me?' attitude."

One gets good insight into why Tom is such a great manager and leader. He is clearly a giver. And giving, in his terms, is an orientation toward others at the expense, to some extent, of yourself. That resonates with the theory that the greatest gifts are those where the giver is giving something that is very dear to oneself, as opposed to something that has little meaning. By extension, it means sublimating one's own ego and being open to the voices of others.

"Consciously thinking about the 'you' and 'we' instead of 'me' takes some attention, because we are all naturally worried and obsessed with ourselves. It reminds me of something I learned from Ernie Arbuckle, who was dean of the Stanford Business School. He had this plaque on his desk that said, 'There's no limit to what the good man can do if he doesn't care who gets the credit.'"

This view was reinforced along the way by other mentors, mentors who Tom says we often seek and find on our own. Mentors like his economics professor at Davis, Erik Gustafson, who took him out after graduation and over pizza and beer advised, "If ever you are making a career decision based solely on money, stop and think of me. Because it is almost certainly the wrong decision."

"I can smell the beer and pizza! There were other influences, too. I became the student assistant to the UC–Davis chancellor Jim Meyer, who grew up in the

Midwest on a farm and had been head of the agriculture school at University of Wisconsin. He was a guy who was entirely service oriented, grounded in his agrarian roots, down-to-earth, and very selfless. He became a mentor and a friend, educating me about life and people.

"During the time I was running Bain, if you asked people how they experienced me, they might say as a zealot—extremely committed. And intense. Yet personally I worked hard to maintain equilibrium in my life, and there were always basic questions: Do I stay in business? Could I see myself in government or a nonprofit? I was continually contemplating other possibilities, parallel tracking."

Again this parallel tracking! Another factor that influences generosity is timing. "I might not have considered making a move like the one to Bridgespan when I was thirty, on the fast track at Bain, and with young kids at home. Timing is everything. With the baby boom generation, we have the healthiest, wealthiest, and most accomplished generation in the history, and I suspect we are going to see more people asking the question 'What can I do with the rest of my life?' Peter Drucker was right in that many of us will have at least two careers."

The amount of talent and money and opportunity for generosity has never been greater. Along with that, unforeseen circumstances can sometimes play a pivotal role.

"I met a guy who had his office in one of the Twin Towers. On the morning of 9/11, he had a meeting out of the office. Of his employees, dozens died. He was very wealthy, but he had never given much money away; he had just accumulated it. He went skiing the winter following 9/11, and on a chairlift, he sat by chance next to someone who led a nonprofit offering after-school programs for poor children. In the course of the lift up the mountain, he got so excited he committed to a multimillion-dollar gift. When I met him, he was incredibly excited about the impact of this spontaneous gift. His actions were not based on analysis; they came directly from his heart. That is often the way of philanthropy."

It is what I call an "ah-ha" event.

"It amazes me that estates over $25 million leave bequests that total four times the cumulative giving of the household's prior ten years. In other words, on average, the wealthy could give away substantially more money during their lifetimes. I just do not understand why more people don't practice giving while living—and enjoy both the process and the results.

"I do believe there are seasons in our lives. In your twenties, you are trying to sort out life and perhaps start a family. In your thirties, you are competitive, you are building, you've perhaps got sharp elbows and are trying to move up some ladder, and often you don't begin to know what you really don't know. At some point in your forties, your kids are older, and you are more satisfied with yourself. There are logical segments in life, and the second half is where various elements most often come together.

"The reality is that the first half of life is challenging. Family life is demanding, some people get divorced and remarried, and careers can be very high-pressure. But the second half's potential is enormous, and the fact that we are living longer opens up all sorts of possibilities. Lots of that potential may be parked behind gated communities or immersed in daily habits; teasing it out is an important challenge.

"This is why Bridgespan started a new subsidiary venture, Bridgestar, as a resource to help facilitate the flow of capable executives into (and within) the nonprofit sector. Over the years, we have heard from hundreds of executives, all with variations on the same question—how do I find more meaning in my professional life? They want to know how I did it and how people like you did it, Peter.

"It's always hard being the first couple of people through the jungle, so to say. But, to the extent a path can be cleared, a road can be built, or a bridge made, and people can see that others have safely traveled that road and crossed that bridge, then more will follow.

"But these are complex personal decisions and there are always competing tensions. In early 2000, when I had announced I was stepping down as CEO of Bain, the stock market was going wild. It was the middle of the feeding frenzy of the Internet era, and an executive search person called. This individual had recruited someone who happened to be on the cover of that week's *Business Week*, and who was now apparently worth $250 million on paper. The conversation went like this: 'Tierney'—remember I had never met this guy—'I can make you $200 million, just like I did for so and so.'"

Sounds like a Faustian moment.

"It was. I went home to tell my wife Karen about this potentially lucrative opportunity. Bridgespan had just gotten up and running. We had taken three or four years to raise the money and had commitments to funders, employees, and clients. I was extremely committed yet somewhat confused. So I went home and said to Karen, 'Am I nuts?' We've got some money in the bank, but we are not super wealthy. If I took this job for four or five years, think of all the money we'd have to give away. Her response was unequivocal: 'Listen, we could be dead in five years. I'd rather we live in a trailer and pursue our passions to serve society than chase after this money. Don't be foolish.'

"I wasn't surprised. Karen grew up in a small town in Kentucky. What's interesting is that the people who have most influenced me—people like my dad, my teachers, the chancellor, and certainly my wife—all have had the same type of advice: stay true to your values. It has served me well. In fact, the company I was asked to run doesn't even exist today, and the 'rich' fellow on the cover of *Business Week* lost everything—further validation of the importance of thoughtful decision making.

"Starting Bridgespan was absolutely the right thing for me to do. It took a lot for us to get it launched; at a certain point I just had to jump off the proverbial cliff. Karen was very supportive and told me later that her real worry was that I would remain caught up in the business world, chasing after big jobs in bigger companies."

Tom does still seem to be chasing something. What is it?

"Perhaps it's the magnets on the table and how to improve the equilibrium in my life, especially as pertains to the pull of public service. I want to contribute as much as I can, every single day, and to strengthen the pull of public service for others."

I wonder if Tom, by any chance, has put together some kind of generosity chart.

"As a matter of fact," says Tom, "I did." (See page 214.)

I admire Tom Tierney's story of how values and leadership come together to make up a life. I also like his Generosity Chart. It only proves that you can take the person out of management consulting but you can't take the world-class management consultant out of the person. There are variations on some of these themes, however, on how one comes to this work that do not lend themselves as easily to organization charts. It is in the realm of spirit and faith.

The Two-Part Conversion

"You have to believe that form follows essence. You should be able to get the essence of your life on the front of a T-shirt, Peter Drucker told me. People have two conversions. The first is from nonbelief to belief; the second leads from belief to integrity, to doing something based on your belief, on the implications of that belief. That is the essence, and it stays constant through life, but the form it takes changes with time and circumstances. You can't plan for it. The best you can do is decide what an opportunity looks like. Opportunity comes in unexpected ways.

"People get lost in things like money, and work, and achievement, but those things are not really the essence of your life, what you're put here to do.

Figure 12.1. Tom Tierney's Generosity Chart

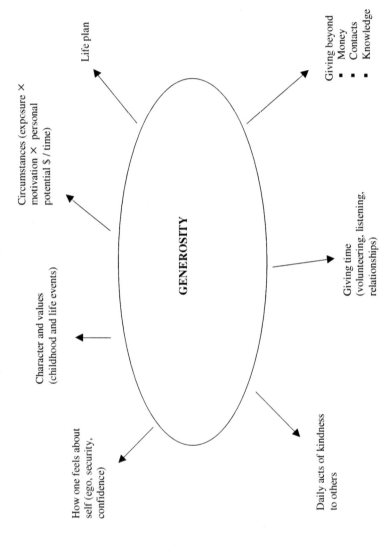

Life plan

Circumstances (exposure × motivation × personal potential $ / time)

Character and values (childhood and life events)

How one feels about self (ego, security, confidence)

GENEROSITY

Giving beyond
- Money
- Contacts
- Knowledge

Giving time (volunteering, listening, relationships)

Daily acts of kindness to others

Defining and finding that is more like archaeology than construction. It is already there, but the task is to uncover it. For me the essence is to transform the latent energy in American Christianity into active energy."

I listen to Bob Buford and am not alone. Half a million people bought his book *Half Time.* Bob defies the stereotype of the evangelical Christian when he preaches about the centrality of community and citizenship. The strategy of singling out the latent energy in American Christianity comes straight out of his success as a cable television entrepreneur. "It's because we have the biggest market share. Among Americans, 85 percent identify themselves as Christians. It just makes sense to go where the market is."

Bob can be even droller. We first met in Dallas in the early 1990s as speakers at a conference of high-end financial planners, he with his message of turning success into significance and me with the significance of strategic philanthropy. The audience of very successful insurance agents and investment professionals was enthusiastic. At some point, Bob got up and announced he was conducting a Vespers service for anyone interested at the close of the day's program.

"Peter," he tapped me after my speech, "if I could deliver you legions of very wealthy Christians, primed to become big-time philanthropists, would you consider converting? Why don't you come to my service?"

Taken aback but game, I went and sat in the back of the room. Bob spoke in his relaxed and informal manner. "Before we begin, I want to welcome my new friend Peter, who is Jewish. I have promised him I would only mention Christ a few times and downplay the Father, Son, and Holy Ghost." Thus began my first and thus far only ecumenical call to Vespers. You can see how Bob Buford might turn a few heads.

"To get the world you want, first figure out what you want to do with your life and treat your money as an extension of that. Then follow your destiny. Every single person alive has one according to the New Testament and the ancients—a calling from God and a task to do, coded into our being. My greatest fear, truly, is being out of alignment with my destiny.

"For me, an important principle is to build on the islands of health and strength. Most philanthropy looks to fulfill a need. I look for people who are strong leaders, who are in the business of fulfilling needs. To change the world, support exceptional people—let them spread the ideas and provide the examples. Be the platform, not the show. It's a matter of letting our work grow up on other people's trees. Don't look for the credit, but back other individuals or organizations to be more effective in *their* work.

"I don't want to be seen as just another big donor to be humored, persuaded, and manipulated. I want to ask social entrepreneurs, 'What can I do to be useful to you?' I want to invest, instead of passing the funds and responsibility on to the future, in the opportunity that is now.

"This is a very personal enterprise. A calling is personal. God doesn't call foundations. He calls individuals. The responsibility is personal. The money and the organization is an extension of the person. They enlarge personal capacity. The central idea is to build trust. Trust is the coin of the realm.

"What draws people together? Draw a triangle on a piece of paper. I've found working with someone of a different race or culture or religion that if we have a common objective, like building a new wing on a hospital, as we draw closer to that objective, we draw closer to each other. We are drawn together by common cause.

"There is no question that today is a time of great spiritual yearning. Robert Fogel, who won the Nobel Prize for Economics in 1983, recently wrote in *The Fourth Great Awakening*, that we are in a period that has at its center human work on spiritual needs. There are other ways to get there, but religion gets you to the spirit faster than anything else."

Bob's Burning Bush program invests in churches that have an entrepreneurial frame, getting them together to share ideas. The group has started new churches in the United States and elsewhere, and these have hosted teaching events for other churches. In the past six years, Bob has led and funded an ongoing major effort to help many of the new megachurches deepen their connection with their communities and, in the process, encourage more broad-based citizen engagement.

Ten years ago, Bob wrote *Halftime*, a plea to people in midlife who had achieved success to transition from success to significance. He defines success as using your knowledge and experience to build up your own portfolio, significance as using the same skills to serve others. His books and his muses on life, society, responsibility, and faith on his blog are attracting a host of "converts."

When TPI presented a conference program called "success to significance" for the World President's Organization (WPO), we asked him and other luminaries, like Sir John Templeton [sponsor of the Templeton Prize] and Gerry Rauenhorst [founding chairman of the Opus Corporation], to come and share their wisdom. Bob's message rang out as clearly authentic.

Bob does not think in terms of magnetic force when he talks about how we come to this work, but attitude is a chief factor, as is balance, just as they are for Tom Tierney.

"What holds people back from the quest is the attitude of what's mine I own. This attitude isolates people from God and from one another. The significance culture is in a very different place than the success culture. Many people don't have enough balance in their lives to aim for significance while they aim for success. Others don't know what the 'transferable core' of their being is. Someone sees oneself as a lawyer, for instance, and can't extract the person who is inside the lawyer costume. They get addicted to their own identity of solutions."

There is no issue that Bob's beliefs are genuine and they have been an enormous support to him. "I lost my only son on January 3, 1987, and it is more than slightly comforting that I know where he is right now and that I will see him again. Ross died when he and two friends tried to swim the Rio Grande River, near Del Rio, and reenter as illegal aliens as a stunt. Of course, twenty-four-year-olds have no conception of danger or death. He and another boy were swept away.

"In his will, he had written that he loved his mother and me, that he had a wonderful life, and that he is in a better place now. It's in present tense, so it is like getting a letter from the other side. He said he would be waiting for me at heaven's gate and even told me how he'd be dressed. He wrote that he was glad that God had given him the chance to write beforehand, or words in that effect, and signed off, 'Thanks, adios, Ross.' Not many people have something like that to hold onto. His message on his answering machine, which I heard after learning of his death was, 'Hello, this is Ross, I'm not here right now. As a matter of fact, I've departed on the greatest epic adventure of all time.' And of course he had done that.

"Christian theology says you've got to face our creator. And I think there are going to be two questions on the final exam. The first question is, What did you believe—what was your theology? And the second question is going to be, What did you do with what I gave you to work with?"

Religion can be channeled, as Bob Buford's is, to bring us closer to the world we want. And, for those who have no answer for the first of his two questions, there is plenty of room left to answer the second.

Sacred Money

> *It is my central premise that whether or not wealth*
> *creates truly transformative change on our planet depends entirely*
> *on the consciousness of the wealth holders and their advisors.*[9]
>
> —TED MALLON

A man is struck by lightening in 1984 and since then has experienced a flow of unusual visions, dreams, and thought patterns. This flow of subtle energy is essentially and intensely spiritual. It allows him to get to a deep inner calmness that surrounds and infuses his rational thinking. At the same time, he continues to observe and experience the tumult and disturbances in the world around us. In his own words, Ted Mallon writes, "One primary outcome is knowing that I live in parallel worlds: the physical world, including the world of money, and the metaphysical world of subtle energies, tones and vibrations."

Parallel tracks and parallel worlds—there must be something in the air.

Ted's experience is out of the ordinary, but not without precedent. Many cultures and religions have long honored wise elders and shamans who have heightened awareness of other levels of consciousness. These esoteric sensibilities are sometimes stimulated by a near-death experience and, remarkably, being struck by lightening is one of the most common, if one can use that word, of these events.

In some cultures, these kinds of experiences are sought. In Ted's case, he did not have a choice in the matter. So now he is responding to a powerful invitation from the realms of the Spirit to pursue his ongoing spiritual journey.

One unlikely aspect of Ted's journey has been wealth, something he never anticipated or desired, but nevertheless earned because of his persistence and entrepreneurial drive. Ted is thus a person of wealth, a person of heightened consciousness, and an individual committed to bringing his insights and wisdom to the spiritual aspects of philanthropy.

About ten years after we met, in the mid-1960s, he began having these experiences, but it took many more years for him to come to terms with what was happening to him. I remember one evening in our living room, I became aware of his tremendous challenge of sustaining a full life of husband, father, businessman, and philanthropist on the ordinary plane with the impinging energies of higher levels of consciousness. For him, the experience has been profoundly life changing.

It led to what Ted calls "masterful philanthropy," a way of experiencing a calling that is "deeply sourced . . . not by the personality and cognitive processes, but through alignment with universal vibratory principles, powerful fields of energy . . . emanating from the Divine . . . that transcend the intellect, time, and space."

Ted defines the Divine as "the formless, unmanifest Ground of Being, the Absolute, God and all the names of God from every tradition. This is the energy of Spirit, the unifying life force of the universe and the energetic basis of all life. It is not tied to a religious dogma, but is the greater unity that connects all souls with each other and with the Divine. In this way, Spirit is a state of consciousness that transcends the physical plane."

Masterful philanthropy actually shares a lot with what we have heard from others on this journey. It is selfless giving that is not about the donor but about the recipient. Unlike transactional philanthropy, this kind of giving is a collaborative, unifying action that allows the recipient to realize potential unfettered by the hubris and power that often spoil the philanthropic act. Ted believes the potential for this kind of lasting and meaningful philanthropic action is boundless.

Ted is one the few people I know who has reflected deeply on the relationship among soul, heart, spirit, love, and generosity.

"For me, it is at a deeply spiritual level that I most feel the interconnectivity of all life, all experience, and all people. I feel as connected to the children in a village in Africa as much as I do to a neighbor's child. This experience of interconnectivity is the essence of humanity. When we fully experience it, we know that what can be accomplished within the realm of thought could be greatly expanded if connected to realms of the spirit."

The psychiatrist David Hawkins writes:

The universe, the very essence of life itself, is highly conscious. Every act, thought and choice adds to a permanent mosaic; our decisions ripple through the universe of consciousness to affect the life of all. Every word, deed and intention creates a permanent record. Every thought is known and recorded forever. There are no secrets; nothing is hidden, nor can be. Our spirits stand naked in time for all to see. Everyone's life, finally, is accountable to the universe.[10]

Accountability can be seen from many perspectives. Ted addresses it with a call for creating a pool of sacred money. *Sacred money* is wealth that is enhanced by "alignment with a higher order of universal principles that would in the end create a field of spiritualized wealth."

Ted's goal is not to sanctify money. What makes it spiritual is that it is based on a cocreative partnership with the Divine. It requires opening to, receiving, and aligning with the universal life force that permeates all existence. These acts resonate with higher levels of consciousness.

"For two thousand years, we have been overly dependent on the cognitive, rational energies of the mind. In our reductionist culture, mental understanding is the primary way of knowing, which makes the human experience very limited. The mind alone misses the river of higher levels of consciousness that permeate the universe and our soul."

What Ted seeks, what he advocates, is to expand our being.

"There is hope for a better world. At the same time, the 'horribles'—global warming, weapons of mass destruction, poverty—are growing. Masculine energies dominate the world. The examples are legion. America oversells itself, and wars threaten to rip apart the world. The other way is to rediscover the energies of the Divine Feminine. Balancing the masculine and feminine within each person is a way to promote healing on the planet. It is an essential precursor to the healthy evolution of consciousness.

"The human world turns on greed and fear that come from the endless needs of the ego. Lodged within, the heart, the soul, one's inner voice and the deeper aspects of the human experience find it difficult to emerge." What Ted seeks is for individuals to become aware of the limiting beliefs of our society and their clamp on most philanthropy.

"If individuals spent more time opening to and aligning with the Divine, the world might begin to transform in ways far beyond what we could even imagine. To begin, we need to slow down, write the poetry, walk in the forest, and play. Those experiences lie below the ego and the personality level, before thought, in an inner space. There we may tap into the collective wisdom, our birthright."

Heart, spirit, and mystery are in Ted's experiences. For us, this may be the metaphysics of reality; for Ted, it is how to seek to live if we are to live well. *Believe* is not the word to use. Only experiences of spirit lead to levels of consciousness the intellect can never know.

Ted is light-years, literally and figuratively, away from the journey to a better world that most travel. But those who believe that listening to our hearts is an important part of that journey may see the value in moving, as best we can, toward our innermost being.

What Ted has done is place the soul at the very heart of the matter. That is his passion, and while I do not pretend to fully understand, I respect Ted for the courage to explore his unique world and find meaning within it.

It seems to me another way to "grow your soul."

A Certain Slant of Life

We all bring what Emily Dickinson called a "certain slant" to life and to all that is within it— listen to these words from the poet:

There's a Certain Slant of Light

On winter afternoons
That oppresses like the heft
Of cathedral tunes

I thought of these hard lines one day last year during time spent in the hills of West Virginia with a successful entrepreneur whose aim is to use his fortune to promote spirituality. He was born a Christian in India and converted as an adult to Hinduism. Educated in India and England, he went on to get a Harvard MBA, became head of the Middle East practice for an international accounting firm, and ended up in the telecommunications business.

At a certain point, when his position as a high-ranking Hindu business leader was at a peak, he became disillusioned with his life. His marriage fell apart, and all the things he had been working for seemed meaningless. He had come to feel that Hinduism, along with all organized religion, was empty; he began exploring other forms of spirituality.

We talked for hours about these experiences and what he had learned.

"What I struggled with were my personal limitations, my loves, my hates, my prejudices, and my angst. For years I could not balance my business life, my personal life, my religious life, and my community life. It is the balance between what Aristotle called 'meanness' that involves an excessive, self-indulgent concern with one's own things and the 'deep-seated desire to ameliorate suffering and promote well-being,' which is the prima facie source of common good. It is the fundamental struggle between the 'I' and the 'we.'"

He slowly recovered from his personal crises, met and married a warm and loving artist from rural West Virginia, and moved there. His satellite business operations continued to prosper. When we met, he was considering an offer to sell his business for more than $150 million.

We talked about his dream of forming a spiritual community on his land based on the little-known wisdom of the elders from the region of the world called the Caucasus, especially Abkhasia—a place where his own ancestors had once lived. His notion was to make it not just a place of contemplation and reflection, but one where people could live and bring up their families. He wanted to use his entrepreneurial skills to build businesses that were compatible with the large tracts of conservation land he owned. He was passionate about this new community being the product of a vision created by the community as a whole, for he had come to respect the values, strength, and character of the impoverished people who lived in those hills. He wanted to help them, but not as a charismatic rich patron. *Servant* and *steward* were the words he used, and he viewed his wealth as a tool. He had finally come to a place that was truly home—this was his destiny.

In the late afternoon, we went for a long walk around his property. After we had reached the crest of a steep hill with the sun setting, the beautiful but rough-hewn countryside around us, he suddenly turned to me and said, "You know, we are all at heart beggars. What we do all of our lives is beg for inner peace, for love, and for salvation."

I was deeply moved by his dramatic plea. It seemed to me an expression of the essential loneliness of being. Educated, worldly, successful, and wealthy though he might be, salvation—spiritual, experiential, or practical—remained elusive. It is not a surprise. So much of what we do in life with our families, our work, and our ongoing search for place and community, love and faith, is because we do not want to be lonely. The world makes it hard to find inner peace and salvation lies who knows where. My West Virginia friend is also not the first person to push back on "the heft of cathedral tunes."

We have heard others speak of wanting to be more in touch with the center of their lives. They seek the alignment of individual convictions and beliefs with a broader community, or social or public purpose. The literal and spiritual journey of this West Virginia transplant has finally found a home and with it a purpose for wealth in a place with great needs. The application of one's knowledge, and skills, and life experience to the issue at hand is another common theme. Seriousness of purpose is also key for those who have made it work—this is not a game. When these elements come together, generosity of self, means, and spirit takes on new meaning.

It is how we come to the work. It is how we find purpose, how we find meaning. My West Virginia friend expressed it one way. There are others.

The Women Religious

Sister Margaret Leonard is, among other things, what might be called a piece of work.

A few years ago I arrived with my friend Dan at Project Hope, the remarkable organization founded in the 1950s by a community of the Little Sisters of the Assumption.

Sister Margaret belongs to this International Community of Women Religious who live and work in poverty neighborhoods in every continent of our world. Project Hope is in Roxbury, Massachusetts.

When family homelessness emerged as a major problem in their community, Sister Margaret and her colleagues opened the doors of their home and invited homeless families to live with them and called it Project Hope. Some of these individuals were part of the genesis of Paul and Phyllis Fireman's One Family Campaign that has the goal of ending family homelessness in the state.

My friend Dan gives generously, and anonymously, to small, community-based projects and had been a long-term supporter of Project Hope. As we walked into the house that feels more like a home than a shelter, Sister Margaret greeted us profusely. She is dramatic, a storyteller who openly shares her own visions, ideas, and knowledge of God's mysterious ways. She can get you to throw up your hands and surrender faster than anyone I know.

"Let me tell you what we need to do here" is all I can remember, except for Dan writing a somewhat bigger check than he had intended.

That is one side of Sister Margaret, the practical missionary and salesperson, who is pretty adept politically as well. And here is another, the side that relates to purpose:

"Visions are in us as constant companions and we move toward their realization inch by inch and sometimes leap by leap. At rare and special times, our efforts reach a tipping point, which catapults us into entirely new ways of thinking and acting. In this way, visions call us into a future yet to unfold."

Sister Margaret's vision is of a world that is more equitable, just, and loving. She has held up this vision for nearly a half century, and it has called, inspired, and moved her to a series of choices. It has sent her to live and stand with families struggling with poverty as neighbor, friend, and colleague. Doing so she has learned the inch-by-inch lessons of HOPE in the work of justice and celebrated the leaps that have graced all of our lives in certain moments of history.

"I believe that justice and equity are inseparable. Justice means that resources are shared in a meaningful way. The pursuit of justice is the way to make that happen. In this sense, *justice* is not a noun but a verb. The reality of where I live and have spent my adult life is that people lack resources, and it has devastating results. Justice is the pursuit of resources to counter the devastation.

"I have learned to look at the world through the basement window, through the lives of people at the bottom. Yesterday, I was talking to a neighborhood mother who has four boys about the new Silver Line buses, which are double-length and have huge windows. 'Everyone is excited about the new buses,' she said, 'but my sixteen-year-old son is afraid to ride the bus for fear that he may be shot.' Why should children have to grow up in neighborhoods where fear for their own safety is paramount, where fear saps their energy and limits their potential?

"I think of the multitude of mothers who live with shame, lack of respect, and blame because they can't provide housing for themselves and their children. Like Matilda, who works forty hours a week at a local bank but lives with her two-year-old in the hallway of an apartment building because she cannot afford housing. She, too, is a victim of fear—fear that if she seeks help, the state will put her child in foster care.

"The faces of beautiful children full of spirit and potential fill my heart. If they were privileged to live in an environment with opportunities for development how different life would be for them. I think of Juan, a creative and artistic young man with a gentle spirit who happened to be in the wrong place at the wrong time and ended up spending his late teens in a federal prison. I think of young mothers of poor families who could become productive leaders in our world, if only they had the chance for quality education, yet are reduced to a life of struggle."

This is life in the basement, and it is a global basement. Throughout the world, we have chosen to structure our national and international institutions and economies in such a way that more and more families lack the resources for human survival. Today we are witnesses to the greatest economic disparity among families in the United States and throughout the world.

"I can't reconcile these differences with a shrug and platitude like 'That's life.'"

If Sister Margaret is motivated by social justice, she is hugely influenced by her faith.

"My vision of the world was forged from the revelations of the Judeo-Christian tradition and the insights emerging from the New Story of the Universe.

"Early in my life, I discovered the God that Jesus called Father and God's dream for humanity 'that we may all be one.' In a deepening personal relationship with my God, I began to see the world through different eyes and to recognize how far we are from the realization of God's dream. I heard the call to strive to make it happen in history in this time and space which is mine and ours.

"I believe that our Creator God, One for whom we have many different names, created each of us with an interior spark of divinity and a mandate to image the One who creates, loves, and frees (Genesis). We are all sisters and brothers, 'siblings with one another and with beast and flower.'[11] Our mission is to create in the time and space which is ours a world, a universe, that is a family dwelling place where there is respect, love, and dignity for all its inhabitants. Genesis awakened me to this true purpose of creation.

"We need to internalize the precious laws of the universe and write them large in our human creations. What are these important laws: Interiority, differentiation, and communion?[12]

"*Interiority* means that every individual reality is its own self-organizing activity, its own interior center. There is a deep mystery at the core of each human being, a spiritual center and source of creative energy. How different our world would be if we reverenced the creative center of everyone and everything.

"*Differentiation* means that everything that is, is different from everything else that is. Difference is the intention of the Creator, and it is gift and blessing. Would incidents of war, racism, prejudice and all the other '-isms' of human history be reduced if we grasped this important truth?

"*Communion* is the third law. As we look at nature, the web of interconnection is everywhere. For every reality of the universe is intimately present to every other reality in the universe and finds its fulfillment in mutual presence. The entire evolutionary process depends on communion. Everything is oriented to communion that they may be One.

"So this is my vision of the world and these are my sources of inspiration and passion. They are within me. Each of us has a unique spiritual center and we must be in touch with that center. When we are, we can sense the civic forms that correspond to the spiritual principles. I don't mean to be too mystical here. We may think we understand how to organize a more just society, but we only know by experimenting and by evaluating the effects of our experiment. We need to ask all the time whether the civic forms are really working for the people who should benefit. We must always seek out new ways to organize communities to achieve justice, equity, and love among people.

"These are the principles by which I live and they are embodied in the organization we call Project Hope."

What would Sister Margaret's benediction be for those of us on this journey? It is this, from Denise Levertov's poem entitled "Beginners":

> We have only begun
> to imagine justice and mercy
> only begun to envision
> how it might be
> to live together as siblings with beast and flower.

Becoming Ruth

When Angelica Berrie, a Philippine national and a Catholic, married her husband Russ, he asked whether she would consider converting to Judaism. Her answer was "I'm a better Jew now than you are! Why should I convert?" Evidence suggests that before Angelica and Russ married, he had not been a very observant Jew, and Angelica, schooled by the nuns in her convent school in Manila, thought that was terrible. Together, they began observing Shabbat every Friday and taking his children to High Holidays. Angelica in earnest and

Russ in love, his Judaism was revitalized in the warmth of family and friends around the Sabbath table.

Russ Berrie died from complications associated with diabetes, and Angelica became president of the Russ Berrie Foundation. One of the principal areas of focus for the foundation is Jewish issues in both the United States and Israel in efforts to bring about transformational change.

Recording something of her own transformation, she wrote regularly to friends and family following his death. This is that story.

"It is unimaginable that he is no longer with me, yet he left a lifetime of happy memories, friends whose loyalty and support have sustained me.

"He also left me to carry on his work. He left me a legacy in the lives transformed, and that is now my work. I know it is just the beginning as I am just beginning to contemplate a future without my other self. It has been like swimming underwater, holding my breath. I am finding my own way, putting one foot reluctantly in front of the other. I feel like an egg that has cracked and I am waiting to see what will emerge. I stay open, waiting for my life to unfold."

"Starting the process of reclaiming my life, I listened to advice 'to discover what gives me joy and do it again and again so I don't forget.' It inspired me to take a flying leap out of a plane. The forty-five-second freefall at ten thousand feet gave me the jolt I needed to jump-start my exploration into the unknown. I felt that flying solo was a symbolic marker in my passage through grief.

"I discovered the Chinese character for *student* means 'to learn to live,' which describes perfectly this stage. As I turn fifty next year, I made up a 'life list' that reflects my intentions: hike through Scotland so I can earn a good night's sleep in a castle; plan a spiritual retreat in Israel while studying for my conversion; learn Chinese; take up Zen Archery; reunite with fifty first cousins from the Philippines, Spain, and the U.S. Gilda Radner said, 'Some stories don't have a clear beginning, middle, and end. Life is about not knowing, having to change, taking the moment, and making the best of it, without knowing what's going to happen next.'"

"As I contemplate a life without Russ, tears mingle with new feelings as I struggle to reconnect the 'wires' in my system, hoping to flip a switch that keeps my consciousness alive and creates that spark of joy.

"As I mark the second year of my loss at Christmastime, I am deeply conscious of the spirit and keeping that spirit powerfully alive by focusing on what matters most, listening to those you love, making time for personal growth and expressing the true spirit of giving by offering the gifts of time, talent, connections, ideas, or energy, to serve those in need around us. . . .

"This has been a year of 'becoming,' of attempting to rebuild a life and finding my own way to fill that life with meaning. It may not seem important that I finally got my driver's license, but the purpose of having a 'life list' is to honor your intentions. My only regret was that it took a life-altering experience of loss to jolt me into soul searching to follow my bliss.

"It was for me a year of spiritual awakening. In January, I had the privilege of joining a delegation of Jewish rabbis to visit the Vatican as a gesture of appreciation for His Holiness Pope John Paul II's efforts to improve the relationship between the Catholic Church and the Jewish people. It was his last Papal Audience. About 160 of us gathered in the Clementine Room, the same room where his body lay in state after his death. Being there made a deep impression. Some of the rabbis could not believe that after centuries of division, such a thing could come to pass. It was a 'can you believe we're here?' moment!

"In India in February, at the ancient Ganesha temple dedicated to the Elephant god, I found pilgrims prostrating themselves lengthwise along the road, marking the spot where their head touched with a stone and beginning their next prostration from that point, making their progress toward the temple in this manner. Dutiful wives followed behind, bending down to massage their husband's feet and offer water.

"Walking through the streets of Jaipur I saw bejeweled kohl-eyed women in gilded saris, camels pulling carts, painted elephants, snake charmers, naked ash-covered Hindu holy men, hundreds of brides and grooms burning dried cow dung patties over ceremonial fires at a mass wedding, families of five loaded on one motorbike.

"In June on a spiritual journey in the Holy Land at a visit to the Technion University in Haifa, I inaugurated the Russell Berrie Nanotechnology Institute. I was in the audience as Nobel Peace Prize winner, Elie Wiesel, received an honorary degree. As my grandchildren toured the science labs, I thought about them returning as adults to see the achievements that will benefit Israel from their Grandpa Russ's Nanotechnology Institute.

"Wearing identical red string kabbalah bracelets, my girlfriends and I spent Shabbat in the mystical city of Safed, where kabbalah originated. We got a lesson in kabbalistic art and met the young commanders of Israel's antiterrorist units. Our host, an American convert, gave us a glimpse of life in the Breslav Orthodox community as one of her guests sang an English translation of an eighteenth-century Russian song about a woman converting, 'listening to that still, small voice inside that told her there must be something more.' Heads covered and bodies wrapped modestly in shawls, we joined the women at synagogue, peeking through a hole poked in plastic wrapping that separated the women upstairs from members of the opposite sex praying below.

"Having made the decision to convert shortly before Russ died, I embarked on that journey in July, spending a month of intensive study in Jerusalem, preparing for my conversion to Judaism. I learned to read Hebrew, studied Torah, Jewish history, and the values associated with each Jewish holiday, 'placing myself in Jewish time.' On weekends, I hiked through the hills of Judea in national parks shaded by pomegranate, fig, pistachio, and almond trees. Feeling alive and free as I put the world on hold.

"I visited the cloisters of the 'Poor Clares,' a contemplative order bound by the vow of silence. Walking respectfully through the premises, I encountered a nun whispering into her cell phone! My guide, Sister Clare Edith, allowed me to photograph her behind the convent grille and related the story of her life as a convert to the Catholic faith and the first native Israeli nun in the order. She explained they get news of the outside world through assigned news 'listeners' who relate events of the day in their daily community prayers. On a tour of the chapel, she emphasized the Church's acknowledgment of Jesus' Jewish origins by pointing out religious paintings depicting Jesus holding a book inscribed in Hebrew, and Joseph in a blue-edged Jewish prayer shawl holding the baby Jesus.

"I returned from Israel armed with a sense of spiritual purpose. My first religious holiday as a 'soon-to-be' Jew was the feast of Sukkot. I decided to build a *sukkah*, a temporary hut that represents the fragility of our lives. I learned that lesson dramatically, when my newly built and beautifully decorated first sukkah, complete with religiously correct *lulav* (a palm frond) and *esrog* (a citrus) gave in to the elements and collapsed after a downpour. It is a feast when Jews pray for rain after the harvest, so I guess we got a good response.

"I completed my conversion process in November by going through a *mikveh*, an immersion akin to baptism. Three modern Orthodox rabbis served as my 'tribunal,' questioning me and testing the steadfastness of my resolve. A female mikveh attendant stood over the bath to ensure I was properly immersed. Her job was to pronounce me 'kosher' three times as I dunked according to complicated instructions. For any aspiring Jewess, 'The Secret to Jewish Femininity' provides a checklist of preparations before immersion. These include instructions to bathe for at least an hour and thoroughly clean and inspect every inch of your body, including your navel and earring holes, for anything that might prevent total body contact with the mikveh waters. These waters must be from a free-flowing source like a spring-fed lake or the sea.

"A woman should not immerse totally upright nor very bent. Rather, she should lean forward slightly as if kneading dough. Having never kneaded dough in my life, I was at a total loss. It took me several hours to comply with all the instructions. I received the Jewish name of the biblical convert, Ruth, and was moved beyond words by the experience. I felt I finally arrived at a place where I always wanted to be. When my rabbi asked if I was ready, I felt my whole being respond, 'I am here.'

"My Catholic-Jewish transition year ended in December when I joined faculty and students at Columbia University to listen to the Dalai Lama. It inspired me to pursue a longtime interest in Tibetan Buddhism and to audit a course under the first Westerner to be ordained a Tibetan Buddhist monk. In summing up my year, I find the words of William Arthur Ward reflective of my journey: 'The adventure of life is to learn. The goal of life is to grow. The nature of life is to change. The challenge of life is to overcome. The essence of life is to care. The secret of life is to dare. The beauty of life is to give. The joy of life is to love.'

"Three years have gone by, and my sense of loss is tempered by the knowledge that growth itself contains the germ of happiness. I learn to measure life by the moments when my spirit has been uplifted, by the challenges I have faced, the adventures I experience along the way. In Israel, I made a commitment to myself to follow where my spirit leads me. In pursuing my way, my essence and my truths, I am discovering my true Self."

Russ Berrie was an extraordinarily generous and gifted man, who began life as a poor kid from the Bronx and built a major business selling, of all things, teddy bears. And I, too, miss him. This is the poem I wrote in his memory.

LARGER THAN LIFE

When a good man dies
The earth nods, heaves a sigh
And goes right back to work.

Perhaps selling improvisations
Or taking on impossible odds,
Grandiose dreams by sheer force
Of will become reality.

Who would have believed this script
In a world where the brisk business
Of birth, death, renewal and chance
Comes in on the money every time.

When a good man dies
The earth nods, heaves a sigh
And just goes back to its work.

You can't trick fate
But you can mold it with passion,
Bend it by ambition
And turn it toward a better world.

Reader's Guide Questions

1. How have you answered the question "Who is my stranger?"?
2. Does a materialistic society like our own need altruism as a counterbalance?
3. Richard Dawkins's *The Selfish Gene* scores on many levels. Could you call this journey and these stories a catalogue of memes?
4. Is the Tit for Tat strategy, a non-zero-sum game, a good explanation why we are generous? Is pure altruism a better one? Are there others?
5. Which of Tom Tierney's magnets most pulls you? Are yours in relative balance?
6. For Tom, tension between his career and public service was constant over many years. Do you identify with that tension? If so, how have you resolved it?
7. What "season" of life are you in? Do you see new careers in the future?
8. When the choice was money or quality of life, which have you chosen?
9. If you put the essence of your life on a T-shirt, what would it say?
10. Bob Buford believes there are two conversions—one to belief and one to integrity. Does that resonate with you?
11. Do you believe in destiny? Are you in alignment with yours?
12. Bob suggests on the "final exam" that you'll be asked what you believe and what you did with what you were given to work with. What are your answers?
13. Ted Mallon writes of living in parallel worlds and multiple dimensions. Have you ever sensed that there is more to our lives than what we discover with our five senses or experienced a higher level of consciousness?

14. Ted experiences "the interconnectivity of all life" at a deeply spiritual level. Do you feel an "interconnectivity"?
15. Ted decries our "reductionistic culture" and sees hope in our feminine, as opposed to masculine, energies. Do you think it can be useful to share things from vastly different perspectives? Are you reluctant to do so?
16. Do you slow down, write poetry, walk in the woods enough, or have another source of inspiration?
17. What is your response to Emily Dickinson's "the heft of cathedral tunes"?
18. Do you agree with the dramatic plea that "we are all at heart beggars"?
19. Sister Margaret Leonard believes that visions are realized "inch by inch." Do you agree, or do you think we can make progress in leaps?
20. What is the difference between justice and equity?
21. Is your faith important to you, as it is to Sister Margaret? If not, what is?
22. How does Angelica Berrie's spiritual journey differ from that of those we have just met? How is it the same?
23. Angelica's loss of her husband jolted her into soul searching. It was her lightening strike. Have you had your soul jolted?
24. Angelica is a learner and a seeker, and unusually ecumenical. Are you?

Notes

1. From Richard Titmuss, *The Gift Relationship* (New York: New Press, 1997), 125, referencing the work of M. Mauss in 1954.
2. Titmuss, *The Gift Relationship*, 145.
3. Titmuss, *The Gift Relationship*.
4. Richard Dawkins, *The Selfish Gene* (New York: Oxford University Press, 1976).
5. Dawkins, *The Selfish Gene*, 3.
6. The Tit for Tat strategy was developed by Anatol Rappaport, a psychologist and game theorist from Toronto.
7. R. Axelrod, *The Evolution of Cooperation* (New York: Basic Books, 1984).
8. Ian Parker, "The Gift," *The New Yorker*, August 2, 2004.
9. Theodore J. Mallon, *The Journey toward Masterful Philanthropy* (self-published).
10. Excerpt cited is from David Hawkins, *Power vs. Force: The Hidden Determinants for Human Behavior* (n.p.: Veritas, 1995).
11. "Beginners," a poem by Denise Levertov.
12. "Exploring a New Cosmology," a video series by Miriam Therese MacGillis, Genesis Farm Learning Center for Earth Studies, founded by the Dominican Sisters of Caldwell, New Jersey.

THE WORLD WE WANT

THE SACRED search for a better world and the transformations that come from people turning their insights and drive into action and progress both lead in the direction we want to go. The stories of spirit, mind, and matter woven together are inspirational. There has been progress, yet is that enough? A continuum that always allows for more. One of the people I spoke with about *The World We Want* said, "I hope it is not all gloom and doom, because I am basically an optimist." But another said, "I am so depressed by what I see in our society, it is impossible not to be pessimistic." For most of us, both statements are true depending on the day, but for me one thing at least is clear. The immense capacity of imaginative individuals to impact the world is both boundless and mysterious.

Mystery

Whenever I visit with Peter White, there is a story that is also a lesson. He is very good at both. This one is about mystery.

"Mystery presents an anomaly, a departure from the logic we prize. We are inclined to dismiss it. But even as mystery troubles our analytic, results-oriented minds, it awakens something within and beckons us to learn.

"The story I am about to relate registers with me as mystery. I learned it long ago, and over the years, as I have told it many times, it has changed, evolving into the story presented here. But its mysterious essence has remained the same:

Many years ago and far away, an aged teacher was strolling contemplatively in the corridor of the dormitory that housed the students of his academy. As he passed the doorway of an especially favored student, he noticed that the young man was preparing for a journey. "Where are you going?" the teacher asked.

233

"*Master, I have heard there is a vicious warlord in a region far from here who is oppressing the people, stealing their land, taxing them into poverty, and enriching himself while they starve. I have prepared myself for mortal combat, and I am going to this region, where I intend to force the warlord to cease his outrageous conduct.*"

Instead of being impressed, as the disciple had hoped, the teacher laughed derisively. "He will brush you away with the back of his hand. You will accomplish nothing but getting yourself killed."

Perplexed, the student thought for a moment. "I know! I will use the power of reason, which I have learned from you, to convince the warlord that his violent ways can only result in an uprising of the people and the overthrow of his regime. Surely reason will prevail!"

Again the master laughed at his well-intentioned disciple. "Your reason will be as effective as reasoning with a river to reverse its course. You will drown!"

Frustrated but ever anxious to find the right answer, the student meditated. Suddenly he smiled and returned to his master's gaze. "I believe I see what you are saying, my esteemed teacher. I must invoke a force greater than my physical strength and my logic to make this wretched man mend his ways. I must invoke the power of God, showing the warlord that God despises the greedy and violent and will surely impose a punishment greater by a thousand times than the material rewards the warlord receives from his oppression."

"Ha, ha, ha!" the old man nearly doubled over in laughter, "The thought of you invoking God, threatening to bring lightening bolts down upon this ruler! Your only hope is that the ridiculous nature of your posturing will move him to ignore you."

Deflated as he had never been before, the student pondered once again and then spoke. "I have it! I will forget force, forget reason, forget even God, and I will go in rags as a beggar. In the mirror of my humility, the warlord will see himself as he truly is and will decide on his own to change his violent ways."

"He will swat you away as an irrelevant insect!" came the master's response, again with derisive laughter.

The student was exasperated. Burning tears flowed down his cheeks and sputtered from his lips, as he cried, "Master, you yourself have said repeatedly that behavior like that of this warlord is wrong and cannot be countenanced. I have committed myself to putting an end to the injustice, to laying down my life if necessary. I have described the best plans I can devise, and you only belittle me and laugh at me. Tell me, please, Master, what must I do?"[1]

"You must fast."[2]

"The first time I heard this story," Peter says, "it didn't suit my logical mind, and it probably won't suit yours, but it pricked my intuition and beckoned me playfully to learn. I have found it a good place to start looking not only at our world but at how we are looking at our world. My conclusion after much thought was this: 'Perhaps we must fast.'"

Early in his career as a lawyer, Peter worked on the Watergate scandal and later joined Fulbright & Jaworski, the high-powered Washington law firm whose senior partner, Leon Jaworski, had been the Watergate special prosecutor. Peter's career took off, and he quickly became successful in the way the world looks at success—lots of money, prestige, and even some fame. But for reasons he could not understand at the time, he was miserable. He became depressed, began drinking heavily, and his life went into a tailspin that ended in a divorce and a career in shambles.

As he slowly put himself back together and emerged from that dark period of time, Peter began a second career, quite unique, counseling very wealthy families about the meaning of wealth. We often work together, discussing and analyzing the issues of wealth, legacy, and responsibility. Peter has a remarkably reflective intelligence, and I like being with him. He brings energy into the room as opposed to taking it out. It is his gift.

Peter's own journey into the depths of despair has given him a unique capacity to empathize with the strange stasis those with immense wealth have to deal with. It may seem odd that those with more money than they will ever need often have great doubt and insecurity about their own self-worth. Often they worry, with good reason, about the impact of wealth on their children. Over twenty years, Peter has perhaps had more deep conversations about these questions with the world's wealthiest families than anyone on earth. One of the things he tells this rarefied clientele is this story of mystery. Today, Peter is vice chairman of U.S. Trust Company, and he spends as much time as he can in his cabin in Montana, where he engages in his own version of "fasting."

I have told Peter White's story because I believe the directive to fast is a powerful metaphor for our journey. To fast is to deny the body, or the soul, or the society, its overly rich menu of largesse. To fast is to bring one closer in spirit to those who have very little, or even nothing. To fast is to cleanse. To fast is to strip out hubris and ego-driven ambition. To fast is to go to the earth and begin again.

If the warlord is a symbol of the tyranny, cruelty, and evil that remains a powerful constant on Earth, a ferocious force difficult to overcome, than fasting is the symbol of the elimination of more than body fat. It is the stripping away of the superfluous in the body and mind to find the essential spirit and soul. And in that reductionist state we become fully present and thereby fortified for the continuation of our journey to the world we want.

Are We Making Progress?

"I believe our hope lies with these, temporizing, delayed, moral learnings. We have slowly and painfully extended the definition of 'human.'"

There is a certain intensity to John Isaacson—flowing beard, narrow pointed face on top of a tall lanky frame. And then there's the way he listens to you, his eyes riveted, hands gesturing slowly as he draws you out. Isaacson is a gifted listener and has used that skill to build, over twenty-five years, one of the largest human resource firms in the country specializing in nonprofit organizations, universities, and foundations. His fascination is with people, which is why he is a superb recruiter, but his passion is history, and he loves dialogue and the tough dialectic of counterintuitive ideas. In another era, he would have been a great Talmudic scholar.

John is from Maine, where his great-grandfather settled in the late 1800s. His grandfather was a lawyer and businessman, and his father still is. "Tough old birds," says John. "I aspire to be one." He grew up part of a small but robust Jewish community in Lewiston-Auburn. He followed his father to Harvard Law School, but took a 90-degree turn on graduation and went into state government in Massachusetts, where he learned headhunting and thrived. His mother is Hungarian and a survivor of Auschwitz.

John offers us a radical perspective on moral learning and its hoped-for progress.

"I am a moralist interested in social and moral learning, over extended periods of time. I believe the learning that constitutes moral progress is independent of religious belief or of political structures or economic forces. I understand that moral progress grows with and through these things, but I am deluded enough to make the case that these learnings have become a kind of modern, sacred foundation, part of a common, increasingly global definition of 'civilized' self."

To judge our "moral progress," John weighs the kinds of violence, official and private, that we sanction against other, "dehumanized" human beings. The things we condone by sanctioning, the evil that we allow to happen to others.

"I accept, as a given, that I may be making a preposterous argument. We have just ended the bloodiest century in human history. Genocide since the end of the Second World War has become more, not less, common, and our own era is dominated by self-righteous suicide bombers (not your conventional warrior) who casually commit war crimes by blowing up unknown civilians.

"Progress is a new idea, a late child of the enlightenment. It crops up in the West as a popular idea in the nineteenth century, when reason and science generated unprecedented wealth. It was linked to the 'spread of civilization,' and it has suffered the same fate as that lofty ambition. I know that both phrases feel antique today. The experience of colonial occupation, colonial rebellion and the early twentieth-century wars made progress, especially 'civilized' progress, an object of ridicule. We no longer use the words with any conviction, and yet there has been progress.

"Let's start with the extreme—cannibalism. We are accustomed, unpleasantly, to the use of the 'other' for economic ends, or simply for self-indulgence, but in the cannibal, a human reduces the human 'other' to mere protein. It is not now part of our moral calculus, though it was once common enough. It may seem ridiculous to call it progress, but we have abolished it as a moral possibility. The human other may be expendable, but not for food."

Is this supposed to be comforting, John?

"It's a start. Something analogous and related emerged in the ancient world for human religious sacrifice and I suspect, in some intuitive way, the two are related. G-d creates man in his image, sacrilizing the body. G-d stays Isaac's hand, a crucial mythical moment, the Torah reading for the Day of Atonement. Gods do not require, perhaps do not permit, the sacrifice of humans to appease them. In the Christian extension, G-d, not men, sacrifices Christ. The central religion of the West deified human religious sacrifice. Jesus saves all who believe. He is of the godhead. No other human sacrifice is required. When the West encountered Inca, Mayan, and Aztec, high civilizations with human sacrifice intact, it recoiled with moral horror. The horror had a certain self-justifying quality and the European invasions spread a pestilence that killed ninety percent of the pre-Colombian population, but the lesson of G-d's word to Isaac, then three thousand years old, persevered. The world has somehow dutifully followed, sacrificing the unconscious urge to murder the young or the mythic urge to murder the powerful, to earn G-d's approval."

With all respect to gaining approval from God, there are other motivations, like the inherent human understanding of what is right and just.

"I agree. In more recent historical time, we have defined our collective ethics in a grappling with slavery. The trade in humans has an ancient pedigree. Virtually all civilizations owned slaves and used them, sometimes marginally, sometimes centrally. The practice grew enormously in the three hundred years, from the early sixteenth through the late nineteenth century, when Western capitalists invested heavily in slave-based, modern agriculture in the Canaries, Brazil, the Caribbean, and southern United States, though not on European soil. There was some shame, even at its height. They produced cash crops for international trade, and in their time, they represented the most innovative, wealth producing parts of the European economy. Historians estimate that the average life span of a plantation field hand in the seventeenth century was seven years. Humans were expendable for economic ends.

"Today, slavery has been universally abolished except for narrow, illegal pockets. It was perfectly compatible with a sophisticated early modern economy. It aided and drove the agricultural and manufacturing modernizations that we inherit and use for our prosperity. It didn't disappear by itself. It wasn't outmoded. The English, at the height of their powers, and their wealth, abolished the international slave trade and the rest of the world slowly followed."

It was moral enlightenment at that time, but it still exists.

"True enough, we have had recent revivals and variations. Slavery was integral to the Soviet gulag and to the German economy of the Second World War. It was part of the Cultural Revolution's political reeducation campaigns, as a kind of afterthought, and there are remnants today, in outlaw totalitarian regimes.

"Child labor, in emerging modern societies approximates slavery, but it is largely an extension of the premodern use of children in the fields and, in general, we have less of that system, not more. Childhood sexual exploitation and the international trade in prostitutes, mostly female, are forms of human trafficking that have grown in recent times. The trade is powered, like its better known economic predecessors, by business opportunity, and the victims are equally expendable. We understand the trade as morally corrupt, but we have effectively tolerated it, and it grows."

I am not sure everyone would agree it is tolerated, as much as difficult to end.

"Perhaps, but I think of the sex trade as a case of incipient and incomplete moral learning. The physical and sexual abuse of women and children has only recently emerged from the domestic closet. We don't yet see prostitution as an extension of intimate violence. We do not routinely call the sexual trade 'slavery,' although it is. It has the feeling of a work in progress, allied to our common understanding of the unconscious and to the liberation of women. Like the other great moral learnings, it moves slowly, though I am pleased to say that in the last couple of years, we have actually made progress in policing the trade.

"In our time, in the last few centuries, I think of moral progress as a scramble to cope with modernization, analogous to giving up drink after an extended binge. We lurch through modernization, a process of rationalizing market-driven commerce that dates from the late fifteenth century to our own time."

It certainly is important, but why so from a moral perspective?

"Because it disrupts as nothing else does. It blows up traditional civilizations. Agricultural production grows exponentially. Land ownership shifts. Population grows, changing all the human landscapes. Efficient manufacture emerges or intrudes. The standard of living rises, but unequally, and people are unhinged from their traditional occupations. Peasants are driven from the land. Artisans and shopkeepers are displaced by factories and efficient retail. Nobles lose status to commercial barons. The clergy are undermined and bellow sin at materialism. Whole classes, peoples, nations, and religions are routinely humiliated by displacement and the occasional economic crash.

"The results are exhilarating and appalling. In the traditional civilization, especially in Europe and Asia, we have witnessed massive disruption and variations on military expansion, aggressive war, social revolution, and occasional genocide. Islam is the last great, traditional civilization to grapple with the process. So far, it has suffered less slaughter than its predecessors."

The picture here is very dark.

"I am actually slightly more optimistic than not. Socialist revolution that demonized the privileged and authorized their elimination has been largely discredited, though Cambodia, Peru, and Nepal should remind us of the power of that idea. Fascist popular war that demonizes the subhuman 'other,' and glorifies the heroic, male, pure, and agrarian past has had a tough century, though it is a resilient disease.

"I think of genocide as the natural extension of slavery but a twentieth-century invention. The authorities, moral or official, define as the 'other' a particular tribal African. Slavs, the Jew, Chinese residents of Nanking, or Tutsis are deemed expendable. Slavery was not always absolute, but it tended to the absolute. In a fully functioning slave system, the owner had the almost universally acknowledged right to work a slave to death, though not always the right to kill. In genocide, murder follows identity."

Then where is the learning that you promised us?

"We have absorbed some learning. The world forgot Armenia, then shuddered at Nuremberg, and then repressed the memory. The mass murder of a half million Indonesians in 1965 was passed off as an incident in the Cold War, the spontaneous destruction of communists, who just happened to be overseas Chinese. The extermination of most Ibo in Biafra in the 1960s left little trace in world memory. The genocide in Cambodia in the early 1970s suddenly reminded us. This happens again and again. It is not clear why, but Cambodia was a turning point in moral learning. Perhaps it was because Eichmann had stood trial in 1960 and the words 'Never again' had become a ritual mumbling, perhaps because Cambodia was linked to Vietnam and the world was watching. Commentators apprehended that another 'Holocaust' had happened, not identical, but comparable. Some significant part of global opinion shuddered. In Rwanda, the globe earned a little shame. We did nothing. We had warning and we failed, but we knew swiftly that we failed and an American president apologized, an astonishing idea, a moment of global moral learning. In Cambodia, it took a few years to absorb the truth, in Rwanda, a few months. Then in Kosovo and in Bosnia and in Darfur, the world struggled to intervene. We did it, and we do it badly, slowly, haltingly, without useful institutions and without much conviction, but for the first time, in the nearly hundred years since the Armenian genocide, we see it, call it by its name, and act, however ineptly."

Slow learning. Very slow. What comes next?

"Here's a wild shot. In the remaining parts of the globe where the power of the market economy has intruded but not yet succeeded, we will see a string of challenges. Maoists will emerge in Nepal or Peru, or similar geographically isolated settings, powered by centuries of peasant and ethnic rage. They could readily veer down a Cambodian path. Islamists will borrow the popular, emotional frames of twentieth-century European fascism and adapt them to a religious, rather than a national or faux racial, history. They will look backward to a 'pure' and triumphant time, when G-d and history's chosen ruled. They will assert that demons, literally 'Great Satans,' are loosed upon the Earth, and they will revive the ancient, male, purifying sword to cut out the modern 'disease' and restore the pride of 'believers.'"

This is beginning to sound like a bad Bollywood movie.

"Well, there is more. In the first world, aging populations and slowly declining standards of living for the young and undereducated will produce a backward-looking, nostalgia-driven nationalism, an attempt to keep 'France for the French,' or an 'English-only' America. We will breed movements to drive the foreign, 'rootless cosmopolitan' out. While that ideology is hopeless and always was, even in Germany in 1933, it can fuel populist, racial/national/religious movements that demonize some mix of 'others' and harness state power for the economic benefit of the 'true French' or their crude first world equivalent.

"We have a demanding time before us, a century or two, for the last great 'modernizing' wave to lap its way around the globe. I don't underestimate the challenges. I think they are real, but in general I believe that for these challenges, these will be easier centuries than the last one. The oldest, richest, largest, and most dangerous civilizations have already lived through the process, invented and discredited the core evils that modernization produces, and made their peace with capitalism. The hardest work was done across the Eurasian landmass fifty years ago with the success of the Allies in the Second World War. We are simply playing out that hand. We will be aided some, when world population stabilizes around midcentury and when Asian wages rise, in roughly the same time frame, to numbers crudely comparable to the West."

Where in your scenario is faith and the learned, the philosopher-kings?

"Alas, we don't have large religious or philosophical systems to support our learning. We are famously in an age of doubt and routinely ridiculed for it. But the doubt was earned; G-d served man in too many unpleasant crusades, and the belief systems of the last century were usefully and morally humiliated. In our time, only economists are full of conviction. Occasionally a political scientist will join an economist and wax prescriptive, but they are increasingly quantitative and appropriately careful. The sociologists are happy to remain contrarian—a useful role—but their statistical tools reach only modestly to history and they refrain, perhaps sensibly, from any sweeping generalizations. By and large, the philosophers, the historians, and the literary critics have become more technical, responding to the increased rigor of the modern academy. If they are public and political, they lean to a postcolonial view, interpreting Western moralizing as self-serving, an excuse for exploitation, a fair critique of the nineteenth century."

And the poets are considering their navels?

"Good question. I didn't even think of poets. Not a good sign. We are left for our moral learning these days, with a motley collection of idealists, religious believers, advocates, and scribblers of every variety who occupy a constantly expanding public sphere. We call them a 'civil society.' It is, I think, a useful term, a utilitarian, sanitized, rediscovery of 'civilization,' without colonial baggage, more a method than a state of being, but still a place to invest moral energy."

Why motley?

"Because it is, I think, a raucous, fractured place for learning. We leap wholesale into civil society ventures. Philanthropists emerge from the unlikeliest corners and place moral bets. We mobilize bits and pieces of one government or another to finance or publicize our disparate views, and the symbolic language of civil society organizations routinely becomes the stuff of cultural and political debate. The entire enterprise has made an intimate alliance with the power of every broad- and narrowcast media. It works. I suspect that the process looks vaguely similar to the antislavery movement or to religious revivals, only in our time, we have made a civic/moral enterprise into an industry."

It is true that no one has elected these players, but are not these ambiguities part of the attraction?

"Yes, but there are also dangers. There is something sloppy in public sphere learning. We tend to forgive tyrants if they emerge from the oppressed. We are easily confused by Third World poverty and its political movements, seeing virtue in the victim's struggle, where there is only pain and rage. We are easily confused by first world working-class intransigence, seeing race clearly but not class. We are aided by the sheer size and variety in civil society and by the strength of the modern academy. The academy sometimes disciplines the worst of the excesses. My hope is that the civil society industry will make our learning faster and more historically accurate. There are no guarantees, but broadly speaking, in the context of a couple of centuries, it looks to me like we are making progress.

And so you end on a qualified note of hope?

"Yes."

Sleepless Nights

What to do with John Isaacson's broad historical and theoretical perspective, which uneases me, despite the originality, the acuity of insight, and the elegance of his expression?

I love the sound and sense of what he says and especially agree with his positioning of the civil society as the place for moral learning in this era. It is exactly what we have seen evidence for on this journey. I take this to be one more person's considered attempt to make sense out of a world that seems too often without sense. It is a kind of op-ed on moral learning. There are not too many of those around.

It is also a scenario that does its best to try to "see around the corner" of what is to come, aside from history being a preface. We know the World We Want, however defined, is not just around the corner. One person I know has formed the Five Centuries Foundation, so his timetable, if you can call it that, for change is aligned with John's.

Yet I have a friend, someone who will see this book, who is so horrified by the trafficking of women and children that she cannot sleep at night. She is often in tears and struggles to maintain her balance, even her mental health, in a world that seems too hard and too cruel for too many. She, like most of us, is not thinking in terms of centuries but of what is in front of her today. I know that John's tone, his brilliant broad brush, will not feel right to her, and the modicum of hope he provides will hardly relieve her concerns.

It is easy to have sleepless nights. Confusion is not what one expects from experience. Experience is supposed to teach one how the world works and lead to greater clarity about how to live one's life. We expect that with age there will be more peace of mind, instead of less. We expect some kind of resolution, a weaving together of the strands of living. We want less cacophony and more harmony. We want to be optimistic, not less confident. We want to believe, and we want leaders who we can believe in.

Otherwise like my friend, we will toss all night, or worse, sleepwalk by the world that needs us.

In the novel *The Sleepwalkers*,[3] the monumental trilogy written by Hermann Broch in the early 1930s, the protagonist suffers from an existential malaise. He is disconnected from reality and unable to cope with the society in which he lives and dreams, harboring a great sense of futility. He is a mirror image of the narrator in Marcel Proust's *Remembrance of Things Past*,[4] which was written in the same era about another society that had lost its way, lost its soul. Proust is not so somnambulant and sleeptalks rather than sleepwalks his way through a hyperconscious, voyeuristic musing on the world around him.[5] And what in his predicament reminds me of our own is that action eludes him. In the same way, or so it seems, that action eludes many who could contribute to society.

Two other recent novels come to mind. Don DeLillo's *Underworld* tells the story of America from the time of the Dodger–Giants game in 1951 when Bobby Thompson's legendary home run became a symbol of an era ended; it was called the "shot heard round the world." The protagonist, a different kind of sleepwalker, drifts aimlessly through fear and denial of the threat of nuclear war while the society around him seems oblivious and materialistic. And Jay Cantor's remarkable novel, *Great Neck*, takes us deep into the turbulent 1960s when radicalism and self-destruction took on a violent life of its own. For those caught up in that time of passion and idealism amid powerful forces of race and class, the sleepwalker woke up, and for some, the dream became a nightmare.

Whenever we read books such as these, with the substance, symbol, and beauty of great narrative, we understand better what it takes to face our own personal demons. We understand more vividly the dilemma of a society that allows its capacity to be "self-correcting"[6] to be diminished. But life is not literature nor are we characters in a book. Most of us would agree with the poet Jane Cooper when she wrote, "I am trying to learn to live a decent life and not want to be a great person, and at the same time know what I have the human right to draw the line at."[7] That is in essence what most of us want. But what does living a decent life mean for you, or for me, if we feel our society has lost its soul or the community in which we live has lost its way? Knowing what is right and having the right to "draw the line" is one thing; exercising it is another.

Action is hard in a society where trust is in short supply and cynicism is pervasive, where too many people are overwhelmed by cultural norms that are offensive to them. Action is hard if one feels powerless in the face of extremism, which is a kind of false faith. The result is what has been described as a "decreasing sense of relationship to the whole."[8] It is what many writers have written about from very different perspectives.[9] When that relationship is lost across an entire society, especially a democratic society dependent on citizen engagement, we give up a lot. We give up too much. Too many citizens are not participating, are not actors on the stage of life.

It is why I am on this journey. It is why I wrote this poem:

ADMONITION

Tell me stories of kinship
Of tropes of caritas effortless
Across a world stage
Tell me what you want to hear

In the face of fury
Moderation is a great fiction
A rhetorical stance subject to guile
Too much is at stake

What good are voices of good will
Sleepwalkers haunt my dream
The cascade of moments has begun
This macrocosm this heart will break

Sometimes you are the only actor
Alone in the audience of your soul
Or your God if you admit to one
You cannot you dare not abdicate

The New Scheherazade

Is Open Sesame a fantasy, another false hope, or is that how we wake up the sleepwalkers among us? We have seen the capacity of creative thinking and sheer human will and it is real. You have seen it in your own experience. The stories seem endless because they are endless. A thousand-thousand stories there for the telling night after night far into future, except the future is now and the medium has arrived. The portal is open! (See http://theworldwewant.org.)

September 2006: more than fifty million blogs and counting; Technorati, the blog-tracking service, estimates the blog universe is doubling every six months. And we are all sitting ducks. Hang onto your seats—irreverence is a given. How do you know something is irreverent, because it makes you pish, squish, and squirm. Blogging is one among the new media that are changing how we communicate, who we communicate with, and what we communicate—it is changing our notions of what is legitimate information. In this free space of bright ideas, no certificate of authenticity is required, it's interactive, informal commentary and conversation "peppered with misspellings, grammatical errors, and forbidden words."[10] Some of the social media is inspired, some is simple and unadorned, all of it is immediate.

Most blogs are noncommercial, and most bloggers are passionate about their subjects. In this new public square, anyone can participate, add their own voice to the din or find their audience, and not be limited to the mainstream media or public relations messaging. There is a saying among bloggers, "We are writing ourselves into existence," and this applies to both individuals and communities. We started the The World We Want blog as a way to engage people in dialogue and catalyze a community of online citizens so we can hash out, together, our values and views.

The World We Want asks:

What is your vision of a better world?

What are the conditions needed to realize it?

What are the obstacles?

Based on your experience, what parts of the vision are realistic, and what ideas, strategies, and plans can make it so?

From the WWW blog we hear the following:

These are all questions about what it means to humanize the earth (the way I interpret "better world" in my life). A better world is one where the human being is the central value, more important than money, more important than power, more important than violence and more important than religion or any other institution.

The most important obstacles for me are the internal ones, my fear of failure, my inability to articulate the deep meaning that I touch on every once in a while for more than a fleeting moment.

Realistic? Well, none of it is actually realistic, but that doesn't make it any less necessary, or in fact mandatory for me to keep working in this direction.—Anonymous

I am a busy executive with better fucking things to do than write an essay for Peter Karoff on "The World We Want." Hey Minim, get your butt in here. Answer these dumb questions for me.—Candidia Cruikshanks, CEO of Wealth Bondage

My vision is a world where heads of state may walk freely and safely alongside citizens, in abiding recognition of the source of their power and legitimacy, all aware that it is delegated, and not an entitlement, with none thinking the arrangement is an abrogation of personal responsibility by any of the parties, where the citizens may be grateful for the service and heads of state appreciative of the opportunity to serve.—Harry

These questions are best answered by the creation of an Augmented Social Network that would build identity and trust into the architecture of the Internet, in the public interest, in order to facilitate introductions between people who share affinities or complimentary capabilities across social networks.—Ken Jordan, Jan Hauser, and Steven Foster

One way to make a better world. Have the Great Djin pull all of our souls out of our bodies and transport them to a huge celestial conference center. Have the Djin tell us we can't leave until we agree on the principals, social arrangements, and political institutions that will govern the planet when we return. Here's the kicker: make it clear that after we finish our deliberations, there will be a random shuffling of bodies and souls. If we were born a poor Arab herdsman, we might return as a wealthy German magnate: if we were a straight Caucasian woman from Mobile, Alabama, with a large family, our avatar might be a gay African American man living with HIV/AIDS in Manhattan. We can't count on our age, gender, marital status, sexual orientation, health, wealth, IQ, religion, political affiliation, or even world-view to survive the shuffle.

I suspect the prospect of inhabiting another person's skin would sharpen our empathetic faculties.—From Behind the Veil

Phil Cubeta is my tutor. He is a financial services executive who maintains and authors a number of blogs, including Gifthub.org and theworldwewant.org. I thank Phil for his insights and an amazing flow of poetry, garbage, and satire, all uncorked for our edification. I like listening to him even when he goes over the top. He speaks from behind many masks, but his own voice is clear.

"What I want as an ordinary citizen is as simple as can be, what I was raised to consider my birthright: a democratic society in which each of us, rich, middling, or poor, takes responsibility for the public good, pledging some of our money, some of our time, and even our own skins if it comes to that to keep the public sphere open, to resist the dark arts of propaganda, to keep our speech free, and even to address the powers that be as equals, for we are all equals in the eyes of God and the Constitution.

"What works, which I have seen, is citizen-to-citizen dialogue in the public square of the Internet where ordinary people discuss the events of the day, connect and reinterpret the disparate bits of mediated news, and begin to tell our stories, creating new narratives that make those of spectacular society seem like bedtime stories for children. It is nothing more than the clamor of democracy, risen from side to side, up from the bottom, and merely overheard from above, often with incredulity, if not unease and mistrust."

Phil studied English language and literature at Yale and has, it seems, total recall of every line he read, particularly Augustan satire, which has at its heart a wounded ideal. His lost Eden, as Phil tells it, was his hometown, Middlebury, Vermont, in the mid-1960s. His father taught at the college on the hill, the Esso station owner coached Little League, the chief selectman ran a backhoe. White clapboard churches surrounded the village green, and citizens had a voice. This was an idealized world, made even more so to a precocious kid by the Harvard dropout, working farmer, and great American poet who lived in nearby Ripton, Robert Frost. "I fed sugar lumps and apples to his old horse." But Phil was never entirely convinced that "nothing gold can stay."[11]

He is a man on a mission, and he is relentless. His mission is to wake us up, and he knows the medium to do it. Meanwhile, he wrestles with demons and friends.

"What is owned by this 'we,' and what is owed to 'them' to 'us' the other human beings? The only 'deal' that matters is the social contract binding us all as citizens of a more just community.

"Democracy is as much about method as it is about topics and outcomes. In the public space, the town meeting, citizens from different walks of life can continue a 'many-to-many' conversation. It is a wonderful thing to say, we are here together to discuss the deepest issues of the day. Most movements start with a journal, a newspaper, or some other semiotic crossroads, a coffeehouse or tavern, where citizens come to hash out their agreements and disagreements, to find voice in conversation, and to gradually draw others in.

"We do not come as Platonic Guardians to conduct a focus group or market-test a sales pitch, not as the high and mighty to give largesse to a faceless crowd. We come as citizens and children of God, as members of Kant's Kingdom of Ends, as individuals endowed by the Creator with certain inalienable rights, to take counsel of one another.

"I love these lines from Pindar about the poet's role—to do justice to his people and his time, and to cultivate human excellence: 'To praise what deserves praise and to sow blame for wrong-doers,' to cultivate our humanity with water and warmth, but also with spade, harrow, and pruning hook.

"Conversation, when we do not go gently at one another is a 'rock tumbler,' in which we as rough-hewn citizens, quarried from very different traditions, abrade one another until we become altered for the better. That is the central idea of the liberal democratic tradition. It underlies democracy, parliamentary debates, a free press, religious freedom, and a free market.

"Moderation is a rhetorical stance—in my opinion, easily trumped by guile. But the rock tumbler is something else. Throw the mild-spoken hypocrites, the marketers, the pollsters, the pundits, the hireling policy wonks, the effete inheritors, the strategic squint-eyed philanthropists into the rock tumbler with the poets, the media, and the bloggers.

"It would be a wonder, a public space where all styles from the polemical, to the satirical, to the lyrical, to the scholarly, to the citizen's outcry are welcome. We would fling all of these words into the conversation with Zarathustra, saying, 'Here is my way; where is yours?' The 'cultural product' would be the conversation itself, a many-to-many conversation of citizens as well as authorities. Pretense, pomposity, and poppycock would be the first casualties."

So, you can see that Phil Cubeta is a dramatist and a democrat and a huge believer in the potential for the Internet and its instruments to be a powerful democratizing force, of which the blog is his "rock tumbler" of choice. Who am I to disagree?

In one of his e-mails, he wrote, "Do you find these techno and market metaphors something like aphasia? We seem to have forgotten the language of our great political, poetic, and spiritual traditions. Note too, Peter, the built-in atomization and anomie of 'personal' as opposed to political or community based solutions." And he constantly pushes against my instinct to paint a rosy picture, believing the more darkness you let into your writings, the stronger they are, and the more they are needed.

I worry about that. I do not want this journey to end as either a shiny bright meaningless Condé-Nast travelogue or a depressing Paul Theroux walk around Great Britain that did nothing and went nowhere.

But I am having trouble ending the flow. It doesn't seem finished.

Variations on the Theme

One of the reasons it is difficult to end the flow is because of the infinite number of variations on these themes. There is an astonishing piano piece by Robert Schumann entitled "Symphonic Etudes (Opus 13)" that takes a very simple theme and builds it over seven movements into a work of great range and imagination, from soft and subtle to big crescendo. The same has been true on this journey, where we have encountered a wide range of imaginative interpretation of the same or similar and often very familiar themes. How could it have been otherwise since so much of what we want the world to be is based on universal aspirations?

Even the words have sometimes been identical. Lucy Bernholz quotes the lovely Tongan proverb, "Whatever happens here, happens to us all," and then weaves it beautifully into the concept of open philanthropy. Rory Francisco-Valentino, in talking about how we as families, communities, and societies are interrelated parts of the whole, goes on to say, "When we see ourselves this way, we accept that what happens to one happens to all." I love these echoes. They reaffirm and bind us in the kind of commonality that leads to hope.

Yet each story is nuanced and different, and makes more precise the remarkable array of individual human response. I think it is always this way. When my father, sixty years ago in his small hardware store in Brockton, Massachusetts, listened so intensely to his customers, you just knew that their concerns—children, spouses, bosses, and the proud joys and sorrows of life therein—were the same but also very different. Every person who bears witness at an Alcohol Anonymous meeting begins the same way: "My name is Dr. Bob, and I am an alcoholic," and while the story that then follows has many of the same challenging elements of every other story, each person's one day at a time version is their own.

If left to my own devices, never mind that of those who are flowing through our recently opened portal, these stories would go on and on, but how many times do you have to hear something and come to believe it is so? Does simply saying it make it true? Sometimes that is exactly what happens if the body of evidence begins to build as it has here, and the persuasiveness of the argument, the case study, so to speak, begins to make sense. We get it, we understand it, and begin to believe in its truth. At a certain point we may not remember how we could have believed anything else. This is how understanding deepens, how change happens, how it becomes internalized.

The violinist Midori Goto introduced us at the beginning of this journey to how learning comes out of deep listening. Perhaps we get to the world we want in that way, and by the close observation of the endlessly fascinating world we live in, the one we pass by but often do not see. Perhaps that is how we bring our own imprint of imagination to the simple and familiar themes that make up the human experience. I wrote this poem during the time I was studying poetry at Columbia, a time of slowing down.

THE TRAIN RIDE HOME[12]

On Friday I go home by train,
moving in a kaleidoscope:
backyards, porches, rusted remains,
bicycles, oil drums, a father's hope

of a garden now overrun by weeds.
Windows on a thousand lives
before life's speed accelerated
and jets sliced the air like knives.

As the train rumbles in slow motion,
I see where New England began.
Suddenly there is the ocean
and winter ice extends the land.

The tiny terns are standing tall,
pencil legs casting shadows on ice.
Old wood boats in frozen overhaul.
I feel closer, a world made precise

by black-billed, arctic-bright swans,
a lone blue heron that wants my hand.
Then houses nested in pale sunlight
in Westerly, Kingston, Cranston.

A light goes on, a woman's face,
then gone. I think she has long hair.
Someone's billowing sheets erase
her silhouette hanging in the air.

Our grand tour has been a kind of kaleidoscope. It is time to return for a final visit to my ordinary room.

Unlocking the Ordinary Room

I am back in the ordinary room. The embers from the fire still glow; the yellow light from the lamp casts soft shadows on the bookcases. It appears I am not alone but have been joined by others. We now have our version of Henry Hampton's *school*. He would have loved to be here with us.

As befits our growing appreciation and understanding of the new era, many have arrived from cyberspace and are busily multitasking, communicating with each other while at the same time listening in. Others we passed along the way have caught up with the flow, and more keep arriving to see what the ruckus is. I like the feeling in the room. It is the world abuzz. It is full and purposeful, a community of interest, part of the network for good. But it is still incomplete.

Certainly I do not pretend these two-score stories, chosen by instinct for a bouillabaisse of ideas, experience and inspiration, are complete. No more than do 250,000 people marching in the streets of Edinburgh to "make poverty history," or 14,000 people on the Omidyar Network, or 50 million blogs and counting complete the potential for the network for good. The elephant in this ordinary room, you see, is that many people who could and should be here have not yet arrived. The heart of the matter is quite clear. It is the awakening of the citizen within that will ultimately determine the world we see, shape, create, protect; see, shape create, protect . . . .

Especially if we take seriously the lessons we have learned on our journey. They do not lend themselves perfectly to a list but here is a sense of some:

Listen to the stories of others before you tell your story.

Acknowledge that people know what they need. Help individuals find their own power and take control of their own destiny.

Seek out the assets that every community has, build on them, and celebrate. Make heroes of those who do this work.

Find the alignment between self-interest and the common good. When
there is none, push back and stand firm.

Make bridges and go across them. Break down silos. Create common
ground. When there is no firm ground, do the right thing.

Go downstream—transformational and top-down change only work
when they become concrete and aligned with individual and community
needs and aspirations.

Break out of the box. Use all available resources and innovation from every
sector— business, citizen, government, nonprofit—to get the work done.

Do whatever it takes—disruption, confrontation, jujitsu, logic, data, advocacy, and traveling the parallel tracks. Tactics and strategies are endless.

Abandon comfort. Raise the bar. Put your whole self in, and hold the
moral conscience of your community dear.

Open it up; open yourself up. Provide building blocks for others to make
their own dreams come true.

The most important transformation is the transformation of the human
heart. To get there means growing your soul. Work on it.

There is still plenty of space in the ordinary room, and you will be welcome as long as you have what Helen Vendler[13] calls a poet's "tones of voice."
It is a unifying element that helps establish the ethical relationship between
poet and reader. Vendler is most interested in a "Utopian" kind of poem that
redefines social expectations rather than argues or confirms them. One seldom thinks of poetry redefining social expectations, but we who have been in
search of the "ultimate good" have been trying to do exactly that. I would
describe the unifying tone of voice from all the voices we have heard as one of
integrity of purpose and integrity of process. The two are intrinsically linked
to the ethical and moral relationship we seek.

As Chattanooga's Jack Murrah said, "When one listens, one must obey."
As Melinda Marble said, "Those at the center of problems need to be at the
center of their solutions. As Stephen Melville wrote, actions are themselves
promises and promises are a serious matter.

Some promises we make to others and some we make to ourselves. All of
the people who we have met are working to make good on their promise to
fulfill a larger purpose in life.

What are the promises you have made? Have you kept them?

The promise I most want to keep is to my four grandchildren. I want
them on this journey with me, and when they are ready, I want the ordinary
room to be there overflowing with stories—your stories.

FALCO PERIGRINUS, A PERSPECTIVE

I'm thinking indemnification,
worrying the irrevocable loss.
True I do have a State Street/Custom House
point of view, bonds routinely issued,
richly resourced, asset guaranteed,
but let me tell you, the fish, schools of fish
that swam thick often swim no more
even the harbor's deep outermost part.
I miss their blue and silver shadows,
Their soft, seamless, choreography.
Someone must stand surety here, but who?

This morning, to clear my head, I fly high.
I love the brilliant Northerly days,
sweeping, soaring, on strong winter winds,
higher, higher, air become thin,
sheaves of particled gold enough to hold,
literally one can see forever—
Nahant's prim little nose, east to Cape Ann,
Casco Bay, south to P-town, Cape Pogue,
Nantucket's soft shoals, the tip of Long Island.
What a gift, this ice-age land meets sea
all sparkling so gloriously!

Reader's Guide Questions

1. Should we fast? What does that mean to you?
2. Are we making progress?
3. Has John Isaacson made a case for "moral learning"? Do you agree with his definition of "moral progress"? What is yours?
4. If Sister Margaret measures inch by inch, John measures by centuries. How do you integrate these views?
5. John is slightly more optimistic than not. Are you?
6. What do you believe will wake the sleepwalkers among us?
7. Is Phil Cubeta's "rock tumbler" vision of democracy new, or is it the medium he is in love with that is new?
8. What are your answers to The World We Want questions?
9. What is your vision of a better world?

10. What are the conditions needed to realize it?
11. Based on your experience, what parts of the vision are realistic, and what ideas, strategies, and plans can make it so?
12. What is your story?

Notes

1. This essay from which this is taken appears as the chapter "Mystery" in *Ecology of Being*, by Peter A. White (Gambier, Ohio: All in All Books, 2006).
2. The story that inspired this story is called "The Fasting of the Heart," which may be found in *The Way of Chuang Tzu* by Thomas Merton (New York: New Directions, 1965).
3. *Sleepwalkers* by Hermann Broch was published in three volumes between 1931 and 1932.
4. *Recherché (Remembrance of Things Past)* by Marcel Proust was published between 1913 and 1932 with the last three volumes appearing after his death.
5. From Rebecca Karoff, "Tropic Containment and Displacement: Reading Style and Consciousness in Broch's *Die Schlafwandler* and Proust's *A la recherché du temps perdu*," Ph.D. diss., University of Wisconsin, 1990.
6. From David K. Shipler, *The Working Poor* (New York: Knopf, 2004).
7. From Jane Copper's essay "Nothing Has Been Used in the Manufacture of This Poetry That Could Have Been Used in the Manufacture of Bread," in *Scaffolding* (Gardiner, Maine: Tilbury House, 1984).
8. Peter White, *Ecology of Being*.
9. See the work of Robert Putnam and Richard Florida.
10. Robert Scoble and Shel Israel, *Naked Conversations* (New York: Wiley, 2006), 1.
11. A line from and the title of Robert Frost's elegiac poem.
12. Published in *Yankee magazine*, February 1991.
13. Helen Vendler in *Invisible Listeners: Lyric Intimacy in Herbert, Whitman and Ashbery* (Princeton, N.J.: Princeton University Press, 2005).

INDEX

About the Authors

PETER KAROFF founded The Philanthropic Initiative (TPI) in 1989. He is a Senior Fellow at the Tisch College of Citizenship and Public Service at Tufts University, a Fellow of the MacDowell Colony and a 2006 Purpose Prize Fellow. Peter has written extensively and has taught, lectured, and motivated hundreds of audiences in the United States and around the globe on the successful practice and art of philanthropy, reflecting his experience through his philosophy, passion, and poetry. He is a graduate of Brandeis University and Columbia University, and he holds an honorary degree from Lesley University.

JANE MADDOX, formerly communications director at TPI, has devoted her career to the development and communication of missions, programs, and ideas for public agencies, nonprofit organizations, and companies, including, for many years, Polaroid Corporation.

About TPI

TPI (The Philanthropic Initiative) is a nonprofit philanthropic consulting firm that provides strategic planning and programmatic services to individual donors, families, foundations, and corporations.

TPI's mission is to increase the impact of philanthropy in society by

- working with donors to make their giving more strategic, effective, and fulfilling;
- crafting creative and productive approaches to important social issues; and
- inspiring and supporting others to invest in their own values, communities, and societies.